THE UNKNOWN GREAT

THE SCOTT AND LAURIE OKI SERIES
IN ASIAN AMERICAN STUDIES

THE UNKNOWN GREAT

Stories of
Japanese Americans
at the Margins
of History

GREG ROBINSON
with **JONATHAN
VAN HARMELEN**

University of Washington Press *Seattle*

The Unknown Great was supported by a grant from the Scott and Laurie Oki Endowment for Books in Asian American Studies.

Copyright © 2023 by Greg Robinson

Composed in Calluna

All rights reserved. No part of this publication may be reproduced or transmitted in any form or by any means, electronic or mechanical, including photocopy, recording, or any information storage or retrieval system, without permission in writing from the publisher.

UNIVERSITY OF WASHINGTON PRESS | uwapress.*uw.edu*

Cataloging information is available from the Library of Congress

LIBRARY OF CONGRESS CONTROL NUMBER 2023942247
ISBN 9780295751887 (hardcover)
ISBN 9780295751894 (paperback)
ISBN 9780295751900 (ebook)

∞ This paper meets the requirements of ANSI/NISO z39.48-1992 (Permanence of Paper).

IN LOVING MEMORY OF

ED ROBINSON (1936–2023)

ALEX ROBINSON-GILDEN (1978–2017)

AND DAVID GILDEN (1950–2021)

CONTENTS

Introduction / Reshaping Japanese American History   xi

A Note from Jonathan van Harmelen   xvii

Chapter 1   **AFRICAN AMERICAN ALLIES**

Erna P. Harris / Champion of Equality	1
Japanese Americans and the Macbeth Legacy	5
Seeking Will Thomas / A Friend of the Nisei	10
Howard Thurman and Japanese Americans / Toward the Blessed Community *with Peter Eisenstadt*	14

Chapter 2   **JAPANESE AMERICANS AND INTERRACIALISM**

From Kenny Murase to Kenji Murase / The Journey of a Nisei Writer, Scholar, and Activist	23
Mari Sabusawa Michener / Champion of Civil Rights and Supporter of the Arts	32
Way Down in Egypt Land / Tamio Wakayama, Civil Rights Photographer	39
Paul Takagi / A Fearless Advocate	46
Toshi Ohta Seeger / The Power behind the Music	50

Chapter 3   **JAPANESE AMERICANS AND AFRICAN AMERICANS**

Stepping Over the Color Line / Nikkei at Historically Black Colleges and Universities   55

African American Scratches on a Nikkei Canvas / Black Characters in Japanese American Literature *with Brian Niiya*   60

The Japanese American Press and the History of the N-Word *with Jonathan van Harmelen*   75

Chapter 4   **THE QUEER HERITAGE OF JAPANESE AMERICANS**

K. T. Takahashi / Transnational Writer and Activist   80

Not Just *A Single Man* / Christopher Isherwood's Nisei Connections   84

Tondemonai / Recovering a Groundbreaking Asian American Play   87

Randy Kikukawa and 1980s Asian American Gay Activism   91

The JACL's Shift to Support for LGBTQ+ Equality   95

Chapter 5   **IN GOOD FAITH**

Laying Down the Law of Love / The 1936 American Tour of Dr. Toyohiko Kagawa *with Bo Tao*   98

Hisaye Yamamoto and the Catholic Worker Movement *with Matthieu Langlois*   103

The Undiscovered History of Japanese Americans and the Church of Jesus Christ of Latter-day Saints *with Christian Heimburger*   110

Nikkei and the Peace Churches / Mennonites and Brethren *with Zacharie Leclair*   118

Chapter 6   MIXED-RACE STORIES

Kinjiro Matsudaira / Mayor of Edmonston, Maryland *with Jonathan van Harmelen*	122
Bernard Spencer Miyaguchi / Ice Skater Extraordinaire	126
Edith deBecker Sebald / Diplomat	128
The Enigma of Marion Saki	131
Ruth Sato Reinhardt / From Chorus Girl to Jazz Momma	137

Chapter 7   MUSIC

Yoichi Hiraoka / Issei Xylophone Virtuoso *with Jonathan van Harmelen*	146
Classical Music in the WRA Camps *with Jonathan van Harmelen*	150
Akira Kikukawa and the Japanese American Orchestra *with Jonathan van Harmelen*	153
Juilliard-Trained Songbird Mariko Mukai Ando Defied Expectations *with Jonathan van Harmelen*	157
Nisei Singer and Civil Rights Activist Ruby Hideko Yoshino *with Jonathan van Harmelen*	160

Chapter 8   LITERATURE AND JOURNALISM

T. John Fujii / Collaborator or Cosmopolitan?	165
Bunji Omura / New York Japanese Antifascist Writer and Publicist *with Jonathan van Harmelen*	173
Iwao Kawakami's Intriguing Elegy for Topaz	178
Eddie Shimano and Gerald Chan Sieg *with James Sun*	182

Florence Crannell Means / The Woman behind
The Moved-Outers — 190

Ayako Ishigaki / Radical Issei Feminist Writer
in 1930s America — 194

Chapter 9 **THE EUROPEAN NIKKEI COMMUNITY**

The French (Nikkei) Connection / Japanese Americans
in Midcentury Paris — 199

Kikou Yamata / Rediscovering the First Nisei Writer — 202

Agnes Miyakawa / The *Toast* of Paris — 206

Toshiko Hasegawa / A Nisei at La Scala — 210

Pioneering Nisei Soprano Tomiko (Tomi) Kanazawa — 213

Foujita Discovers the Americas / An Artist's Tour
with Seth Jacobowitz — 217

Epilogue   229

Acknowledgments   233

Notes   235

Selected Bibliography   239

Credits   245

Index   249

Introduction
RESHAPING JAPANESE AMERICAN HISTORY

I am glad to welcome readers to *The Unknown Great*, a new anthology of my newspaper columns and blog posts about Japanese American history. This is the third collection of my short articles to be published. As with its two predecessors, this book is made up of "sketches," readable (and fun) stories of unheralded figures in Japanese American history, ranging from the turn of the twentieth century through the mass confinement of the community during World War II and up to the present day. Yet beyond being entertaining, my sketches have a serious purpose: by focusing on exceptional people and things, they challenge stereotypes of Nikkei (ethnic Japanese) in popular culture as colorless and suggest the diversity of the group's experience.

Indeed, even more than in my previous work, *The Unknown Great* offers a radically different account of the history of ethnic Japanese in the United States, underlining the cosmopolitan nature of their experience. According to the *Merriam-Webster Dictionary*, two main definitions of *cosmopolitan* are "having wide international sophistication" and "composed of persons . . . from all or many parts of the world."[1] First, from the outset, the Japanese community not only comprised people from another continent—Japan—but included many who had spent time in nations such as Hawaii (independent before 1898), Canada, and Latin America before settling in the United States. The community was made up of a diverse population, including Okinawans, ethnic Koreans, and *Burakumin* (Japanese "untouchables"). Their children and grandchildren were an even more far-flung group, whose members migrated to different areas of North America or went to live in Europe or Asia—particularly the Japanese empire.

As for being "sophisticated," a visible fraction of the immigrants, especially those who settled in New York and Chicago, were businesspeople and artists. They felt at home in the larger society and were able to mix more or less freely with white associates. Even those in West Coast communities were exposed to other cultures and drew from elements of Western and Asian civilizations in their lives. Issei women, in particular, were on average far more educated than their white counterparts. They were passionate readers, composed poetry, and wrote diaries in their limited free time. They encouraged their children to study and to develop intellectually and culturally. The Nisei generation, in turn, would boast a stunning proportion of writers, artists, and musicians as well as consumers of books, films, and jazz or classical music.

What is more, *The Unknown Great* stands apart from the historical literature in its focus on new and undiscovered themes within the Nikkei experience. These are marginal areas in being not only less documented, but also difficult and sometimes uncomfortable to unravel. They involve sensitive and even taboo subjects such as race and interracial relationships, sexuality, religious faith, and national identity.

First, a central aspect of the book is devoted to the long-standing interactions between African Americans and Japanese Americans. Historically, African Americans, as the most visible and influential nonwhite minority in America, have provided a model for Japanese Americans to follow in structuring their communities and building institutions in the face of discrimination. Yet as Brian Niiya and I explain in our chapter herein, the powerful (and ambivalent) interactions between members of the two groups have too often been effaced from the conscious history of the Nikkei. To be sure, various scholars have done important work on parts of this history, and I have discussed aspects of it in the past, but much more remains to be uncovered.[2] One particularly important area I explore here is the collaborations forged among individual Black artists, writers, and activists and their ethnic Japanese allies. I also explore the diverse nature of representations of African Americans in Nikkei art and literature.

At the same time, *The Unknown Great* innovates in its complex presentation of Nikkei sexuality and family arrangements. Historians have generally assumed that mixed white-Japanese couples and their *hapa* (mixed-race) descendants were exceptional and unwelcome within Nikkei society, at least until recent years. In fact, early Japanese communities, notably outside the West Coast, included numerous people of mixed ancestry who comprised a significant fraction of the group's writers, artists, and performers. While there has been an explosion of *hapa* studies by scholars from Paul Spickard onward, plus anthologies such as Duncan Ryūken Williams's *Hapa Japan* (and even the *Journal of Critical Mixed Race Studies*), the full contributions of mixed couples and their children still remain to be discovered.[3] In broader terms, conventional narratives of Japanese American history focus on nuclear family groups and pass over the Issei "bachelors" (with their largely same-sex domestic arrangements) and other unmarried people who long composed a significant share of the group's population.

Indeed, in regard to sexuality, perhaps the most strikingly original aspect of this book is its exploration of the queer history of Japanese Americans. This area can be well described as the "black hole" of Japanese American life because of the stigmatized nature of the subject and the difficulty of finding and interpreting source material. Yet LGBTQ+ people have always been present within Japanese communities, and their hidden past richly deserves rediscovery. Here my book adds to the small volume of existing literature on the queer history of Japanese Americans by Amy Sueyoshi, Andrew Leong, John Howard, Eric Wat, and others.[4]

The Great Unknown consists of eight chapters, each of which brings together multiple articles under a common theme. The first chapters center on historical encounters between African Americans and Japanese Americans. Chapter 1 recovers the stories of remarkable Black Americans, including Hugh Macbeth (Sr. and Jr.), Erna P. Harris, and Howard Thurman, who championed the rights of Japanese Americans in the face of wartime racial prejudice and hysteria against them. Chapter 2 deals with their counterparts: the progressive Nisei who supported equal rights for other minorities and embraced intergroup activism and coalition building. A highlight of the chapter is a study of Tamio Wakayama, a Japanese Canadian who joined the civil rights movement in the early 1960s and became official photographer for the Student Nonviolent Coordinating Committee (SNCC). Chapter 3 examines further connections between African Americans and ethnic Japanese, including the history of Nikkei at historically Black colleges and universities (HBCUs). The highlight of this section is my extended study, cowritten with Brian Niiya, of African American characters in Japanese American literature.

The fourth chapter, on the queer history of Japanese Americans, sheds light on alternative sexualities within Nikkei communities, from the nineteenth century though the post-Stonewall age. Some highlights of this chapter include studies of groundbreaking queer works of literature by K. T. Takahashi, Christopher Isherwood, and Soon-Tek Oh, as well as the affirmation of Asian American gay identities and the birth of LGBTQ+ Asian social and activism in the 1980s.

Chapter 5 of *The Unknown Great* deals with the interaction of Issei and Nisei with different communities of faith. Beyond the everyday religious practice of individuals in Buddhist and mainstream Protestant congregations, Japanese community members have interacted—sometimes as converts but more often as beneficiaries of support—with diverse religious minorities, including Christians, Jews, and others. A highlight of this section is my column, cowritten with Christian Heimburger, that traces the unsung but indispensable role played by members of the Church of Jesus Christ of Latter-day Saints (popularly called Mormons) in the growth of Nikkei communities and their survival during World War II. I also include a collaboration with Zacharie Leclair on the Anabaptist "peace churches." A special feature of this section is my joint article with Matthieu Langlois, written especially for this volume, on the writer-activist Hisaye Yamamoto's involvement with Dorothy Day and the Catholic Worker movement.

Chapter 6 offers stories of mixed-race Japanese Americans. I single out some exceptional *hapa* public figures who distinguished themselves over the first half of the twentieth century by their international connections and mainstream success. One highlight of this chapter is the extraordinary story of Kinjiro Matsudaira, who first became mayor of Edmonston, Maryland, in 1927—the first Asian American elected official on the United States mainland.

Chapter 7, produced in collaboration with Jonathan van Harmelen, covers the unknown history of Japanese Americans in classical music. Numerous ethnic Japanese performers pursued concert careers with support from their communities, although mainstream orchestras were slow to hire Asian instrumentalists, and opera companies relegated Nikkei singers to small parts (or typecast sopranos in the role of Cio-Cio-San in Puccini's opera *Madama Butterfly*). One highlight of this section is a meditation on the unique career of international xylophone virtuoso Yoichi Hiraoka.

Chapter 8 brings together tales of Japanese American writers and journalists. One highlight is a study, cowritten with James Sun, of Eddie Shimano and Gerald Chan Sieg, two writers employed by the New Deal–era Federal Writers' Project (FWP) during the 1930s. A special feature is a study of the white writer Florence Crannell Means, author of the first published novel on the camps. The final chapter is perhaps the most unorthodox. It centers on the vital but unheralded presence of Issei and Nisei in Europe, notably France. Entries in this chapter include stories of Nisei sopranos Agnes Miyakawa, Toshiko Hasegawa, and Tomi Kanazawa, who performed in Europe and across the globe.

I wish to offer a word of warning to the reader. My main goal in delving into these unexplored aspects of Nikkei history is to break new scholarly ground. My studies are limited in scope, and the conclusions I draw from them are meant to be tentative rather than definitive. My hope is to open conversations and trace directions for future researchers who will expand on what I have uncovered and examined in these pages—and correct whatever errors of fact or interpretation I have made! Because these articles were originally written and published independently, occasionally different aspects of the same events are discussed in separate chapters, while the grouping of pieces by theme can seem arbitrary in some cases.

Let me add a final word about my sources: as I explain further in the epilogue, a large majority of the pieces included in this volume were written in the period 2020–21, at a time when the COVID-19 pandemic severely restricted my access to archives and libraries. As a result, I was forced to work from home, using research I had accumulated over previous years. The main repositories I drew from were the Library of Congress, National Archives, UCLA Young Research Library, Harvard University Libraries, Franklin D. Roosevelt Library, and Tamiment Library at New York University. The rest of my research I did by internet: my ability to find so much of what I needed online is a marvel of technology that testifies to the dedicated efforts of scholars and librarians, inside and outside Japanese communities, to digitize and make available historical materials. The Hoji Shinbun Digital Collection at the Hoover Institution, which includes scans of the prewar Japanese American press, was my most frequent reference, and I also made heavy use of the Densho digital archive; the Online Archive of California; the Japanese Evacuation Research Survey (JERS) digital archive at the Bancroft Library, University of California (UC), Berkeley; the California Digital News Archive; and the Library of Congress digital databases Chronicling America and Japanese-American Internment Camp Newspapers. Among commercial databases, I was especially glad to use ProQuest Historical Newspapers, which afforded me access to popular dailies like the *New York Times*, *Washington Post*, and *Los Angeles Times*, and America's Historical Newspapers and Newspapers.com for back files of smaller-size and foreign-language newspapers. Through Ancestry.com I reviewed census forms, shipping and immigration records, marriage records, and school yearbooks. I used Archive.org and Google Books to study magazines, yearbooks, and digitized book contents. While I did not conduct formal interviews or oral histories of any individuals, in a few cases I drew on notes of conversations with the small number of subjects whom I had met in person or whose family members provided me with information. In order to promote easy reading by nonspecialists, I have limited the number of notes. Those needing specific information on citations are invited to contact me at robinson.greg@uqam.ca.

A NOTE FROM JONATHAN VAN HARMELEN

Greg Robinson has graciously invited me, as his collaborator, to add a few words in my own voice. As Greg notes in his introduction, the columns that make up this book are meant to inform and entertain readers by presenting a wide range of unconventional narratives, ranging from music to politics. In our dual roles as historians and community journalists, we write not only to document the past but also to use it to challenge readers to rethink their understanding of the Japanese American experience as a whole and of the diverse individuals who left their mark on areas of American life.

For me *The Unknown Great* captures the partnership that Greg and I have built up over the last five years. Not only does the book include a selection of our joint columns, but Greg insists that even his solo writings bear a certain stamp of our discussions, as he and I have developed the practice of proofreading and commenting on each other's drafts before publication. Still, it is the coauthored pieces that stand out most highly for me. The special beauty of our collaboration, as we have learned, lies not only in our mutual interest in the subjects we write about but also in how we together found inspiration from our different backgrounds.

Perhaps the best example of this is our section on Japanese American musicians. Greg, a devoted listener of opera and a specialist in African American history, suggested that we spotlight singers Mariko Mukai (Ando) and Ruby Yoshino, two talented singers who wielded their stardom as a tool for civil rights advocacy. As a classical percussionist, I found in Yoichi Hiraoka two stories that spoke to me: first, that of a performer who used his musical talent to bridge the cultural gap between Japan and the United States; and second, as an innovative percussionist who transformed the marimba and xylophone into centerpieces of orchestral performance. In the case of Kinjiro Matsudaira, we both drew from our knowledge of Meiji Japan and Washington, DC, to understand how a former circus performer came to be elected as mayor of Edmonston, Maryland. In each case we sought to uncover stories about Japanese Americans that defied traditional narratives of race and immigration and challenged our assumptions about US history.

Beyond our coauthored pieces, Greg's articles reprinted in *The Unknown Great* add a new twist to the existing historiography on Japanese Americans. Beyond being enjoyable in its own right, each section either sets the groundwork for further research or complements new trends in Japanese American history. The sections dedicated to interracial coalition building and queer history are invaluable resources for future scholarship on Japanese American activism and in sexuality studies. Chapter 5 offers enlightening stories about religious leaders from across the United States (or in Toyohiko Kagawa's case, around the globe) who mobilized to support Japanese Americans amid difficult times. Like Duncan Ryūken Williams and Emily Andersons's recent exhibit and book for the Japanese American National Museum (JANM), *Sutra and Bible*, it forms part of a new and transformative wave of scholarship on religion and Japanese Americans. Finally, as a scholar who looks beyond national boundaries and has studied the relationship between Europe and Japanese America, I particularly appreciate the remarkable transnational nature of so many of the articles in *The Unknown Great*, especially those that make up chapter 9. Greg's deft exploration of the Japanese American expats who lived in Paris and other European cities forms the groundwork for something greater.

The Unknown Great, as Greg reminds us, is not to be seen as definitive; rather, it is the beginning of something new. For any historian, the greatest honor they can receive is the knowledge that their work inspires others. I hope that you enjoy these stories as I have and are inspired by them to see Japanese American history in a new way.

THE
UNKNOWN
GREAT

Chapter 1

AFRICAN AMERICAN ALLIES

ERNA P. HARRIS / CHAMPION OF EQUALITY

One part of the history of Japanese American wartime confinement that has been curiously neglected is the disproportionate support offered by Black Americans. Victims of racial injustice themselves, African Americans demonstrated different forms of solidarity to their Nikkei counterparts in the wake of Executive Order 9066. (Issued by President Franklin Roosevelt on February 19, 1942, this order authorized the army to exclude or confine all persons on the West Coast deemed a threat to national security and led to the forced removal of some 110,000 US citizens and long-term resident aliens of Japanese ancestry from the region and their mass confinement in a network of camps inland.) In particular, numerous African American writers and journalists spoke out in support of the rights of Japanese Americans. The celebrated poet Langston Hughes devoted several columns in the *Chicago Defender* to opposing the government's policy as racist and tyrannical. The critic and novelist George Schuyler not only supported the rights of Japanese Americans in his articles for the *Pittsburgh Courier* but offered funds from his own pocket to help found a New York chapter of the Japanese American Citizens League (JACL), the organization's first interracial branch.

One outstanding dissident was columnist Erna P. Harris of the *Los Angeles Tribune*. Erna Prather Harris was born on June 29, 1908, in Kingfisher, Oklahoma, a small town about forty miles northwest of Oklahoma City. After attending segregated schools in Oklahoma, she enrolled at Wichita State University, where she served as a reporter and editor of the school's newspaper, the *Sunflower* (according to one source, she won a journalism award, but when the town newspaper came to take a picture of the prize-winning student and discovered that she was Black, they decided to cancel the shoot). Upon graduating with a bachelor of arts degree in journalism in 1936, she had difficulty finding a position as a reporter, so she decided to start her own weekly newspaper, the

Kansas Journal. It operated for three and a half years. However, when Harris ran an editorial in October 1939 opposing conscription, she angered readers and advertisers and was forced to close her newspaper.

In 1941 Harris moved to Los Angeles and was hired as a reporter for the *Los Angeles Tribune*, the newest (and least established) of the city's three African American newspapers. Since the *Tribune* had a female editor, Almena Davis, it might have been easier for Harris as a woman to gain employment. Once at the *Tribune*, Harris wrote features and began an editorial column, Reflections in a Crackt Mirror. Outside of her newspaper work, she also was active with the local chapter of the nonviolent human relations group Fellowship of Reconciliation (FOR).

In spring 1942 the *Los Angeles Tribune* distinguished itself as the sole Los Angeles newspaper to formally oppose mass removal. Harris was particularly outraged by Executive Order 9066. As she later recalled in her column, "Ever since the evacuation of Americans of Japanese ancestry and Japanese along the Pacific Coast was proposed, I have pointed out that the issue was one of race and on that basis affected anyone who was physically distinguishable as 'colored'" (February 7, 1944). Worse, it was a government action that thereby gave official approval to prejudice. As Harris wrote in spring 1942, "To visit evacuation [evacuated] neighborhoods and talk with neighbors of the 'evil, treacherous, fifth column menaces' who are being summarily moved away, who have been adjudged guilty without any trial at which to claim innocence was to acknowledge an event with all earmarks of a legalized community lynching." Harris's position was scored by popular syndicated columnist Westbrook Pegler, who dismissed "E.P.H." as naive. Pegler's attack had the effect of publicizing Harris's views nationwide.

Once mass removal took place, Harris seems not to have spoken about government actions toward Japanese Americans, though she mentioned Nisei among the ranks of racial minorities deserving justice. In late November 1943 reports of rioting among "disloyal Japanese" at the government's "segregation center" at Tule Lake brought anti–Japanese American sentiment in Southern California to a climax. Politicians and organizations called for a military takeover of the camps and for the end of resettlement. In a column Harris decried the hysteria over "disloyalty," laying into the bigots and expressing sympathy for Japanese Americans who had been "set on" as part of the inflammatory campaigns of the Hearst press:

Eighteen months ago the evacuation of the Issei and Nisei was being called a matter of military necessity on threat of imminent invasion. In a few months it was called protective custody for their own safety—such cannibals are we, their erstwhile neighbors, alleged to be. But now, as the interests which have long wanted them eliminated from California in the hysteria of war-bred hatred dare to come out into the open, there comes the call for their permanent exclusion from California, for treating them as war prisoners, for depriving them of citizenship, and from a man pledged to enforce the law, [Los Angeles County] Sheriff [Eugene] Biscailuz, comes a plea for sending many of them to Japan in exchange for prisoners of war. Such a move would involve some American citizens. If citizenship is to become a matter of racial or national predeterminism or of periodic authoritarian changes, who will be safe from the whims of the powerful? (Reflections, *Los Angeles Tribune*, November 22, 1943)

In the months that followed, Harris devoted several more columns to defending Japanese Americans. In her January 3, 1944, column, for example, she denounced an anti-Nisei Christmas cartoon by *Los Angeles Times* cartoonist Ed Leffingwell. Harris snapped, "Friends, this is how Hitler made little Nazis: by reaching the children and youth through stories and pictures, he taught them to fear and hate certain groups." Harris explained her own insight into the question:

> Through friends and newspapers I have maintained a fairly close contact with the evacuee-victims of our lack of confidence in American education and government agencies. On Christmas Eve it was my pleasure to have as a houseguest an old friend who is teaching in the relocation center at Poston. I hasten to suggest that Mr. Leffingwell could find among the Japanese and Nisei internees some real characters whose story, recounted by him in picture, would set before his small readers an example of courage, sensitivity, forgiveness and humility such as would set his cartoon aside from the petty humdrum of its fellows.

Harris's concern over the treatment of Japanese Americans reflected her larger interest in struggles against discrimination by minorities, including Jews, Mexican Americans, and Asians. In an article in late 1944 in a new multiracial magazine, *Pacific Pathfinder*, she deplored the racial bias of white nativists such as the Native Sons of the Golden West and scored John Sinclair, a state official with the American Legion, for making a speech in Santa Barbara calling for pressure to discourage Japanese Americans from returning to the Pacific Coast and for openly affirming, "I would like to keep this a country for Caucasians." Harris warned of the dangerous implications of such attitudes for all minorities: "Americans of Chinese ancestry share in disproportionate measure the apprehension of other non-Whites with regard to the summary treatment of Americans of Japanese ancestry. Tightening of residential restrictions against them, for instance, in the neighborhood surrounding San Francisco's 'Chinatown' gives basis for their fears." In February 1946 she complained in her *Los Angeles Tribune* column that all the events for Brotherhood Week that year were being hosted by whites seeking to reach out to Blacks. Harris insisted that African Americans should hold their own events and reach out to others: "Joint hosts on the negroes' invitation would be Nisei, American Indians and other Americans whose physical characteristics make them detectable. I have heard of no such observance during Brotherhood week."

During the postwar years, Harris welcomed a group of outstanding Nisei who joined her on the staff of the *Tribune*. They included Hisaye Yamamoto, who started as a columnist and editorial writer in June 1945 (at the modest salary of thirty-five dollars per week), and later sports editor Chester "Cheddar" Yamauchi and his wife, the future playwright Wakako Yamauchi.

In 1952 Harris left Los Angeles and moved to Berkeley, California, where she operated a print shop and continued to be active in a number of peace and civil rights organizations. She was appointed to the National Board of the Women's International League for Peace and Freedom (WILPF) in 1956 and regularly traveled to WILPF congresses in Europe and Asia, including one in Birmingham, England, in 1956. She was a member of the WILPF delegation that visited the USSR in 1964 to participate in the US-Soviet Women's Seminar in Moscow. Harris also grew active in cooperatives in the Berkeley area and in February 1983 was elected to the board of directors of the Berkeley Co-Op, the nation's largest cooperative. Erna P. Harris died on March 9, 1995. She was subsequently honored by the naming of a public housing project, Erna P. Harris Court, in the city of Berkeley.

Although a less renowned figure than George Schuyler or Langston Hughes, Erna Harris was among the earliest Black critics of the treatment of Japanese Americans and arguably the most forthright and brave. In the process she proved that African Americans, themselves victims of racism, could reach out effectively to other minority groups.

JAPANESE AMERICANS AND THE MACBETH LEGACY

Hugh Macbeth Jr., who died in fall 2019 at the age of one hundred, was an extraordinary figure. On a personal level, he was a distinguished lawyer and judge—a prime member of a generation of African Americans who achieved mainstream success, despite the formidable obstacles in their path. On a symbolic level, Hugh bore the historical legacy of the remarkable Macbeth family, most notably the father whose name he shared. For Japanese Americans, the name Macbeth stands as a title of particular honor, given the heroic support and friendship that Hugh Sr. provided the community and that his son then carried on and extended.

Hugh Macbeth Jr. was born in Los Angeles on June 21, 1919, to Edwina and Hugh Ellwood Macbeth. Hugh Macbeth Sr. was the product of an elite Black family from Charleston, South Carolina, and the son of Arthur Macbeth, an early African American photographer. After graduating from Harvard Law School, Hugh Sr. spent some years in Baltimore as a muckraking journalist, then moved to Los Angeles in 1914. There he established a law partnership with his brother Gobert and made a name for himself as an independent-minded attorney who represented white clients as well as Blacks and reached out across different communities. In 1938 Hugh Sr. was appointed executive secretary of the new California Race Relations Commission.

Hugh Macbeth Sr. settled his new family in the Jefferson Park district of Los Angeles, then a largely Japanese area. Hugh Jr. later recalled that as a child he had attended Japanese school with his Nisei friends, since otherwise he would have no other children in the neighborhood to play with once the regular school day finished. There he studied Japanese language and judo—and also absorbed some endemic community prejudices against Chinese and Filipinos. Meanwhile, the Macbeth family informally took in an orphaned Nisei boy, Kenji Horita, who celebrated all his birthdays with his adopted family and established a lasting bond with Mrs. Macbeth. After graduating high school in Los Angeles, Hugh Jr. attended UCLA, where he was elected to Phi Beta Kappa. In fall 1941 Hugh Jr. enrolled at UC Berkeley's Boalt Hall Law School (today UC Berkeley School of Law). There he studied with the well-known legal scholar

Hugh Macbeth Jr. and Maxine Macbeth at their home in San Francisco, 2012. Author's collection.

Dudley McGovney and became active with the Berkeley branch of International House. In 1943 Gobert Macbeth passed away. In 1944, after completing law school, Hugh Jr. was invited to return to Los Angeles and serve as his father's law partner. He was admitted to the California bar in January 1945.

While his son was away at school, Hugh Sr. threw himself into defending Japanese Americans in the aftermath of Pearl Harbor, believing that pressure for mass removal was a classic case of official racism. During spring 1942 he appealed to West Coast commanding general John DeWitt not to institute mass exclusion, visited Japanese American friends confined at Santa Anita, and corresponded extensively with Norman Thomas, the US Socialist Party leader, who was the only national political leader to oppose Executive Order 9066. It was Macbeth who furnished Thomas with the bulk of his information about the conditions facing West Coast Japanese Americans. Macbeth even traveled to Washington, DC, and attempted to secure a meeting with President Roosevelt (according to Hugh Jr., his father used a White House cook as an attempted back channel to the Oval Office). Most of all, in partnership with American Civil Liberties Union (ACLU) lawyer A. L. Wirin, Hugh Macbeth Sr. joined in legal cases challenging Executive Order 9066 and legal discrimination. He helped argue the habeas corpus petitions on behalf of Ernest Kinzo and Toki Wakayama, who had protested their confinement in camps. When the

Hirabayashi and *Korematsu* cases were heard before the US Supreme Court, Macbeth signed the JACL's brief on behalf of the defendants. He also helped draft the JACL's amicus brief in *Regan v. King*, a US Appeals Court case in which nativist groups challenged Nisei voting and citizenship rights on racial grounds.

Once Hugh Jr. became a partner in his father's firm, he began work with Japanese Americans as well. In 1945 he became engaged in *People v. Oyama*, a California superior court case in which California's government sought to seize the farm property of the Oyama family under the Alien Land Act. Hugh Sr. joined A. L. Wirin in presenting the case that the Alien Land Act was racist and unconstitutional and distinguished himself in oral argument. After the Oyamas lost their case, they appealed in federal court, and eventually the case (renamed *Oyama v. California*) was taken up to the US Supreme Court. While the Macbeth firm withdrew from the case, it remained vitally interested in it. It was Hugh Jr. (taking a tip from his old professor Dudley McGovney) who proposed to Wirin what became the appellate strategy, namely, that the case be argued on the basis of the law's discriminatory impact on American citizens of Japanese ancestry. In January 1948 the Supreme Court ruled in favor of the Oyamas. Their victory not only halted enforcement of the Alien Land Act against Japanese Americans but established the legal grounds for future Supreme Court civil rights cases.

In addition to his work on the *Oyama* case, Hugh Jr. found other ways to support Japanese Americans. In 1946 he signed the ACLU amicus brief in the California supreme court case of Issei fisherman Torao Takahashi, who had been denied a state fishing license on racial grounds. In 1947 he and his father hired Chiyoko Sakamoto, the first Nisei woman admitted to the State Bar of California, as an associate in their firm. Hugh Jr. even sat for a portrait photo by the esteemed Nikkei photographer Toyo Miyatake.

In the years after World War II, Hugh Macbeth Jr. left his father's firm and built a prosperous law practice. During these years he married and had two children, Hugh III and Douglas. He also took on responsibility for aiding his mother, especially after Hugh Sr. died in 1956. While his direct involvement with Japanese American legal cases wound down after 1949, he maintained close connections with Nikkei communities. During the 1950s Hugh Jr. and his son Douglas became active participants in a social group of Japanese American fathers and sons. Hugh Jr. was pleased to connect with a circle of Nisei friends, as he had in his childhood years, and in the years that followed he attended events and went on several vacation trips with his new buddies. In 1975 Hugh was named a commissioner and judge on the Los Angeles Superior Court. He remained on the bench for a number of years and even presided over the well-publicized divorce proceedings of boxer Mike Tyson and actor Robin Givens. Following his retirement, Hugh Jr. moved to San Francisco, where he lived with his second wife, Maxine (the two had first met decades earlier, at International House, but did not marry until 1994).

In his later years Hugh Jr. was honored for his and his father's outstanding wartime support of Japanese Americans. In 2009, for example, he was invited to be candleholder at a Day of Remembrance (DOR) ceremony in San Francisco (there he met the Nisei activist Kiku Funabiki, who had grown up in the same area of Los Angeles, and the two became fond friends). He was similarly included when the organizers of the annual Manzanar Pilgrimage paid tribute to Hugh Macbeth Sr. in 2013 and again two years later, when he was commemorated at the Los Angeles DOR. Filmmaker Jeffrey Gee Chin and the Little Tokyo Historical Society consulted him as part of their long-term research project on Nikkei editor Sei Fujii and his prewar collaboration with Hugh Macbeth Sr., which eventuated in their 2022 biography of Fujii, *A Rebel's Outcry*.

I first met Hugh Macbeth Jr. early in 2005. Sometime before, while reading through the microfilm papers of Socialist Party leader Norman Thomas, I had come across his extended correspondence with Hugh E. Macbeth of Los Angeles, in which Macbeth furnished him with detailed information about the conditions facing West Coast Japanese Americans. I determined to find out who this Hugh Macbeth was and began collecting papers on him.

While meeting with the veteran attorney and JACL activist Frank Chuman, I asked whether he had ever met Macbeth. Chuman responded with a smile that he had indeed known Macbeth, who was a lawyer of his own generation. This comment puzzled me for some days—I knew that Chuman had been in his mid-twenties during World War II. Finally, it occurred to me that there might be a junior Macbeth. Upon googling, I discovered, in fact, that there were a "Mr. and Mrs. Hugh Macbeth Jr." who were funders of International House in Berkeley. I checked the white pages for the Bay Area and found a listing for a Hugh Macbeth in the Richmond district of San Francisco. I thereupon called and reached Hugh. He confirmed his identity and gladly agreed to let me interview him, and I set an appointment for my next trip to San Francisco.

When I arrived at his house, Hugh greeted me warmly and brought me inside, where I met his wife, Maxine. I sat down with them in their living room, where Hugh's prized portrait by the photographer Toyo Miyatake occupied a prominent place. I explained that I had begun research into the brave efforts of Hugh Sr. to defend Japanese Americans and brought out copies of documents that I had collected, notably the Norman Thomas correspondence. Like the good lawyer and judge that he was, Hugh examined the evidence closely, then sat up and turned to me. In a voice of wonder, mixed with pride, he told me that while he had of course known something of his father's efforts on behalf of Japanese Americans during the time that they were in practice together, he had had no idea of the depth and varied nature of his father's support—especially in the first part of the war years, when Hugh Jr. had been away at law school. He was modest about his own contributions, however, which he said were nothing out of the way.

This first encounter set a pattern for future visits. Whenever I visited San Francisco, I would stop by Hugh and Maxine's house. I would have a drink, or they would make me lunch, and we would chat about life and our activities. They were always glad to talk about their families, and sometimes I met friends or grandchildren there. On one visit, when I told the Macbeths that I was looking for housing for my next trip, they offered to put me up in their guest room. While I felt that I should not burden an elderly couple, I was touched by their friendship and hospitality. After the social part of the visit was over, I would sit down with Hugh in the living room and brief him on my latest researches into his family. He would always marvel over my discoveries—he seemed to radiate gratification and joy. I would ask him for anything he remembered of the history I was tracing. While Hugh usually claimed that he could not recall much, his responses actually provided me a good deal of useful insight into events. He also shared photos and documents with me. I was amazed when he took me to his back office and showed me volumes of the original series of reports by the War Relocation Authority (WRA) on Japanese Americans, a set that he had saved ever since the war years—I was greatly touched when he gave me two of the books as a gift. He also let me look over his family scrapbooks and offered me copies of his official portraits. When I asked whether I might reproduce his prized Toyo Miyatake portrait photo for my 2012 book, *After Camp*, Hugh not only kindly consented but authorized my assistant, Michael Massing, to take the photo out of its frame to make a high-resolution scan of it.

The last time I saw Hugh and Maxine was in 2014. Unlike my other visits, it was a purely social call, with no research or work talk. By that time Hugh was in his mid-nineties, and his health was increasingly frail. I came over in the early evening and brought in Chinese food for us all to eat, so that they would not have to host. It was still nice to spend a little time and chat with them. In the last years, my trips to San Francisco grew more sporadic and rushed. I did not make time to go see the Macbeths again, though I exchanged an occasional email with Maxine.

I will miss Hugh. Though he was already at an advanced age by the time I met him, I feel that my researches enabled me to form a special bond with him. I was honored to bring to public notice the story of his father's heroic defense of Japanese Americans. Hugh told me repeatedly that I had found so much that he had never even suspected about his father. Indeed, at one point he confessed to me that my discoveries had helped him change his own views. Hugh Jr. explained that he had tended to think of his late father mainly as an impractical man who did not concentrate sufficiently on earning money and providing for his wife and family. However, learning of his father's actions, and seeing the friendship and gratitude Japanese Americans expressed to him once those actions became publicly known, had given Hugh a new feeling of admiration and pride in his parent. I can only hope that he recognized, in turn, how much I admired him and how his friendship helped shape my life and career.

SEEKING WILL THOMAS / A FRIEND OF THE NISEI

Beginning in the last decades of the twentieth century, the Asian American experience became a topic of interest in mainstream American society and in the process was enshrined in the nation's literary production. Books by authors of all backgrounds were published, and authors such as Amy Tan, Jhumpa Lahiri, and Viet Thanh Nguyen became bestsellers. During this time the wartime confinement of Japanese Americans, which had already achieved pride of place as the most-studied subject in Asian American history, became a subject for popular literature in many different genres, featuring books produced by Japanese Americans as well as those from other backgrounds. From David Guterson's *Snow Falling on Cedars*, Julie Otsuka's *When the Emperor Was Divine*, and Jamie Ford's *Hotel on the Corner of Bitter and Sweet* to Danielle Steel's *Silent Honor*, numerous authors of mainstream books were inspired to dramatize the wartime events.

In vivid contrast, during the postwar decades, Asian Americans occupied at least as marginal a place in American literature as they did in the writing of the nation's history. Not only were Japanese American novelists unable to make a breakthrough into literary circles, but the group's very existence was ignored

Will Thomas's portrait photo for *The Seeking* (1953).

in the pages of books by the nation's mainstream authors. Even the drama of mass removal and confinement of Japanese Americans failed to stir the hearts of the nation's readers and writers. John Okada's 1957 novel, *No-No Boy*, which has since become a classic work of American ethnic literature, was rejected by mainstream publishing houses. The initial edition was published by Charles Tuttle, a small press, then all but ignored. True, a handful of books produced by mainstream presses during these years told the story of the camps, such as Florence Crannell Means's *The Moved-Outers* (1945), Karon Kehoe's *City in the Sun* (1946), and James Edmiston's *Home Again* (1955), but they remained outside the American canon and are largely forgotten today.

Most prominent (and enduring) among the small selection of postwar literature that referenced the wartime treatment of Japanese Americans were works written by Black American authors. Victims of racial violence and legalized discrimination themselves, African Americans were attentive to racism against other minorities and eloquent in discussing its impact. Chester Himes's 1945 novel *If He Hollers, Let Him Go* includes a powerful indictment of racism against Japanese Americans, crystallized by the narrator's description of a Japanese American child, Riki Oyana, singing "God Bless America" just before he is led off to Santa Anita with his parents. Maya Angelou's memoir *I Know Why the Caged Bird Sings* (1969) speaks in more neutral (or ironic) tones of the mysterious disappearance of Japanese Americans from wartime San Francisco and adds that it was a matter about which African Americans newcomers to the city seemed largely indifferent.

One striking, if little known, piece of African American literature to reference Japanese Americans was the fictionalized memoir *The Seeking* (1953), by author Will Thomas (the pen name of William "Bill" Smith). The book recounts the story of the author's life and his experience dealing with racial prejudice. Because of the pain he suffers in the United States, Thomas is at the point of moving to Haiti with his wife, Helen, and their three young children. Instead, they make a last attempt to find a place for themselves by relocating to Vermont, to which they are drawn by the state's historical opposition to slavery (in 1777 the founding Vermont Constitution abolished slavery—the first state in the United States to do so) and its proximity to Canada. As the only African American family in the village of Westford, Vermont, writes Thomas, they could live a life as human beings, not based on race.

An especially poignant section of the book is devoted to the author's years in Los Angeles in the early 1940s, before he settles in Vermont. Thomas describes how he buys a house in West LA, on a rare street free of restrictive covenants. He and his wife then grow friendly with the Suzukis, a Japanese American family living next door, who teach him how to weed his lawn and plant flowers.

Thomas is stunned by the Pearl Harbor attack (though he notes a sneaking sense of pleasure among many Black friends at seeing a "little Yellow nation" knock white Americans off of their comfortable sense of racial superiority) and dismayed by the rapid emergence of general hostility and suspicion against Japanese Americans.

Two days after the attack, Johnny Suzuki, the family's teenaged son, attempts to enlist in the US Army but is barred on racial grounds. He returns heartbroken and sits out in his backyard wracked with sobs. Thomas is sympathetic to his neighbor's sense of injustice but also ambivalent, given the fact that prewar Japanese Americans, especially in the South, had received what he termed beneficial treatment compared to Blacks. "I tried to soothe the boy, to explain, but my heart wasn't in it and I guess he knew it. Yet I'm sure he didn't understand the irony of my even trying to do so, for probably he did not realize that although browner by far than I, and of alien ancestry, he enjoyed greater general acceptance in my native land than I."

Yet such resentment melts away in the wake of Executive Order 9066. Thomas recounts how outraged he and many African Americans were that his neighbors were being placed in facilities akin to "concentration camps" because of their racial ancestry. Thomas describes saying goodbye to the Suzukis as they are herded off in an army truck to Santa Anita. "When the truck roared up, Mr. Suzuki said in an odd, stilted voice, 'If we never come back, you keep everything, Mist' Thomas. And thank you very much.' Only he said, 'sank you.' 'You'll be back,' I assured him, 'and your things will be right here, waiting.' Our garage and attic were crammed with Suzuki possessions." Thomas describes how he remains haunted by the sight of the removal and the sad resignation of the Suzukis as "the ruin of a golden dream of a sweet land of liberty where freedom rang. Only not for them. Nor, alas, for me."

By the latter part of the book, the author's previous ambivalence toward Japanese Americans as privileged has melted away entirely, and his sense of empathy is displayed in its fullest measure. Thomas is invited to speak at a forum on race relations in a nearby Vermont town. There he meets Samuel Ishikawa, a Nisei from Los Angeles who had been confined in an American concentration camp during the war. "Behind Sam's placid exterior, his grave mien, his solemn manner of speaking, there was a subtle humor which gave sharp point to some of the things he told his audience; and sometimes there was sadness in his words, a wistfulness which bespoke a deep yearning to be accepted as an American in his native land, to discover that America was, after all, the land of the free. How well I understood that."

Upon its publication in 1953, *The Seeking* was crowned with a measure of success. Due in part to the advocacy of Thomas's neighbor, the writer Dorothy Canfield Fisher (who wrote an introduction to the book), *The Seeking* was chosen as a selection by the influential Book-of-the Month Club and became a club bestseller. It received widespread and respectful reviews in the African American press. *Jet* magazine stated that "*The Seeking* has a beautiful message of hope, an omen of the future in race relationships in the US." Dora Reynolds Gebo, speaking in the *Journal of Negro History*, offered praise for Thomas and "the depth of his emotions as he recalls the effect that such incidents as the relocation of the Nisei and the bombing of Hiroshima and Nagasaki had upon him."

After many years in obscurity, the book reappeared in a reprint edition in 2013, with a new afterword by Mark J. Madigan and Dan Gediman that deals with the author's life after *The Seeking*. It remains worth reading for its view of American life and the author's gift for description.

HOWARD THURMAN AND JAPANESE AMERICANS / TOWARD THE BLESSED COMMUNITY *with Peter Eisenstadt*

During the early 1940s, Howard Thurman, a noted orator and writer, was dean of chapel and professor of religion at Howard University, a historically Black university in Washington, DC. He usually spent his summers on the road, traveling to conference centers, retreats, and churches. Despite the wartime conditions, the summer of 1942 was no different. That July his journeys took him as far west as California, where he attended a ten-day Race Relations Institute at Whittier College. During that trip he made it his business to visit an "Assembly Center" for Japanese Americans, presumably at Santa Anita Park, the thoroughbred racetrack in Arcadia, California. As he wrote to a friend: "I saw some of the Japanese internment centers for the Japanese. They are behind eight feet of barbed wire with the outside patrolled day and night with United States soldiers with machine guns. The point that I saw was a former racetrack and houses about 26,000 Japanese. [That number is probably somewhat high.] The horse stalls have been renovated, but I understand that it still smells horsey."

Thurman was born in Florida in 1899 and spent his boyhood in Daytona as the vise of Jim Crow was tightening on the state's Black residents. His was a poor family, headed by his grandmother and mother after his father died when he was eight years old. By dint of his intelligence, ambition, and more than a little luck, he obtained an excellent education, attending the historically Black Morehouse College in Atlanta from 1919 to 1923 and Rochester Theological Seminary in Upstate New York from 1923 to 1926. He was ordained a Baptist minister, but denominations did not matter to him. He was a mystic and thought that the direct experience of God was more important than any religious creed. In the years that followed, he became a popular speaker before both white and Black audiences.

Thurman deserves recognition as the first prominent African American advocate of radical Gandhian nonviolence. In 1935 he headed a four-person "Negro Delegation" to India, Ceylon, and Burma, during which time he was one of the first African Americans to meet with Mahatma Gandhi, the leader of the Indian independence movement. He was a longtime member of the prominent Christian pacifist organization the Fellowship of Reconciliation. In 1940 he became a national vice chair of FOR and would continue in that position during the years of World War II, when it became one of the few

Howard Thurman in later years.
Howard Gotlieb Archival Research Center, Boston University.

national organizations to protest the wartime removal and confinement of Japanese Americans.

Thurman was an opponent of militarism and imperialism of all kinds, including that of Japan. In July 1937, shortly after the commencement of full-scale hostilities between Japan and China, Juanita Harris, a Howard University undergraduate, wrote Thurman a letter stating that she supported Japan's invasion of China because, she insisted, if the Japanese didn't conquer China, "the white man will." Thurman responded that he completely agreed that "the predominant attitude of the white races towards the darker races" was to "hold the darker races in subjection, if not servitude." However, he considered Japan to be the aggressor, adding, "I am fundamentally opposed to imperialism, whether the imperialist be black, yellow, white, or any other color." His pacifism and hatred of imperialism and the subordination of nonwhite peoples would shape his attitudes toward Japanese American confinement.

Thurman's summer 1942 visit to the Assembly Center was not his initial encounter with the wartime plight of Japanese Americans. Several weeks earlier, in April 1942, Kenny Murase, a student at the University of California who was active on the executive committee of the local YMCA Race Relations group, wrote Thurman: "The exigencies of an all-out, total war has made it necessary for me, an American-born Japanese, to withdraw from the University of California to enroll in a university in the east." A friend of Thurman had advised

Murase to apply to Howard University, which, he was told, "would be glad to receive me." Murase continued: "It may seem singularly odd that a Japanese student should be interested in attending a college primarily for Negroes, but . . . belonging personally to a racial minority group presents one concrete basis for my ambitions." (As mentioned in the article on Kenny Murase in this volume, Howard ultimately took no action on Murase's application and scholarship request, and the young man was forced into confinement at Poston).

In April 1943 Thurman received a letter from Emiko Hinoki, a graduate of Mills College in Oakland, California, who was secretary of the Young People's Church Council of the Granada Christian Church in the Granada (Amache) camp. Hinoki asked if he could possibly include a stop there during his summer travels, for "you no doubt have a great and inspiring message to give to [a] minority group such as the Japanese Americans." The leaders of the Amache chapter of the FOR also wrote him asking him to visit. Thurman responded, "I shall be operating on a very close margin of time, but be assured that if it is in the range of human possibility, I shall certainly do this [visit Amache.]" Thurman saw it as a deep obligation to visit the incarcerated Japanese. By May, Thurman had made plans to go from Los Angeles, detour to Amache for a quick stop, and then travel on to Oakland. However, it is unclear if his schedule permitted him to make the stop.

In August 1943, in an article "The Will to Segregation," published in *Fellowship*, the journal of the Fellowship of Reconciliation, Thurman wrote, "The fact that we were attacked by Japan has aggravated greatly the tension between the races. I am not suggesting that the war between Japan and the United States is a race war, but certainly many people have thought of it in terms of a non-white race 'daring' to attack a white race. This has given excellent justification for the expression of the prejudices against non-white people just under the surface of the American consciousness," leading to, on the part of whites, "increasing bitterness, intolerance, and hatred" and often, on the part of Blacks, "reactions in kind."

Nevertheless, while Thurman remained in Washington, DC, his contacts with Japanese Americans and with the realities of mass confinement and its consequences remained rather limited. This changed in the summer of 1944, when he moved to San Francisco as co-pastor of the Church for the Fellowship of All Peoples in San Francisco, one of the first churches in the United States consciously organized on an interracial and interdenominational basis. When Thurman arrived in San Francisco, he immediately realized he had moved to a center of anti-Japanese racism, as he later wrote: "It was not infrequent that one saw billboard caricatures of the Japanese: grotesque faces, huge buck teeth, large dark-rimmed thick-lensed eyeglasses." The point was, in effect, "to read the Japanese out of the human race; they were construed as monsters and as such stood in immediate candidacy for destruction. They were so defined as to be placed in a category to which ordinary decent behavior did not apply. ... It was open season for their potential destruction."

As was the case in many West Coast cities, it was only during World War II that African Americans moved to San Francisco in large numbers. Blacks, lured by opportunities in the defense industry, settled into former Japanese neighborhoods, thereby retaining the formal and informal distinctions between "white" and "nonwhite" neighborhoods. The wartime surge in San Francisco's Black population created a number of social dislocations. The city's new Black neighborhood rapidly became badly overcrowded. Alfred Cleage, who would become the assistant minister to Fellowship Church in early 1944, wrote that "twenty thousand Negroes were crowded into make-shift rooming houses and apartment houses which had accommodated about eight thousand Japanese." Joseph James, a founding member of the Fellowship Church who was also a distinguished concert baritone and shipyard worker, wrote in 1945: "Caucasian San Francisco turned the machinery at hand [formal and informal means of discrimination] for the subjugation of the Oriental and applied it to the Negro." As chairman of San Francisco's NAACP branch, James would concentrate his efforts on welcoming returning Japanese Americans. In mid-1944 the San Francisco NAACP passed a resolution drawn up by James "calling for fair treatment of loyal Japanese-Americans and condemning efforts of reactionary interests to incite suspicion among Americans of African ancestry for Americans of Japanese ancestry." The following year James joined a delegation that met with state attorney general Robert Kenny to discuss ways to end violence against Japanese American resettlers.

As Japanese Americans moved back to San Francisco, Thurman found ways to support them. In fall 1944 the Japanese American Citizens League petitioned the Western Defense Command for permission to open a San Francisco office, and in October 1944 JACL president Saburo Kido met with the West Coast defense commander, Gen. Charles Bonesteel, who authorized the JACL to open its office as soon as the US Army lifted the official exclusion of Japanese Americans from the West Coast. With Bonesteel's consent, the JACL sent Teiko Ishida, who had been serving as office manager and fundraiser at the wartime

JACL offices in Salt Lake City and New York, to San Francisco to prepare. Once Ishida arrived, Howard Thurman offered her a job as a temporary secretary, and she worked with him until January 1945, when the new office formally opened its doors. He declared that Ishida, besides bringing "order to the chronic chaos in which I have been living and functioning," participated in the life of the church. In December 1944 there was a dinner with what Thurman called an "interracial menu." Thurman cooked 122 pieces of fried chicken—he was an excellent cook—and "a Filipino gentleman prepared the Filipino sauce in which the chicken was steeped, and Miss Ishida, our temporary secretary, prepared the rice."

In December 1944, after the US Army announced that the official exclusion of Japanese Americans from the West Coast would be lifted, the Gannon Committee, a California state assembly "fact-finding" committee, publicly declared that the "overwhelming opinion" of Californians was against the return of Japanese Americans and warned of violence against resettlers. Thurman signed a petition prepared by the Pacific Coast Committee on American Principles and Fair Play that refuted such claims and denounced the committee for its "gospel of fear" in predicting violence. In 1945 Thurman and Joe Grant Masaoka of the Japanese American Citizens League attended together the eleventh anniversary celebration of the Northern California Chapter of the American Civil Liberties Union, where they reported on the problems facing African Americans and Japanese Americans. In December 1946 Thurman was principal speaker at the annual dinner of the California State Council for Civic Unity, a San Francisco–based interracial group heavily engaged in promoting Japanese American resettlement. According to the Nisei newspaper *Progressive News*, Thurman "stressed the importance of continuing the tremendous gains in race unity which grow directly out of wartime conditions, into all future programs of inter-race relations." By the following year Thurman had joined the board of the organization, renamed the California Federation for Civic Unity.

Thurman's support was greatly appreciated by Japanese Americans. Tomi Fujino, who heard Thurman speak at a national convention of the Young Women's Christian Association in San Francisco in March 1947, described him as "inspiring." Japanese Canadian Norah Fujita, who was sponsored by the activist group Japanese Canadian Committee for Democracy to attend an interracial workshop in Washington, DC, in summer 1947, reported in the *New Canadian* that she was particularly inspired by hearing Thurman's words comparing the sufferings of African Americans under Jim Crow with those of the Apostle Paul when set upon by mobs and Roman police. "And the depth of loyalty, charity, and forgiveness of the American Negro Christians is something before which we can all stand in shame."

It was as co-pastor of the Fellowship Church that Howard Thurman made his greatest contribution to working with Japanese Americans. As mentioned previously, in 1944 Thurman was invited to join a white minister, Alfred Fisk, as co-pastor of the new church, which was one of the first churches in the United States organized on an intentionally interracial and interreligious basis. The assignment was sufficiently noteworthy that on his departure from Howard in May 1944, Thurman was feted at a gala in which the guest speaker, First Lady Eleanor Roosevelt, wished him success in the undertaking. Mrs. Roosevelt would remain a "national associate and donor" of the Fellowship Church.

Although ethnic Japanese, excluded from the West Coast and confined by official order, formed a rather ghostly presence in San Francisco at the time of Thurman's initial arrival, the local Japanese community was critical to the history of the Fellowship Church. The first home of the church was the small Japanese Presbyterian church in the prewar Japanese neighborhood dubbed "Little Osaka." The church was formed, in turn, with help from a group of young female college graduates who lived together in a Gandhian commune, or ashram. Their collective was known as the Sakai group because they lived together in a house formerly owned by a Mr. Sakai.

From its founding in early 1944, the Fellowship Church was concerned with the plight of San Francisco's Japanese Americans. One of the founding members of the church was Annie Clo Watson, leader of the International Institute of San Francisco, an offshoot of the YWCA. In addition to her efforts to win better treatment for Japanese Americans in the camps, she published an article on the subject, "Americans on the Fringes," in the *Journal of Educational Sociology*. By the fall of 1944, when Thurman's wife, Sue Bailey Thurman, joined its board of directors, the International Institute was gearing up to help prepare for the return of the former inmates to the city. In May 1945 Sue Bailey Thurman likewise reported to the *Chicago Defender* on her work attending sessions of the San Francisco organizing conference of the United Nations and sitting in the "dress circle" of the San Francisco Opera House as a "national observer." In repeating dialogue among observers about Japanese Americans, she took the opportunity to remind her readers about the 17,600 soldiers of Japanese ancestry fighting for the United Nations, especially the exploits of the 100th Battalion in Italy.

Beginning in January 1945, as exclusion was lifted and the WRA camps began to close, the former Japanese residents of San Francisco, plus others who had formerly lived in rural areas, started to trickle into the city in hopes of restarting their interrupted lives. The Fellowship Church made a special effort to welcome the returnees, holding a dinner in February 1945 for 24 Japanese Americans, who were the guests of honor at a dinner alongside 130 Fellowship Church members and friends. In June 1945 the church hosted Hugh E. Macbeth, an African American lawyer from Los Angeles deeply involved in the struggle for Japanese American rights (as explained further in the article on Macbeth in this volume), as the guest speaker on a Sunday morning.

As they returned, Japanese Americans soon became a crucial part of the Fellowship Church. In March 1945, answering an urgent appeal by Thurman, the church hired Ayoka Murota, recently returned from the camps, as its secretary. Thurman would later write in his autobiography that a few months later, he would take the time to sit in his office and hold her hand, "from 8:30 in the morning until 2:00 in the afternoon while the tidings of Hiroshima were coming across the air. Her aunts, her uncles, her nephews were all there. Now and then, the grip of my hand would tighten on hers, or the grip of her hand would tighten in mine. There were no words for words were raspy noises, unuttered in the discipline that would make manifest what was stirring in our hearts."

By the end of 1945, Dave Tatsuno, president of the San Francisco chapter of the Japanese American Citizens League (and later creator of an award-winning film, *Topaz*, about his experience in camp), had joined the church's board of trustees. Under his leadership, Thurman would write, "the Sunday school was largely Japanese-American with a few Caucasians and a few Negroes." Japanese American attendance declined over the next few years. Even as the Fellowship Church moved to a new building outside the Japanese district, the prewar Japanese churches reopened, and many Japanese churchgoers chose to return to their former congregations. Still, by 1948, according to an article in the *Atlanta Daily World*, a Sunday service held by Thurman drew "250 men and women of all races. . . . Half the congregation was white, a third Negro, and the rest Japanese, Chinese, and Filipinos."

One of Thurman's strongest Japanese American connections was with John Yamashita, a Nisei Methodist minister. Even before moving to San Francisco, Thurman was already acquainted with the Yamashita family. In summer 1942 John's sister Kay had attended a race relations institute at Mills College where

Thurman was a guest speaker. Then, in February 1945, John met up with Thurman in Ann Arbor, Michigan, while traveling through the East. In 1947 and 1948 John Yamashita as engaged by the Fellowship Church as an assistant minister, preaching one Sunday per month. In hopes of obtaining his services, Thurman wrote to a Methodist minister in May 1947:

> Because of the general climate on the Pacific Coast that in some ways is not congenial to Japanese Americans, we are particularly anxious to provide an experience of complete integration within our religious fellowship on all levels of participation in what we are doing. It would be a very great thing if there were at least one church on the Pacific Coast in which these people shared the leadership and membership participation as a part of a fellowship of heterogenous people. I need not tell you that they have sustained a profound injury both spiritually and psychologically from which it is extraordinarily difficult for them to emerge with some measure of vitality and health as American citizens.

Thurman's approach to this sort of dislocation, for African Americans, for Japanese Americans, for any minority group, was not to pity nor to try to "help" from a position of authority and superiority but to include them as equals, as is clear in this description of a meeting of a young adult group in the church from 1947: "An open fire cracked and popped. Hearthside rays glanced from an East Indian reflected to the intense faces—the faces of young people in discussion—all young Americans—a Negro sailor from Chicago, a Nisei girl, a native San Franciscan, a Caucasian from a southern state, a Filipino youth leader.... Questions, answers, opinions flew back and forth. Suddenly the mugs of cocoa appeared, the discussion drew to a close.... The whole group joined in laughter, song, and fun."

In August 1952 the old Booker T. Washington Community Center, a long-standing community center for African Americans that had moved into a former Japanese language school building during World War II, opened a new facility to be used as a community center by people of all races and creeds. Howard Thurman, presiding at the dedication, stated: "There is not a person here tonight who could hold a straight and honest face if we were dedicating a center—a community center—for one race at the exclusion of another. Since the First World War, the whole idea of people being separate has changed. And so tonight I am able to join with you of many races in opening a center for the whole community."

Within a year after that night, Thurman left San Francisco and the Fellowship Church to take up a position as dean of chapel at Boston University, remaining in that position until his retirement in 1965. After his retirement he returned to San Francisco, where he maintained an active schedule of writing, preaching, and lecturing until shortly before his death in April 1981. His commitment to Gandhian nonviolence and social change influenced Dr. Martin Luther King Jr. and other civil rights activists.

Apart from occasional visits with the Yamashitas, Thurman had little direct contact with Japanese Americans in his later years. Yet he retained the spirit of his Fellowship Church and spent his life trying to create a world community in which different peoples and different religions would draw strength from their differences. In 1960 he visited Japan, where he connected with peace activists who were "opposed to anything that might portend a future Hiroshima for themselves, or mankind anywhere." Thurman concluded his philosophical masterwork, *The Search for Common Ground* (1971), by saying that "community cannot feed on itself, it can only flourish where always the boundaries are giving way to the coming of others beyond them."

Howard Thurman was a shy man who avoided the spotlight and did not lead large protests or write best-selling books. It is to be hoped that the publication in recent years of several volumes of his papers and speeches will help make his remarkable career and ideas better known.

Chapter 2

JAPANESE AMERICANS AND INTERRACIALISM

FROM KENNY MURASE TO KENJI MURASE / THE JOURNEY OF A NISEI WRITER, SCHOLAR, AND ACTIVIST

The life of Kenji Murase, a Nisei litterateur, activist, and social scientist, illustrates some of the challenges faced by Nisei intellectuals in the mid-twentieth century. Although he came from a poor farming family and had to scramble to get an education, Murase threw himself into progressive literary and political movements. Years later, even after he became a distinguished professor, he retained his focus on community empowerment.

Kenji Kenneth Murase was born in Parlier, California, near Fresno, in January 1920 (while his birth and marriage certificates listed January 9 as his date of birth, Murase claimed January 3 as his birthday). Known in his youth as "Kenny," he was the second of three sons of Mantsuchi (Manzuchi) and Moto Murase, Japanese immigrants who eked out a living as sharecroppers working in the grape fields. According to the later testimony of his daughter Emily Murase, the family had so little money that they made clothing at home, sewing shirts from rice sacks. Murase attended Parlier Union High School, where he joined the track and basketball teams. He graduated in 1938 as co-valedictorian. During his teen years he became interested in writing and published an essay in *Scholastic* magazine.

Murase later recounted that he did not go directly to college after graduating high school, due to family opposition and financial concerns. Instead, he worked as a farm laborer during the day and wrote in the evening. During this time he made contacts with Nisei in Los Angeles and soon started working as a columnist and fiction writer for the local Nisei press. In June 1939 he published a short story, "Resurrection," in *Kashū Mainichi*. It was the tale of a Nisei, embittered by prejudice, who is shocked to discover the more severe discrimination faced by Blacks. (This story is discussed more fully in the section "African American Scratches on a Nikkei Canvas" in this volume.) He followed

Kenji Murase in a casual snapshot. Courtesy of the family of Kanji Murase.

that in October 1939 with "Gummed Up," a baseball story, and in December 1939 with a satirical romance entitled "By the Time You Read This." Meanwhile, he began a regular column for *Kashū Mainichi*, dubbed "Perpetual Notion." In its pages he pursued a mock feud with "Napoleon," his friend and fellow columnist Hisaye Yamamoto, who blasted Murase as a pimply-faced stuffed shirt. The young Kenny also contributed a short story about Nisei farmers to the 1940 new year issue of *Nichi Bei* (around that time the Murase family bought a farm near Reedley, California, and relocated there).

By the beginning of 1940, Murase enrolled at UCLA. During this period he expanded his press activity. He penned a short story, "That Old Indian Summer," for *Rafu Shimpo*, wrote a regular column for the short-lived Nisei newspaper *Japanese American Mirror*, and in November 1940 began a new column for *Nichi Bei* (first called "Nocturne" and later "The Sixth Column"). He likewise contributed articles to James Omura's monthly magazine, *Current Life*. Murase's piece in the October 1940 issue, "Who's Who in the Nisei Literary World," was a jokey guide to the circles of West Coast Japanese American litterateurs. For example, he described his close friend and fellow progressive activist Warren Tsuneishi as "an ultra-reactionary and rugged individualist (weak emphasis on 'rugged') [who] adores girls with 'exquisite lips.'" In later issues he analyzed the work of popular Armenian American author William Saroyan, whom he claimed as a model for second-generation creative artists.

Even as he threw himself into literature, Kenny Murase became absorbed in progressive politics, and he connected his creative vision with his commitment to racial equality. In November 1940 the *Fresno Bee* published his letter scoring racial discrimination against "American-born Japanese." In the letter he contended that "American society has failed to function properly in relation to its diverse racial elements" because of the general tendency by hostile whites to assume that those of foreign ancestry were attached to their ancestral nations. Murase countered that the Nisei were loyal to the United States and democracy: "[We] cannot accept the totalitarianism which is rampant in the country of our ancestors. We recognize the war in China for what it is, an imperialistic war of aggression, and we will have none of it." In a period when the Nikkei press generally either supported Japanese foreign policy or remained silent, this was a powerful statement of opposition.

At the same time as he defended Nikkei to outsiders, Kenny Murase addressed his fellow Nisei. In several articles he underlined the responsibility of Nisei writers to offer leadership to the rest of the community, even as writers from other racial and ethnic groups had done, and win Japanese Americans outside recognition as a dynamic minority. For the new year 1941 issue of *Nichi Bei*, he penned a column with a daring title, "What I Saw in a Hashish Dream." It was a frank exploration of the plight of the Nisei in which he excoriated group members for their insularity and stifling group consciousness. "The immediate security and congenial relations that [the Nisei] has found among his fellow nisei has perhaps satisfied him; but at the same time, it has built around him an impenetrable shell of indifference to the existence of other racial minorities and their problems which are not exactly diametrically opposite. As long as the nisei insists . . . upon clinging to the myopic viewpoint of working only among his own group and ignoring the Italians, Poles, Jews, Chinese, Negroes, and other minorities, his will be a lonely and a futile cry in the vast wilderness of apathy and scorn." The solution, he contended, lay in organizing through churches and in political action. Murase respectfully critiqued the JACL, which he found too patriotic and insufficiently focused on intergroup action. "We have known JACL workers to be earnest, conscientious, and unquestionably sincere; but at the same time, we have also known JACL leaders to be opportunists and lacking in a clarity of vision. It is not in them wholly, however, that the ailment of the JACL lies; it is in their program that we find inadequacy and misdirection."

In 1941 Murase enrolled at UC Berkeley as an English major. He scaled back his writing for the daily Nisei press, though he continued to contribute to *Current Life*. He rapidly joined assorted progressive on-campus clubs such as the Welfare Council of the Associated Students of the University of California and was named to the executive committee of the local YMCA Race Relations group. Around this time Murase joined the Nisei Young Democrats of Oakland and was named the group's educational chairman. Through the Nisei Young Democrats, he collaborated actively with African American attorney Walter Gordon in his campaign against restrictive covenants in the East Bay that limited housing opportunities for minorities.

Because of his literary flair and progressive political interests, Murase became a point man connecting Nisei outsiders on campus. Murase grew especially close with James Sakoda, then a graduate student, with whom he moved together into a shack in Berkeley. He soon also connected with other socially minded Nisei such as Tamotsu Shibutani, Warren Tsuneishi, and Charles Kikuchi. In fall 1941 Kikuchi and Murase collaborated on a review of Louis Adamic's book *Two Way Passage* for *Rafu Shimpo*, and the two friends led a symposium in Berkeley on Nisei and labor. Murase moderated the meeting, and Kikuchi presented the findings of his survey of Nisei employment.

Following the Pearl Harbor attack and the outbreak of the Pacific War, Kenny Murase was invited to join the Nisei Writers and Artists Mobilization for Democracy (NWAMD). On behalf of the NWAMD, he wrote a column for *Nichi Bei* in March 1942 expressing frustration over anti-Nisei discrimination and impending mass removal, which was occurring because, he said, "our folks are considered in the camp of the enemy and the Army can't afford to take chances with us." Still, he reminded his readers that in an Axis country they risked being sent to real concentration camps. He further suggested that the wartime events had an unexpected benefit in permitting the Nisei to emancipate themselves at a single stroke from Issei leaders, who had delayed their entry into the American social and economic mainstream. The Nisei, he proclaimed, should look beyond their personal interest and join the struggle to destroy the Axis powers.

As mass removal turned into mass confinement, Murase's resentment over the injustice to the group mounted. In a letter to author Carey McWilliams, he noted: "We are not going to camp because of 'military necessity.' We know that such a reason is groundless. We are going because groups of native American fascists were able to mislead an uninformed American public, and this partly because we were uninformed and unaware of our responsibility as one integral part of the democratic process." During early 1942 he published a pair of letters in the *Fresno Bee* defending the Americanism of the Nisei (and immigrants generally) against racist attacks on their loyalty.

Sometime before the end of the spring 1942 term, Murase left Berkeley and returned to his family farm in Reedley. Reedley lay in Military Area 2, outside of the main West Coast excluded zone, so the Murase family was not taken away to the Assembly Centers during spring 1942. Because of his interest in race relations, Murase applied to transfer to Howard University, an African American university in Washington, DC. He had no money for his studies, so he also applied for a scholarship. Howard officials failed to act on his request. Their official reason was that they were not certain whether Nisei students could be admitted into the East Coast Defense zone. It seems plausible, however, that they also failed to act because they were less than enthusiastic about admitting him in the face of widespread prejudice against Japanese Americans.

Even after the West Coast Defense Command announced that, contrary to their previous promise, Military Area 2 would be emptied of its ethnic Japanese population, Murase hoped to move out and continue his education. Soon after, Murase was invited by Rev. Owen Geer, the pastor of the Mt. Olivet Baptist Church in Dearborn, Michigan, to join an interracial work camp there, and he applied to the Army Provost Marshal's Office for permission to leave, but he was turned down. Facing confinement, Murase applied to go to Tule Lake, where he could join the Japanese Evacuation Research Survey project there. However, the authorities sent him to the Poston camp.

In August 1942 Kenny Murase arrived at Poston with his parents and brothers. He soon was invited to join the Bureau of Sociological Research (BSR), where he worked under the direction of Dr. Alexander Leighton. He also volunteered to assist JERS researcher Tamie Tsuchiyama. Meanwhile, Murase returned to journalism. First, he took the position of acting city editor of the *Poston III Press Bulletin*. In addition to his editing work, he was invited to write for the *Pacific Citizen* by editor Larry Tajiri (whom Murase had gotten to know in San Francisco when they both worked with the NWAMD). During September and October 1942 Murase produced several installments of a column, Whistling in the Dark. The column featured "Little Esteban," an imaginary Mexican Native American "sagebrush imp" who was a form of resident spirit of Poston and who appeared to the narrator and engaged him in a series of dialogues.

Murase used these dialogues to speak on such topics as avoiding useless divisions between the inmates and obtaining recreational facilities for confined children. Murase was so concerned about the lack of equipment and the danger of juvenile delinquency and demoralization if youngsters in Poston lacked recreational outlets that he sent a letter to the *San Francisco Chronicle* appealing for donations of equipment, including sporting goods, toys, and games. The letter appeared in the *Chronicle*'s September 18, 1942, issue and led to the creation among Bay Area white supporters of a "Murase baseball fund" to purchase extra play equipment.

In the end Murase was able to leave Poston in early October 1942, barely two months following his arrival. Even in confinement, Murase did not cease his efforts to transfer to an outside college. In early September he wrote in a letter to M. Margaret Anderson, editor of the magazine *Common Ground*, that he was planning to enroll at the University of Nebraska as one of the first three Poston Nisei admitted to outside colleges through the new National Japanese American Student Relocation Council (NJASRC). In order to leave, he required FBI clearance and an armed escort out of the camp. Hoping to get to join the work camp in Dearborn that had previously accepted him, Murase initially applied for admission to Wayne State University in nearby Detroit and was granted a scholarship there. Reverend Geer proposed bringing Murase to resettle there. The Dearborn Safety Commission vetoed the plan, and when Reverend Geer requested an open hearing on the matter, three hundred local residents attended the meeting to protest the idea. In the face of public hostility, Wayne State University withdrew its acceptance. Soon after, Murase was accepted by Haverford University, an elite Quaker institution in the suburbs of Philadelphia. Within a week of his arrival, though, he decided that Haverford was not a good fit for him—he later described his feelings of discomfort upon moving into a residence with a servant who made his bed every day. With help from a local professor, he transferred to Temple University in Center City Philadelphia.

Murase spent two years at Temple. His studies were funded by a scholarship offered through the American Baptist Home Missionary Society, and he worked as a janitor at a settlement house and also as a staffer for the NJASRC.

Murase became well known on campus after he contributed an essay, entitled "What Are We Fighting For?" that won second prize in a campus contest and was published in Temple's student newspaper. Murase sent back a handful of articles for publication in the *Pacific Citizen* and the *Poston Chronicle* (articles that were reprinted in the Japanese Canadian newspaper *New Canadian*). His letter to Carey McWilliams from 1942 was cited in the article "The Nisei Speak" in the magazine *Common Ground*. In 1943 he participated in an Institute on Minorities sponsored by the Youth Committee for Democracy and led a discussion on "Economic Factors in Minority Problems."

While at Temple, Murase become reacquainted with Kimi Tanaka, whom he had first met at Poston, and the two became a couple. They lived in an interracial cooperative in Philadelphia called Brudercoop. After Murase completed a bachelor of arts degree in sociology at Temple in February 1944, the couple married and moved to New York, where Murase was hired as an aide in a social service agency. He also worked as a feature writer and rewrite man for the *News Letter* of the antifascist Japanese American Committee for Democracy (JACD). In 1945, after the West Coast reopened to Japanese Americans, Murase returned to Reedley with his wife and worked on the family farm. He later explained that he felt duty-bound to replace his two brothers, who were in military service. (Though Murase was quoted in an April 1943 Associated Press article that he was anxious to enlist, he did not serve during the war.)

After several months, the Murases moved back to New York. At first Kenny was excited about reuniting with the dynamic progressive Japanese Americans he had known before the war, such as Joe Oyama, Dyke Miyagawa, Chiye Mori, Eddie Shimano, and Ernest and Chizu Iiyama. Murase attended meetings of the Nisei Progressives and wrote articles and assisted with production of the short-lived newspaper the *Nisei Weekender*. However, he found that Nisei circles in New York were too diffuse and lacked the cohesive energy of prewar groups such as the Oakland Nisei Democrats.

During this period Murase enrolled in Columbia University's School of Social Work. He later recalled that one of his first assignments as a student was as a fieldworker in a welfare office in a Black community in Brooklyn and that seeing the oppressive living and working conditions his African American clients faced strongly shaped his ideas. After receiving his master's degree in 1947, Kenneth Murase (as he then called himself) worked as a social worker in the psychiatric division of King County Hospital, then later moved to the children's court in Manhattan, which he considered a very rich experience.

He separated from his wife during this period and took up residence in the East Village.

After 1951 Kenneth Murase turned to teaching and academics. His first teaching job was as a lecturer in the School of Social Work at the University of Minnesota. In 1952 he was named as the first American Fulbright Scholar in Japan (it is not clear whether he was also the first Nisei Fulbright Scholar). He spent that year as a visiting professor of social welfare at Osaka University. Although he originally planned to do research on juvenile delinquents, he ended up studying the needs of war orphans and teaching social work. Following his return to the United States, he took a position as assistant professor at the School of Social Work at the University of Washington. He remained there for three years. During this period he published a set of professional articles and book reviews in *Social Service Review*, beginning with the study "Some Considerations for Programs of Social and Technical Assistance" in the September 1955 issue. He also met a Japanese-born student named Miyako Ohno. The two were married in Oregon in 1954.

In 1956 Murase returned to New York and enrolled once more at Columbia University for his doctoral studies. He served as a teaching fellow at the New York School of Social Work at the same time. He received a doctorate in social work in 1961 from Columbia. His dissertation, entitled "International Students in Education for Social Work," traced the experiences of foreign students in US doctoral programs in social work during the previous decade.

After graduation, Murase served as the director of the Intercountry Social Services Research Project at Columbia University. He worked with the Mobilization for Youth Project, which involved low-income, ethnic minority households in Manhattan's Lower East Side. In 1965 he was hired by the American Friends Service Committee. During this period he married his third wife, Seiko. The couple had three children, daughters Emily and Miriam and son Geoffrey.

In 1967 Dr. Kenji Murase (he switched in these years to using his Japanese name) was recruited as one of the first faculty members at the newly formed Graduate School of Social Work & Social Research at San Francisco State University, where he taught for twenty-three years. He later founded its Institute for Multicultural Research and Social Work Practice. While at San Francisco State, Murase coauthored the guide *Social Work Practice with Asian Americans* (1993) and contributed to the anthology *Community Organizing with People of Color* (1991).

In addition to mentoring students and publishing scholarly research,

Kenji Murase devoted his time to helping meet the social service and mental health needs of Asian American communities. He did this not only through his scholarship but also through his grant writing and executive board work with nonprofits. For example, Murase wrote the grant application to the United Way that resulted in the founding of the San Francisco–based social service programs United Japanese Community Services, the Japanese Community Youth Council, and Kimochi, Inc. He produced a guide to health care services, *Home Care: A Help Guide to Japanese American Seniors and Their Families* (1994).

Murase also worked with the Pacific Asian Mental Health Research Project. In particular, he directed a study under its auspices, "Alternative Service Delivery Models in Pacific / Asian American Communities" (1981), which analyzed fifty community-based agencies providing mental health–related services to Pacific / Asian American communities in Seattle, the San Francisco Bay Area, San Diego, and Los Angeles. Murase took a special interest in the health needs of Southeast Asian refugees. In 1991 he codirected a survey for San Francisco's Department of Public Health that took as its subject Southeast Asians living in San Francisco's Tenderloin district and their level of information concerning AIDS and the means of preventing its transmission. The result was a text coauthored with Susan Sung and Vu-Duc Vuong, *AIDS Knowledge, Attitudes, Beliefs and Behaviors in Southeast Asian Communities in San Francisco* (1991). Released at a time when same-sex sexuality in immigrant communities was stigmatized and free discussions rare, this was an especially important study.

Murase never forgot his camp experience and the scholarship he had obtained through the NJASRC, which had made it possible for him to attend Temple University. In 1980 he and other beneficiaries created the Nisei Student Relocation Commemorative Fund as a way of passing on the gift. The fund-raised money for college scholarships for children of Southeast Asian refugee families who had arrived in the United States without funds. He later stated that his work with the fund was the most satisfying of all his community activities.

In his later years Murase returned to his intellectual roots by working to preserve and further the cultural heritage of Japanese Americans. In a 1996 panel discussion, Murase defined Japanese American cultural heritage as "those cultural values which were transmitted from the Issei generation to the succeeding generations." Such values, he added, contributed to the Nikkei having the highest per capita and median family income among Asian Americans and also the most education, the lowest rates of crime, mental illness, alcoholism, drug addiction, and AIDS as well as the longest life spans. As part of this mission, he collaborated with the Japanese Cultural and Community Center of Northern California, of which he was a founder, and wrote historical articles for *Nikkei Heritage*, the magazine of the National Japanese American Historical Society. His article on the death of Seiichi Nakahara, an Issei taken into custody in 1942 as an "enemy alien," was also featured in *Discover Nikkei*. On June 2, 2009, at the age of eighty-nine, Dr. Kenji Murase died of cancer at his San Francisco home.

MARI SABUSAWA MICHENER / CHAMPION OF CIVIL RIGHTS AND SUPPORTER OF THE ARTS

One arena of public life in which Japanese Americans have achieved great visibility during the twentieth century is the visual arts. A constellation of brilliant Nisei creators—among them Isamu Noguchi, Ruth Asawa, George Nakashima, Shinkichi Tajiri, Frank Okada, and Satoru Abe—achieved fame on the national and international level for their work. Curiously, one outstanding Nisei contributor to the American artistic and literary scene was Mari Sabusawa Michener, a woman who seems never to have produced any artwork or creative fiction on her own. Rather, she and her husband, the prolific novelist James A. Michener, built up a vast collection of contemporary American art and donated an estimated $100 million in money and artwork to museums, universities, and other institutions. Yet before her years as writer's muse and philanthropist, Mari Sabusawa Michener built an impressive career as an activist and civil rights advocate, a mission that strongly influenced her later development.

Mari Yoriko Sabusawa was born on June 17, 1920, in Las Animas, Colorado, the daughter of Sutakichi Sabusawa, a melon farmer and housecleaner who died in 1929. In 1936 Mary Sabusawa, as she was then known, moved with her family to Long Beach, California. It is unclear whether the Sabusawas were connected to the Sugihara family, who had moved from Las Animas to Long Beach earlier, but it seems likely. The Sugiharas operated a produce market in Long Beach, while Mary's older brother Harry was listed in census reports as a produce market worker. Mary attended the same church and school as Ina Sugihara, a year her senior—a woman who would herself go on to make important contributions as a journalist and civil rights activist in New York City. Mary Sabusawa attended high school at Long Beach Polytechnic and was part of its Japanese Friendship Circle. She also joined the Nipponettes, a local Nisei girls club. Meanwhile, she became active in Long Beach's Japanese Presbyterian church, serving as secretary and chairman of the local branch of Christian Endeavor. She served as art director for the church's young people's biweekly magazine, the *Sea-Shell*. She played a part in a Christian play, *The Cross Triumphant*, that was performed there.

After graduating from high school, in 1938, Mary Sabusawa attended Long Beach Junior College. During this period she became active with the local JACL, serving as an officer. Her fellow Nisei remarked on her intelligence and leadership skills. In September 1941 she won the Southern District JACL oratorical contest. The topic of her address was "What Is Our Part in the Present Emergency?"

Sabusawa hoped to enroll at UC Berkeley, where Ina Sugihara had taken up studies. However, in spring 1942, following Executive Order 9066, Sabusawa was sent with her family into confinement at Santa Anita and then to the Amache camp in Colorado (ironically, it was located only fifty miles from her hometown of Las Animas). Almost no sooner did Sabusawa arrive in camp, however, than she was permitted to leave. Through the efforts of John W. Thomas of the American Baptist Home Mission Society, she was offered a scholarship at Antioch College in Yellow Springs, Ohio.

Sabusawa, the first-ever Japanese American student at Antioch, majored in political science and international relations there. She served as chairman of Antioch's College Race Relations Committee for two quarters, during which she helped raise scholarship funds to bring three outstanding Black students to attend the school (one of the three students was Edythe Scott, who was joined at Antioch soon after by her younger sister, the future activist Coretta Scott King). As a student representative on the Community Council, Sabusawa delivered talks on Japanese Americans at outside venues. In October 1944, for example, she and her fellow student Nao Okuda spoke before the Co-operative Club in Xenia, Ohio, on the social, economic, and political problems faced by resettlers.

Through Antioch's cooperative job program, Sabusawa spent a term in Washington, DC, where she analyzed Japanese news and propaganda for the Foreign Broadcast Intelligence Service. In 1944–45 she moved to Chicago, where she was hired by the American Council on Race Relations (ACRR), a newly formed race relations clearing house and lobbying group. At ACRR Sabusawa worked with its director, Robert Weaver, a Harvard-trained economist who in 1965 would become the first African American cabinet officer, serving as the initial secretary of the new Department of Housing and Urban Development under President Lyndon B. Johnson.

In 1946, following the end of World War II, Mari Sabusawa (as she now called herself) enrolled in a graduate sociology program at the University of Chicago, specializing in race relations. Around the same time, she was hired as assistant director of ACRR—in the process becoming a full-time professional in race relations work. During her tenure the ACRR sponsored studies on housing and job discrimination against African Americans and other minorities and provided information to the general public. For example, the ACRR engaged sociologist Setsuko Matsunaga Nishi, Sabusawa's fellow graduate student at University of Chicago, to compile an antiracist pamphlet, *Facts about Japanese Americans*. In 1946 Sabusawa returned to Antioch to speak at a conference on "Techniques for Good Race Relations," on behalf of the ACRR. In 1947 she hosted a summer institute at the University of Chicago on "Race Relations and Community Organization," jointly sponsored by the university and the ACRR. In addition to her duties as a host, she was assigned to conduct preliminary research work in preparation for the institute. One year later she was invited by Mary McLeod Bethune, director of the National Council Negro Women (NCNW), to serve as an ACRR representative on a national human relations committee sponsored by the NCNW.

No doubt because of her experiences at Antioch and with the ACRR, Sabusawa took a broader view of racial questions. Longtime *Pacific Citizen* editor Harry Honda, who had known her from prewar days, described Sabusawa as "liberal minded with reference to minorities in the United States. She was a very outgoing person, very intelligent, interested in all kinds of issues, not necessarily Nisei issues but overall, including national politics." Following a 1947 interview with Sabusawa in the *PC* (which was then reprinted in the Canadian newspaper *Nisei Affairs*), author John Kitasako described her orientation: "As far as the Nisei are concerned, Mari thinks that many of them should overcome the tendency of regarding themselves as an isolated issue, an attitude stemming from the glaring spotlight as on the discrimination of the Nisei during the war years. They should realize that their problems are not wholly distinct but are also the problems with which other minorities must cope."

Within her larger focus, Sabusawa supported resettlement and equal rights for Nisei, especially through the JACL. In 1947 she became the first chair of the new JACL Midwest District Council and proceeded to organize several new chapters in areas surrounding Chicago. The following year she was elected president of the league's Chicago chapter. Also at this time, she joined the JACL's national board and served as national secretary for two years. In 1950 Sabusawa held the position of public relations chair for the eleventh JACL national conference, held in Chicago. Four years later she served on the committee that selected the Nisei of the Biennium. During 1954–55 she represented the JACL on the board of Chicago's Council Against Discrimination.

In 1950 the ACRR folded, and Sabusawa took up a new job as assistant editor of the American Library Association's *Bulletin*. However, she remained engaged in community work. It was Sabusawa's activism that led to a dramatic shift in her life. During the early 1950s she volunteered for work with a Chicago committee that assisted with resettlement of GIs who had married Japanese women. In late 1954 she was one of a group of local JACL members who were invited to a lunch sponsored by *Life* magazine, whose editors had commissioned a story on Japanese "war brides" in the Chicago area. There Sabusawa met the best-selling novelist James A. Michener, who had been commissioned by *Life* to write the story. Michener had gained fame through books such as *Tales of the South Pacific* and *Sayonara* that featured white-Asian couples and explored the harmful impact of racism. She told the author candidly that she disapproved of the sad conclusion of *Sayonara*, which seemed to suggest that interracial couples such as those in the novel faced a tragic end. The two hit it off nonetheless, and they corresponded over the months that followed, during which time Michener was traveling abroad.

Following Michener's return to the United States, in 1955, he and Mari Sabusawa became a serious couple. The two were an odd match in certain respects. James A. Michener was forty-eight years old, had already been twice married and divorced, and was generally known as a rather self-contained and private person. Mari Sabusawa was in her mid-thirties, and while she had previously had relationships with other men—she was publicly linked with famed Chicago novelist Nelson Algren—she had never been married. She had an outgoing personality and loved socializing and gossip. Friends described her as warmhearted but also frank and straightforward. (According to one source, Michener joked obliquely over Mari's outspoken character: "I would like to get my hands on the fellow who said that Oriental women were submissive.") Yet the pair had many common tastes and interests, such as in literature, theater, and art, and were both strong advocates of racial democracy. More importantly, both were ready to defy conventional social stigmas against interracial marriage. On October 23, 1955, the Micheners were married in the Graham Taylor Chapel of the University of Chicago by the reverend Jitsuo Morikawa, pastor of the First Baptist Church. The wedding was reported in dozens of American newspapers. The Micheners would remain happily married for thirty-nine years.

Following their wedding, James and Mari Michener went on an extended honeymoon in Hawaii and Australia. In the period that followed, they moved to Hawaii, where James A. Michener did research for his best-selling 1959 novel, *Hawaii*. However, two years later, the couple unleashed a storm of controversy when the *New York Post* journalist Joseph Wershba ran an article quoting Michener as saying that the couple had been forced to leave Hawaii as a result of racism against his Nisei wife: "On the day-to-day operating level at which my wife and I had to live, we met with more racial discrimination in Hawaii than we did in Eastern Pennsylvania." Friends pointed to an incident in which, as a result of racial discrimination, they had been unable to buy a house in an exclusive district of Honolulu. Michener later tried to calm the controversy, stating that while he stood by his comments, he also believed that Hawaiian society had made enviable strides toward achieving social integration among its diverse racial and ethnic groups.

In any case, after 1961 the Micheners settled in Bucks County, Pennsylvania, near James A. Michener's hometown of Doylestown. Mari Michener accompanied her husband on his frequent travels around the world to conduct research for his books. The two spent extended periods in Japan (where Mari obtained a certificate from the Sogetsu school of flower arranging). In 1982, following an invitation to Michener from Texas governor William Clements to write a novel about the Lone Star State, the couple took a house in Austin, near the University of Texas. A few years later, after Michener announced his intention to write a novel about Alaska, the couple were invited to take up a residency at Sheldon Jackson College in Sitka. Mari Michener made an exploratory trip to Alaska, and the couple ended up living there several years.

During her married years, Mari Michener focused her attention on attending to the routine details of life, so that her husband could concentrate on his research and writing, and watching over her husband's health (especially after he suffered a heart attack in 1965). She read her husband's completed manuscripts. In 1960 she performed with him in a New Jersey summer stock production of the musical *South Pacific* (which was adapted from stories in Michener's book *Tales of the South Pacific*) and also played a small role in the 1978 TV miniseries *Centennial*, adapted from the Michener novel of the same name on the history of her home state of Colorado.

Mari Sabusawa Michener also supported her husband in his unsuccessful candidacy for Congress on the Democratic ticket in 1962, although she told a journalist frankly that she had opposed his running: "I did everything I could to talk him out of it, because I felt we had enough pressures in our life. I felt that being in politics would add a serious responsibility to an already overcrowded program. I knew how politicians campaign, and I was concerned about Mitch's health. He decided to run, so now I'm in the campaign with him." She attended political rallies and made five political talks on her own as well as helping with fundraising and handling his campaign correspondence and scheduling.

Throughout her married life, and especially in her later years, Mari Sabusawa Michener explored and often initiated charitable donations, in both her and her husband's names. One of the main fields of their philanthropy was art. During their long life together, the couple assembled a large collection of American and Japanese art. (James A. Michener, an admirer of Japanese prints, wrote a pair of books on the subject.) In the 1950s they gifted a valuable collection of nineteenth-century Japanese wood-block prints to the Honolulu Academy of Art. The couple donated the Michener Art Collection, made up of some 376 works of twentieth-century American art, to the University of Texas. Mari Michener remained active in advising the curator of the collection on further acquisitions.

The center of the Micheners' giving and involvement was the James A. Michener Art Museum, which opened its doors in Doylestown in 1988. It featured works by artists from Pennsylvania and around the world. From its early days, Mari Michener was active with the museum. She established the Mari Sabusawa Michener Endowment, which funded all the educational programs held there, and provided a Mari Michener Docent Award to the teacher, lecturer, or tour guide who put in the most hours. (According to one source, she would ask the museum gift store for posters of the collection to hang in her house because she and her husband had given away the largest part of their holdings!) Her most important gift to the Michener Art Museum was a $1.5 million legacy she granted in 1994, which provided most of the needed funding for a gallery celebrating local Bucks County artists in all media. The two-story addition, named the Mari Sabusawa Michener Wing, opened in October 1996.

Mari Sabusawa Michener's spirit was also reflected in the decision by the museum trustees to create a memorial to the famed Nisei woodworker and furniture designer George Nakashima. In 1992, two years after Nakashima's death, the Michener Museum commissioned his daughter, Mira Nakashima, to create the George Nakashima Memorial Reading Room, a place of respite and contemplation for visitors to the museum that would feature examples of Nakashima's wood furniture. Opened in 1993, the room was immediately hailed as the "jewel" of the museum.

Another area where the two Micheners offered massive financial support was higher education. Their joint charitable donations totaled more than one hundred million dollars. They included support to the Iowa Writers Workshop and Swarthmore College. The Micheners also donated sixty-seven million dollars to the University of Texas, the largest sum that it received from any private individuals. In particular, beginning with a gift of one million dollars in 1986, the couple provided generous support to establish and support the Texas Writers Center (later the Michener Center for Writers), which provided full financial support for participants. Their donations would later inspire the university to create the Mari Sabusawa Michener Chair of Creative Writing.

Beyond her partnership with her husband, Mari Sabusawa Michener made additional gifts in her own name. She served as alumni fundraising chair for Antioch College, her alma mater, and ultimately donated two million dollars to the college. A donation to the University of Northern Colorado in Greeley helped foster the creation of the Mari Michener Gallery (located on campus, inside the James A. Michener Library). In a move that recalled her efforts to recruit African American students at Antioch College during World War II, she created the Mari Sabusawa Scholarship Fund at Eckerd College in St. Petersburg, Florida, where her husband taught creative writing classes in his last years. The fund (apparently the only one of her gifts that was endowed in her maiden name) was designed to provide scholarships for racial and ethnic minority students over several years. Meanwhile, to honor John W. Thomas, who had arranged the scholarship at Antioch College by which she had left camp, Michener made a bequest to the American Baptist Churches, USA, to establish a scholarship fund to assist American Baptists in attending seminars, conferences, and continuing education programs as well as encouraging diversity.

Although Mari Sabusawa Michener retreated from active involvement with Japanese Americans and civil rights after her marriage, she retained ties with the JACL. At the 1957 Eastern District Council-Midwest District Council convention, she was appointed as a special JACL representative on her tour of Hawaii, Guam, and Singapore and remained a semiofficial roving JACL goodwill ambassador. Both alone and with her husband, she attended JACL banquets.

Sometime before 1983, she endowed the Mari and James Michener Scholarship for freshman college students under JACL auspices.

Mari Sabusawa Michener also found ways to express her feelings about the wartime confinement of Japanese Americans. In 1969 she wrote a review of Bill Hosokawa's historical study *Nisei: The Quiet Americans* for the *Chicago Tribune*. In speaking of Executive Order 9066, she stated frankly that on "Easter Sunday 1942 my family and I were sent to a concentration camp." Yet for all that, she sounded an oddly positive note. "A great tragedy could have resulted. Fortunately this is a sensible nation and the Japanese-Americans are a sensible people. Both behaved rather well, and in the end a new relationship was established." She was not always so free from rancor. Speaking of the Michener Art Collection in her last years, she told an interviewer that one reason they had chosen the University of Texas to house it was that "I was in a detention camp on the West Coast and we had no interest in seeing it go to the West."

Mari Sabusawa Michener died of pancreatic cancer on September 25, 1994, three years before her husband.

WAY DOWN IN EGYPT LAND / TAMIO WAKAYAMA, CIVIL RIGHTS PHOTOGRAPHER

In a column I once wrote on the Nisei photographer Yoichi Okamoto, who served as Lyndon Johnson's White House photographer, I mentioned that photographs can go beyond documentation of history or political propaganda and shine as art. This is certainly true in the case of Tamio Wakayama, another Nikkei whose camera captured the history of 1960s America. Tamio was not only a witness who documented the events surrounding him in inspired fashion, but his very presence touched them.

Tamio Wakayama had an unusual life story. Born to a Japanese immigrant family in British Columbia in 1941, he was the youngest of six children (one of whom died in infancy). His parents hailed from Shida, a small fishing village in Kyushu. They had immigrated to Canada in 1921. After years of working in the logging industry, the senior Mr. Wakayama had bought a farmhouse near the sawmill town of Port Hammond, British Columbia, east of Vancouver. He opened a grocery store on the house's main floor, where he also made tofu for sale. Tamio was only a baby when the Pacific War broke out. Like other Japanese Canadians, the Wakayama family was taken from their home and

Maryka Omatsu, Greg Robinson, Tamio Wakayama, and Mayumi Takasaki at dinner in Vancouver, ca. 2013. Author's collection.

herded into long-term confinement in eastern British Columbia, where they were housed in the newly built camp of Tashme. While they were confined, they suffered the official confiscation of their family home, car, and other possessions by the Canadian government. As the war drew to a close, confined Japanese Canadians were confronted with a stark choice: agree to leave camp and resettle eastward at their own expense or be deported to Japan once the war was over. The Wakayama family made the difficult choice to risk moving east and migrated to southwestern Ontario, where they eventually settled in the small town of Chatham. The Wakayamas were able to find a house in the town's Black ghetto (sold to them by a kindly Mormon neighbor), and Mr. Wakayama found work in a fertilizer factory and tannery.

Life for the Wakayamas, as for other Asian arrivals in the area, was difficult. Chatham had a rich history in the nineteenth century as a place of refuge for the Black Americans who had fled slavery using the Underground Railroad (a history that is nicely documented today in the Chatham-Kent Black Historical Society & Black Mecca Museum). However, even if the refugees found freedom in Canada, they were forced to fight both poverty and discrimination there in the following decades. As Tamio later put it, "The squalor and abject poverty of our neighborhood was sorry proof that the descendants of those runaways had fared no better than their Afro-American brothers."

By the time the Wakayamas arrived after World War II, Chatham was a town deeply segregated by race and class. For Tamio, mixed in with happy childhood memories was the trauma of racist insults and humiliations. He later said in an unpublished memoir:

> Much of my own life has been spent in coming to terms with the memory of growing up in Chatham. I remember the cries of "Jap go home" and a judo teacher who warded off his tormentors with a perfectly executed series of hip and shoulder throws. I remember my own battles to and from school fought with little skill and even lesser glory. I remember the first day of classes and the ordeal of registration—sitting at my desk, the lone Asian waiting in agony for the moment when I would have to interrupt the litany of genteel white names and voice aloud the alien syllables of my father's name.

When Tamio was still only a teenager, his father died tragically during his commute home from work, when his bicycle was hit by a drunk driver. In the wake of his father's death, Tamio was left without a major source of support. He managed to complete high school, then enrolled at the University of Western Ontario in nearby London, Ontario. During his third year of college, 1962–63, he fell deeply for a fellow student, a young woman of Russian ancestry, and suffered the pangs of first love. At the end of the school year, she broke off the relationship with him, which left the young man devastated. He returned home, as he put it, "to lick my wounds." In the following weeks, even as he groped to put together the pieces of his life and his broken heart, he followed the news of the civil rights movement then reaching its peak in the southern United States. After seeing reports of a lunch counter sit-in in Danville, Virginia, where peaceful protesters were pelted with eggs and liquids, he felt a stirring of empathy for the movement and a need to join. Thus, in early September he jumped in his newly bought Volkswagen Beetle and drove south. He arrived in Birmingham, Alabama, on September 12, right after the terrorist bombing of the Sixteenth Street Baptist Church that killed four girls. In the following days, Tamio managed to meet John Lewis and Julian Bond, the leaders of the Student Nonviolent Coordinating Committee, and drove them back to their Atlanta headquarters. Upon arriving in Atlanta, he was put to work for SNCC, successively as janitor and driver, and soon became a full-fledged paid staffer.

During his time at the SNCC home office, Tamio put together a flyer for an upcoming rally. Danny Lyon, a SNCC photographer, was impressed by the flyer and encouraged Tamio to take photographs. Tamio started bringing a camera to demonstrations and other events. He did not go out on assignments to take photos, partly because he believed that other photographers (especially African Americans) should have priority and partly because he was needed in Atlanta to operate the darkroom. Finally, in fall 1964, in the wake of the Mississippi Freedom Summer, Tamio got his chance. Another photographer, tired out by repeated beatings and by the destruction of his equipment, left the project. Tamio traveled to Mississippi and was sent to Neshoba County (where three civil rights workers, James Cheney, Andrew Goodman, and Michael Schwerner, had been kidnapped and murdered earlier that year). He worked there over the next months, capturing images, witnessing events, and keeping out of trouble, so as to be able to leave with his body and photos intact. As he later put it, "In the terror and beauty of the Black Belt South, I learned to be a photographer." His images of local people, of civil rights protests, and of the landscape all immortalized a time and place, rendering it uniquely tangible to future viewers.

After spending two years in the South, Tamio returned to Canada. He was inspired by the lessons of the Black freedom movement to document racial and ethnic oppression and to push for affirmation of minorities against racism and marginalization. He continued his photographic work, documenting life among Native communities of Saskatchewan and the Doukhobors—Russian sectarian Christians notable for pacifist beliefs—in eastern British Columbia (in the process, he returned to the region where his family had been confined during World War II). He also produced a book of art photographs, *Signs of Life* (1969).

In the 1970s Tamio settled in Vancouver, where he set up a photographic studio. In Vancouver, Tamio took the lead in a project marking the centennial of Japanese Canadians. The product was a traveling exhibition of photographs honoring the Issei in Canada and telling the story of Japanese in Canada. It was then transformed into a book, *A Dream of Riches: Japanese Canadians, 1877–1977*. The book was notable not only for its rich display of historic photographs but also for its trilingual (English-French-Japanese) text—until recent times it was the only published historical work on Japanese Canadians available in French.

By dramatizing the injustice of mass removal, the work helped buttress the Japanese Canadian campaign for reparations that resulted in a redress settlement a decade later.

During this period Tamio made two connections that would remain central for the rest of his life. One was with Mayumi Takasaki. Mayu had grown up in the Vancouver area, in the old Japanese Canadian fishing and cannery village of Steveston. The two would remain together for forty years. As Tamio put it archly, "Mayumi Takasaki [was] a sweet innocent Sansei from Steveston whom I seduced into my evil clutches or so everyone thought when we first got together. Our relationship has outlasted all those naysayers." In association with Mayu, Tamio became involved in the Powell Street Festival. The festival, first held in 1977, symbolizes the homecoming by Japanese Canadians to Powell Street, the city's historic Japantown, which was destroyed by mass removal in 1942. It is an annual event that mixes visual and performance art, martial arts, food fairs, and Japanese community events such as historic walking tours. Tamio worked on documenting the festival. His 1992 book, *Kikyō—Coming Home to Powell Street*, combined photos from the first dozen years of the festival with oral histories by participants. In addition to his collaboration on the Powell Street Festival, Tamio provided photographs for the *Bulletin*, the newspaper of the Vancouver Japanese Canadian Citizens' Association. He also served as editor of its English-language section.

In his final years Tamio lived in semiretirement and worked on a memoir of his civil rights days, which he called (with a nod to Eldridge Cleaver) "Soul on Rice." Tamio participated in multiple commemorations and tributes to the Black freedom movement and lectured about his experiences. His powerful photos of the civil rights movement were featured in an exhibition and in a powerful book, *This Light of Ours: Activist Photographers of the Civil Rights Movement*. His photos were also featured in exhibitions at the Japanese American National Museum and the Japanese Cultural and Community Centre of Toronto, among others. He passed away on March 23, 2018.

I cannot recall precisely when I first heard of Tamio Wakayama. Although I owned a copy of *A Dream of Riches* and had looked through his 1992 book, *Kikyō—Coming Home to Powell Street*, I had only a rather vague sense of him until around 2010, when I began hearing about a Japanese Canadian who had been active in the civil rights movement. As a historian focused on connections between Blacks and Japanese Americans, I was definitely interested. I spoke about Tamio with Allyson Nakamoto, director of educational programs at the

Japanese American National Museum. She had joined with Tamio on a program commemorating the fiftieth anniversary of the Freedom Rides. At my request she wrote an email putting us into contact. I followed up by writing Tamio. I informed him that I habitually visited Vancouver once or twice per year and asked if I could interview him the next time that I came to town.

Thus it was that I got to meet Tamio on my next trip to Vancouver, in February 2012. He agreed to come downtown for a chat-interview with me and my partner, Heng Wee. In order for me to better prepare questions, he sent me a draft of his unpublished memoir. Knowing of his long career as photographer and activist, I initially felt a bit intimidated about meeting him.

As Tamio came into the café where we had agreed to meet, I caught my first glimpse of him and involuntarily shook my head. I think that I must have been expecting a venerable and polished public figure. He was already seventy years old by that time but looked to be in his early fifties. He wore baggy, comfortable clothes, topped by an aged and slightly misshapen slouch hat, which I soon learned was his trademark. Another trademark was the well-worn bicycle on which he relied for most of his transport within the city. Even in inclement weather, he insisted on pedaling to his destinations. Eventually, he was able to buy an electric bike, which made going up the city's hills much easier for him. Whenever he went out, Tamio wore a yellow-orange reflective vest, which gave him the look of a construction worker. I thought of this as amusingly eccentric behavior on his part until I discovered that his late father had been killed while riding home one night, when his bicycle was hit by a car whose driver had not seen him.

From the beginning, Tamio was quite open and engaging. While he expressed his sincere affection and regard for the people he had met in the Black freedom movement and he was clearly proud of his contributions, I saw that he was a quiet man who was reticent about speaking of himself. In fact, he expressed greater interest in asking about my researches on Blacks and Asians and in getting me to talk. I also saw that he did not take himself too seriously. Instead, he played the curmudgeon and soon had me laughing at his views of people and things. Even more, he was fascinated by ramen and thereby bonded with Heng Wee, a passionate ramen aficionado. Tamio shared with us his favorite restaurants and discussed his methods of preparing ramen at home.

A month later I traveled to the Japanese Cultural and Community Centre in Toronto to attend the Keisho conference on Japanese Canadians and World War II that Tamio's older brother Peter Wakayama had helped organize. There

I saw Tamio, who had come east to attend. He was there with his partner, Mayu, whom I instantly adored. Mayu's warmth and vivaciousness perfectly complemented Tamio's mordant wit and taciturnity, and they shared many interests. (In seeing their complementarity and close connection, I thought of Ralph Martin's comment about Larry and Guyo Tajiri, the husband-and-wife team of Nisei journalists, to the effect that sometimes it was hard to tell where Larry ended and Guyo began.) A highlight of the conference presentations was the premiere of filmmaker Chris Hope's documentary *Hatsumi*. After the screening I spent a lovely evening over drinks with Tamio, Mayu, Chris, and Peter. The next day I gave a brief talk mentioning the need for an additional conference on Japanese Canadians in the postwar years. Tamio chimed in publicly to express his agreement and left me bursting with extra pride when he referred to "Greg Robinson, who is fast becoming an old friend."

I next saw Tamio and Mayu several months later, when I returned to Vancouver with Heng Wee. We met for dinner as a foursome and hit it off. During our evening together, I discovered that Tamio and Mayu were close to Judge Maryka Omatsu, an important legal scholar and Canadian redress advocate. I was an admirer of Maryka's, and so I wangled an invitation to meet her and her husband, Frank Cunningham, in Tamio and Mayu's company. Heng Wee and I had such a good time that we began the practice of triple dating with the two couples whenever we were all in Vancouver.

Another interesting connection that I made through Tamio was with Ed Nakawatase, a Japanese American from Seabrook, New Jersey, who had gone South to join SNCC during the civil rights movement, then later became an Asian American activist in Philadelphia. Ed was the only other Nikkei that Tamio had seen in the Black freedom movement. The two worked together, and they remained so close that Tamio referred to him affectionately as "Brother Ed." I later had the chance to meet Ed in Philadelphia, and he proved to be a wise and engaging person.

The only time that I actually worked with Tamio was when we both spoke at the JANM conference in Seattle in mid-2013. I was tapped to serve on a panel on multiracial activism, alongside Tamio, Diane Fujino, and Daryl Maeda. Tamio thought that it would be a great opportunity to deliver a section of his unpublished memoir, "Soul on Rice," and to show slides of his photos. However, there was no AV system available at the conference hotel, and rentals were prohibitive. Tamio finally resigned himself to being unable to show images at the conference. Luckily, some time before it started, he met up with his old friends Nelson Dong and Diane Wong. Nelson was a distinguished international attorney in Seattle. When Tamio explained his predicament, Nelson kindly offered to lend his company's slide projector. So, with Nelson as donor and Mayu as projector operator, Tamio was able to present at the conference and to illustrate his talk with his striking images. Truth forces me to confess that Tamio stole the show with his wit and his wonderful stories of his civil rights days—the rest of us on the panel were quite overshadowed.

I think that my favorite moment with Tamio was our evening together in January 2015. While usually we would all go out to eat, this time he and Mayu invited Heng Wee and me to dinner at their home in Vancouver. It was a small apartment located in a housing complex near the city's historic Chinatown. Books and Tamio's photos were piled all around in cozy disorder. Tamio and Mayu made delicious Japanese food. We sat around with them and their other friends and talked and laughed. I had a delightful time. I recognized that it was the first (and so far only) time that I had ever visited a private house in Vancouver or eaten a home-cooked meal there. By the same token, I realize now that while I had met and liked a number of Canadians of Japanese ancestry, Tamio and Mayu were the first ones whom I thought of as real friends. The last time I saw Tamio was in January 2017. Fittingly, we went out for ramen in Vancouver—Tamio and Mayu took us to a newly opened restaurant near their house. It was just before Donald Trump's inauguration, and at first the mood was a bit somber, but as we ate and enjoyed the food and conversation, the mood lightened. Once we were finished, we went for coffee and dessert at a nearby café. Tamio told me that he was in negotiations to turn over his photo collection to an archive. I knew that it would entail an enormous effort of packing and classification, but I was glad that the photos would be preserved and made publicly accessible. I was taken by surprise by the news of his sudden passing a year later and felt a real sense of loss. Although the man has passed away, I continue to feel his legacy, both professionally and personally.

PAUL TAKAGI / A FEARLESS ADVOCATE

Many notable events of 1969—the first landing on the moon, the Woodstock rock festival, the Stonewall riots, and the New York Mets World Series victory, among others—were recently the subject of widespread commemoration, as their respective fiftieth anniversaries dawned and people took stock of the diverse legacies of that monumental year. Asian American studies scholars, for their part, celebrated the fiftieth anniversary of the birth of the field. Popular attention tended to focus on the student strikes at San Francisco State University that ushered in the first ethnic studies programs there. Less known is the story of the outstanding Asian American studies course that debuted that year across the Bay at UC Berkeley, and that of the professor who taught the course, the formidable scholar and advocate Paul Takagi.

Paul Takao Takagi was born in May 1923 in Auburn, California, one of three surviving children of Tomokichi and Yasu Takagi. His younger sister, Hannah Tomiko (Takagi) Holmes, who lost her hearing at the age of two, later became a prominent activist. Paul Takagi grew up in the Sacramento Valley, where his father operated a fifty-acre strawberry farm (the farm would be seized by the California state government during World War II and sold off for property taxes). He later recalled that he attended a two-room schoolhouse, where he encountered supportive public school teachers. He attended Elk Grove High School, where he graduated in 1941, then started junior college in Sacramento.

Soon after, in spring 1942, the Takagi family was incarcerated at the Manzanar camp. While at Manzanar, the young Takagi was employed as a medical orderly. He was at the camp hospital in December 1942 when Jim Kanagawa, who had been shot by Military Police during the so-called Manzanar riot, was brought in. Takagi remained on duty overnight as Kanagawa's life ebbed away amid the inadequate medical facilities. Traumatized by the experience, Takagi left his job and took a position on the editorial staff of the *Manzanar Free Press*. In mid-1943 he resettled outside camp. (The rest of the family moved to Tule Lake so that Hannah could attend a new school for the deaf that the WRA had opened there, but when the school proved disappointing, they relocated to Chicago.) Paul departed Manzanar with the declared goal of attending a trade school in Iowa but ended up settling instead in Cleveland. There he worked as a "swamper," loading and unloading trucks. Through his job he joined an American Federation of Labor union. "I was happy working outdoors and meeting people I've only read about—Jews, Pollocks (not my word, theirs), Greeks, and people from the Ukraine—all of us getting the same pay," he later recalled.

Not long after arriving in Cleveland, Takagi joined the US Army and was assigned to the renowned 442nd Regimental Combat team. He underwent basic training at Camp Shelby in Mississippi, but just before his unit was to go overseas, he was transferred to the Military Intelligence School at Fort Snelling. There he specialized in the study of German. He was discharged in October 1945, following the end of the Pacific war.

Following his discharge, Takagi enrolled at the University of Illinois, with support from the GI Bill. There he experienced discrimination—a writing assignment that Takagi produced on his experience in the hospital at Manzanar received a poor grade from a bigoted professor—which led him to withdraw from the university after a single year. He moved to Chicago to be near his family and found a job in a milk bottle factory. He later recalled that he would work the late shift and would then go downtown to frequent bars and listen to music by the jazz bassist Pops Foster and the blues guitarist T-Bone Walker. In 1947 Takagi moved back to California and completed a bachelor's degree in psychology (he was mentored by Timothy Leary, the future professor and LSD advocate, who was then a Berkeley graduate student). In the following years, Takagi married Mary Ann Takagi and had two daughters, Tani and Dana—Dana Y. Takagi would later become a distinguished professor of sociology and Zen priest.

After graduating from UC Berkeley in 1949, Paul Takagi worked as a prison guard at San Quentin, which led ultimately to his becoming a parole officer for the California State Department of Corrections. In 1952 he was engaged as a deputy probation officer in Alameda County, in part supervising adult offenders placed on probation. Although he was honored, he later explained, to make history as the first ethnic Japanese probation officer in the state's history, he increasingly found the work meaningless. Thus he transferred to Los Angeles, where he asked for and received a caseload of people who had gone to prison for heroin possession, sale, or use. His service there caused him to rethink his ideas on race and social control. As he later explained, "The state became alarmed by the drug problem and they picked me—the expert—to conduct a survey.... I realized then doing research was what I wanted to do, and I went back to school as a graduate student at Stanford."

Takagi was already nearly forty years old when he enrolled at Stanford, but he persevered and ultimately received his doctorate in criminology in 1967. Even before he completed his degree, he was recruited by UC Berkeley's School of Criminology—Takagi was a rare individual who had both academic credentials and "field experience."

Over the following years, as professor and associate dean of the Criminology Department, Takagi helped transform Berkeley's school into a center of the "crime and social justice" approach of radical criminology, which examined crime in the context of class and racial conflict. He helped found and edited the journal *Social Justice*. In lectures nationwide and in his writings, which included the books *Punishment and Penal Discipline* (1980) and *Crime and Social Justice* (1981), both written with Tony Platt, Takagi examined the impact of racism and poverty on attitudes toward the law. He also made a name for himself as an advocate for prisoners' rights and as an influential critic of systemic police brutality. Takagi and a colleague alienated California governor Ronald Reagan and state authorities so deeply by their commitment to the rights of nonwhite communities that the School of Criminology was eliminated in 1974. Takagi then moved to Berkeley's School of Education, where he remained for the rest of his teaching career.

Even as he worked in criminology, Takagi branched out into other areas. In spring 1969, working together with students, he designed and led the experimental class Asian Studies 100X-Berkeley's first-ever Asian American studies class. While the university paid Takagi's salary, he raised outside money for guest speakers, bringing in community figures such as activist Karl Yoneda to address students. Takagi also sponsored a lecture by Supreme Court resister Fred Korematsu (Korematsu, who was shy in those years about speaking publicly about his court case, apparently did not make a favorable impression on students). According to Takagi, Emil Guzman, the son of a Philippine farmworker, arranged a get-together of students and farmworkers at the United Farm Workers headquarters in Delano, where the group was welcomed by the famed labor activist Philip Vera Cruz.

Takagi subsequently published signal work in the area of comparative ethnic studies. Various of his students, including Ling-Chi Wang and Gregory Mark, went on to be distinguished teachers and scholars.

In connection with his Asian American studies classes, Takagi encouraged students to reach out to local communities. He provided a strong model when he became centrally involved in the effort to save the "bachelor hotels" in San Francisco's Little Manila. Takagi also was an outspoken supporter of the Black Panthers (whose first minister of information, Richard Aoki, had been his student). In 1971 Takagi announced support for a controversial referendum proposal to divide Berkeley into separate racial zones, so that white police—whom he charged had frequently used excessive force on African Americans—would no longer patrol Black neighborhoods. In 1975, when Wendy Yoshimura, a Japanese American associated with the Symbionese Liberation Army (SLA), was arrested (alongside fellow member Patty Hearst) on charges of weapons possession, her bail was set at the astronomical figure of $500,000. Takagi befriended her family and offered to serve as her sponsor so that she could be released from prison, which he considered essential for her legal defense. In the end Yoshimura's bail was reduced on the condition that she live with the Takagi family at their Berkeley house, and she remained there throughout her trial (she was ultimately convicted and spent some three years in prison).

Takagi retired from teaching in 1989, four years after his wife's death. On the occasion of his retirement, he had the signal honor of receiving a tribute by California congressman Ronald Dellums, delivered on the floor of the House of Representatives. He enjoyed recognition for his contributions. For example, in 2007 he was honored by the National Council on Crime and Delinquency for his contributions to the field. He was also invited to speak that year at the Manzanar Pilgrimage. In 2008 the Association for Asian American Studies honored him with its Lifetime Achievement Award, and he made a sentimental return journey to Chicago to receive the award. In later years he worked on various research projects, notably on the history of eugenics in early twentieth century America. His book, *Paul T. Takagi: Recollections and Writings*, coauthored with Gregory Shank, appeared in 2012, three years before his death.

TOSHI OHTA SEEGER / THE POWER BEHIND THE MUSIC

Toshi Ohta Seeger was a remarkable Nisei who collaborated with her longtime husband, Pete Seeger, in his musical career and support for progressive causes. However, both because she was an Asian American woman and because she preferred to shun the spotlight and work in the background, she has not historically received the attention she is really due. It is therefore essential not only to bring her remarkable career "out of the shadows" but to use the example of her life to better understand the larger context within which that erasure occurred.

She was the daughter of Takashi Ueda Ohta, the son of an elite Japanese family, and Virginia Harper Berry, a white American from Virginia. Takashi presented a version of his unusual story in *The Golden Wind* (1929), a well-received semiautobiographical novel he produced together with American writer Margaret Sperry. In it he asserted that his father, Sumiwo Ohta, who had been one of the first Japanese to study in Europe, had been radicalized after witnessing the Paris Commune of 1871. In later life the elder Ohta had translated works by Karl Marx into Japanese and raised money for Sun Yat-sen to start a revolution in China. When Sumiwo was sentenced to banishment for his political activities, young Takashi agreed to leave Japan in place of his father, as was then possible under Japanese law. Following periods of residence in China, South Africa, South America, and Europe, Takashi came to the United States. Once in the United States, he gravitated to New York, where he worked as a set designer for the famous theater troupe the Provincetown Players. During this time he met Virginia. The two married in 1921, then left the country when Virginia became pregnant.

Toshi-Aline Ohta, their first child, was born in Munich, Germany, on July 1, 1922, and entered the United States with her mother at the age of six months. As the daughter of a white American (although technically Virginia Ohta had lost her US citizenship by marrying an "alien ineligible to citizenship"), she was allowed in and was recognized as a US citizen. After a stay in Philadelphia, where Toshi's younger brother, Allen Homorei Ohta, was born, the family settled in New York's Greenwich Village. There Takashi worked as a painter and supported himself by various jobs, including caretaker at the Henry Street Settlement House.

In 1928 Takashi was hired as set designer and scenic director at the Maverick Theatre, located around the Woodstock artists' colony in Upstate New York, and the family moved up with him. Toshi attended the Bearsville school. At Christmas 1932, ten-year-old Toshi played a shepherd in the Woodstock Community Christmas Festival. In the depths of the Great Depression, the Ohtas lived off what they could grow and sell.

By 1935 the Ohta family left Woodstock and moved back to Manhattan. Takashi was offered a dramatic role as a Japanese conference delegate in Rev. John Haynes Holmes's anti-war drama *If This Be Treason* (he returned to Broadway eight years later, in Victor Wofson's Chinese drama *The Family*). During these years Toshi attended the progressive Little Red School House in New York City, then enrolled at the High School of Music and Art. In 1939, while still in high school, she met the folk singer and activist Pete Seeger at a square dance and agreed soon after to help him put together a book of labor songs. Soon the two started dating. Meanwhile, under the name "Toshi Ota," she contributed three works, *Grandma*, *Schoolgirl*, and *Head*, to a show of painting and sculpture by Issei and Nisei, dubbed "The Younger Group of Japanese Artists," held in mid-1939 at International House, near Columbia University.

In the period following Pearl Harbor, the young Toshi joined the newly founded Japanese American Committee for Democracy. As with the 1939 art show, it would be one of the few times in her career that she engaged in activities within the Japanese community. According to the *JACD News Letter*, in

June 1942 she hosted a tea party at her home for Nisei girls to encourage them to become active in the war effort. Shortly after, she was elected to the JACD Executive Board and served as a program committee volunteer.

Even as Toshi remained active in the JACD, her fiancé, Pete Seeger, was interrogated over her associations. According to a 2015 article in *Rafu Shimpo*, based on documents obtained from Seeger's FBI file, the singer sent a letter to the American Legion in fall 1942 vehemently opposing the Legion's resolution calling for Japanese Americans to be stripped of citizenship and deported after the war. The FBI then launched an investigation of Seeger, who reported that his fiancée was a loyal American whose father had come to the United States because he disagreed with Japanese militarists and who was working for the JACD: "This organization, according to [Seeger], was organized for the purpose of showing this country that the Japanese who were born here are one hundred percent American."

In 1943 Toshi married Pete Seeger, then on furlough from the army. She seems to have withdrawn from the leadership of the JACD, although it may have been Toshi who persuaded the folk singers Leadbelly and Woody Guthrie to perform at JACD dances. In 1944 she gave birth to a son, Peter. He lived just six months and never met his father, who was stationed overseas.

In the first years after World War II, Toshi was primarily involved in caring for her home and her family. During this period the Seegers had three more children, Mika, Tinya, and Daniel. In 1949 the family moved to Beacon, New York, where they built their own cabin, at first with no electricity or running water. (Takashi came to live with the family, most likely after Virginia's death in 1958, and remained there until his own passing in 1970.) Still, Toshi joined her husband in various political activities, including campaigning for Henry Wallace's 1948 Progressive Party presidential candidacy and attending political protests. The Seeger family attended singer Paul Robeson's controversial 1949 concert in Peekskill, New York, where their car was attacked and windows broken by right-wing vigilantes.

After 1950 Pete Seeger became increasingly renowned as a folk music performer, first as a member of the popular singing group the Weavers, later as a soloist. Toshi was the main supporter for Pete Seeger's career. She served as his producer, booking agent, and publicist, and also helped answer mail and handle financial affairs for him. She ultimately branched out to serve as booking agent for other musicians as well.

During the late 1950s, Pete Seeger was blacklisted for his left-wing associations. In 1961 he was sentenced to a year in prison for contempt of Congress, a sentence that was overturned on appeal. He was largely unemployable as a concert artist at this time. Tohi collaborated with Pete and later their son, Dan, in ethnomusicology and filmmaking. In 1951 the Seegers helped record folk music at a Texas prison. In 1956 it was released as an LP, *Negro Prison Camp Work Songs*. In the early 1960s they took a trip around the world and visited folk musicians on several continents. Although untrained in cinematography and filmmaking, Toshi coproduced, directed, shot, and edited short films of folk music taken during the visit, including pieces set in Ireland, Italy, and other places. For example, the Seegers' film *Duke Tritton, Australian Sheep-Shearer* featured an interview with a legendary composer of sheep songs. Their 1964 film, *The Singing Fishermen of Ghana*, features songs created by fishermen in the West African coast town of Winneba. After returning to the United States, Toshi continued her filmmaking in travels with her husband around the country. Their 1966 film, *Afro-American Work Songs in a Texas Prison*, depicts music made by inmates. The Seegers also produced *The Many-Colored Paper* and *The Country Fiddle*. (Their films were later collected into the DVD *A Musical Journey*.)

In 1965–66, by which time Pete Seeger was no longer banned from television, Toshi directed and produced his public television show, *Rainbow Quest*. In 1968 the two were coproducers of *Circle of Lights*, a televised holiday songfest.

In addition to working with her husband, Toshi served as chief organizer of the Newport Folk Festival in its early years. Before the first festival in 1959, according to one source, she not only produced a list of performers but established the principle that no performer, whether a star or an unknown, would be paid more than fifty dollars for their work. Meanwhile, she attended civil rights demonstrations in the South and marched with Dr. Martin Luther King from Selma to Montgomery in 1965. Her support for singer-activist Bernice Johnson Reagon, a leader in the Albany, Georgia, civil rights campaign, led Reagon to name her daughter, the future singer Toshi Reagon, in honor of Toshi Seeger.

Beginning in the 1970s, Toshi Seeger became best known for her work with the Hudson River Sloop Clearwater organization, a nonprofit organization that the Seegers founded to advance the goal of cleaning the polluted Hudson River. Organizers used a replica of an eighteenth-century sailing ship as a vehicle for raising funds and publicity. (According to one story, it was Toshi who steered the boat and who first taught her husband to sail.) She organized the annual Clearwater Great Hudson River Revival, a folk music festival and seedbed of activism, ran the events—such as dropping the stone in the "stone soup" symbolizing community cooperation—and recruited performers for benefit concerts.

In later years Toshi continued her efforts. In 1990 the Seegers were jointly presented the WESPAC Foundation's Peace and Justice Award. Toshi Seeger was likewise honored by being appointed to the New York State Arts Council. In 2007, at age eighty-five, she served as executive producer of an Emmy Award–winning documentary on her husband, *Pete Seeger: The Power of Song*. She created a new version for children of Pete Seeger's song "Turn! Turn! Turn!" which was featured in Dan Zanes and Elizabeth Mitchell's 2013 album of that name. Toshi Ohta Seeger died in July 2013, one year before her husband. Shortly after, the Pete and Toshi Seeger Riverside Park was named in their honor in their hometown of Beacon, New York.

Chapter 3

JAPANESE AMERICANS AND AFRICAN AMERICANS

STEPPING OVER THE COLOR LINE / NIKKEI AT HISTORICALLY BLACK COLLEGES AND UNIVERSITIES

One pillar of American education is the network of historically Black colleges and universities, known as HBCUs. Founded to give free Blacks access to higher education in the century following Emancipation, a period when African American students remained largely excluded from mainstream universities, these institutions sprang up all through the Old South and border states. Among the most prestigious are Howard University, a federally-funded institution in Washington, DC, and the group of institutions run by the American Missionary Association, including Hampton University (originally known as Hampton Institute) in Virginia; Fisk University in Nashville, Tennessee; and Atlanta University in Georgia. Today, over fifty years after the civil rights movement, there are some one hundred HBCUs, both public and private, still in operation in the United States.

Even though their primary mission was to educate African Americans, these universities did not close their doors to non-Blacks, either as students or professors. For example, Howard University admitted numerous white students during its early decades (some of them children of Howard professors). One source states that in 1887 the student body at Howard's law school was one-third white—its low tuition costs and accessibility made it especially attractive. Meanwhile, Hampton Institute in Virginia admitted large numbers of Native Americans in the late nineteenth century. HBCUs also attracted a significant international population. Kwame Nkrumah, first president of Ghana, studied at Lincoln University in Pennsylvania, while Nnami Azikiwe, first president of Nigeria, was an alumnus of Howard University.

Given all these facts, it is intriguing to inquire about the past relationship of Japanese and Japanese Americans with HBCUs—what was the Nikkei presence at these institutions during the Jim Crow era? While the evidence that I have collected so far is fragmentary, it does hint at diverse kinds of contacts.

One especially significant early connection was that formed by Jenichiro Oyabe (Koyabe). Oyabe, a Japanese Christian from Hokkaido, came to the United States in 1888. His goal, as he later recounted in his 1898 memoir, *A Japanese Robinson Crusoe*, was to seek education so that he could uplift the Ainu (Japanese aborigines). He was particularly interested by the opportunity to work with Native American students. After his arrival in the United States, Oyabe was invited by Gen. Samuel Chapman Armstrong, president of Hampton Institute, to enroll there as a special student. Oyabe spent the next two years at Hampton. Curiously, Oyabe does not mention in his memoir the fact that Hampton was an African American school. Not only did he state in his memoir that studying there was a wonderful experience for him, but he appears to have remained attached to the school in later years, following his return to Japan. In 1903 he was interviewed in the Hampton journal the *Southern Workman* about his missionary efforts with the Ainu in Hokkaido, which included the building of an industrial school on the Hampton model.

In 1890 Oyabe transferred from Hampton to Howard University, where he studied for a degree in theology. At Howard he became a protégé and companion of president Jeremiah Rankin, who nicknamed him "Isaiah" and invited him to live in the president's house with him. Again, Oyabe lauded the school in his memoir but was silent about his African American classmates. In 1933 Oyabe was invited by Howard president Mordechai Johnson to attend commencement. He declined the invitation but sent a warm reminiscence about his years at the university that was duly published.

Jenichiro Oyabe was not the only Japanese student at Hampton and Howard at the turn of the century. As historian Yujin Yaguchi discovered, while at Hampton Oyabe shared a dorm room with two other students from Japan, Seijiro Saito and Genta Sakamoto (as well as a Chinese student, Loo Kee Chung). Interestingly enough, Saito and his wife would later serve as assistants to Hampton professor Alice Mabel Bacon in preparing a revised second edition of her book *Japanese Girls and Women* (1902). As for Howard, Keisaburo Watanabe, a student from Nagoya, attended the university's dental school during those years. When Watanabe graduated, in 1897, he was offered special congratulations at commencement by President Rankin and by the dean of dentistry.

In the first years of the twentieth century, Booker T. Washington, president of Tuskegee Institute in Alabama, became the nation's most powerful spokes-

Jenichiro Oyabe, frontispiece photo from *A Japanese Robinson Crusoe* (1898).

man for African Americans. The "Wizard of Tuskegee" formed important connections with Japan and Japanese. As Brian McLure details in his PhD dissertation, "Educating the Globe: Foreign Students and Cultural Exchange at Tuskegee Institute, 1898–1935," Japanese visitors such as Samuro Kakiuchi and Professor Rishoji of the Imperial University of Tokyo toured Tuskegee on several occasions to study the school's teaching and farming methods. According to McClure, the first Japanese student to study at Tuskegee was Iwana Kawahara, who arrived from Tokyo sometime in 1906 and graduated in 1908. Kawahara so appreciated his Tuskegee education that he arranged for his sister, Nobu Kawahara, to be admitted to the school. However, her guardian refused to believe that an American college would admit a woman—ultimately, Booker T. Washington was obliged to write a letter to the American ambassador in Tokyo, confirming that she would be welcomed. Once she arrived at Tuskegee, she quickly integrated into school activities and made close connections with other students. She graduated in 1911. Perhaps in response to the presence and success of these Japanese students, the Japanese community of Seattle organized to honor Booker T. Washington when he visited the city in 1913 and amassed funds to endow a scholarship for a Tuskegee student.

In the wake of Tuskegee's experience, Fisk University in Nashville was inspired to consider attracting Japanese students. However, Fisk president George Augustus Gates felt uneasy about the prospect, due to Tennessee state laws that specifically forbade "Negroes" from attending school in company with other races. In December 1911 Fisk announced that Nashville's city attorney had issued an opinion that enrollment of any Asian students would be illegal, and the university thereby was obliged to deny admission to a Japanese student. It is not clear how widespread such interpretations of law were. However, by 1916–18, when the magazine the *Japanese Student* put out a directory of Nikkei students attending universities nationwide, none were listed as attending African American institutions. One source states that Dr. S. Tamanaka attended Southern University in Baton Rouge, Louisiana, in the 1920s, but this is unverified.

What is clear is that in the interwar decades there were only sporadic contacts between Nikkei and HBCUs. In 1924 Howard University's baseball team hosted a visiting squad from Meiji University of Tokyo and prevailed four to three. The following year Howard's nine played a game against a group of Japanese former college athletes at Griffith Stadium. Robert Russa Moton, president of Tuskegee, toured Japan in 1927, as did the famed sociologist W. E. B. Du Bois, then at Atlanta University, nine years later. In 1940 Kaju Nakamura, a member of the Japanese Parliament and president of the Oriental Culture Society, made a lecture tour of African American institutions. He spoke on "Oriental culture" at such institutions as Morgan State University in Baltimore and Dillard University in New Orleans and tried to recruit African American students to travel to Japan. During these years the West Coast Nikkei press reprinted reports from Tuskegee on lynchings. In 1941 Jay T. Wright, director of the Trinity School, an African American high school in Athens, Alabama, run by the American Missionary Association, hired Issei minister Tsuyoshi Matsumoto as a music teacher.

The coming of World War II and the mass removal of West Coast Japanese Americans catalyzed the founding of the National Japanese American Student Relocation Council, whose mission was to arrange and secure funding for Nisei students to transfer to colleges outside the excluded zone. In 1942 Fisk University indicated it would be open to such transfers, and the War Department placed it on the authorized list. However, the East Coast [executive] committee of the NJASRC decided not to authorize admission of Japanese American students to any African American school, for fear of arousing white opposition. (As discussed in the article on Kenny Murase in his volume, in spring 1942 Murase applied to Howard University for admission and a scholarship, but Howard took no action on his application before he was sent to confinement.)

Despite the ban, HBCUs looked for different ways to offer support. In 1943 Jay T. Wright, by then dean of LeMoyne College in Memphis, wrote to the WRA to ask its officers to recommend qualified Japanese American candidates for the position of professor of English. Shortly afterward, Hampton Institute president R. O'Hara Lanier asked the WRA about the possibility of hiring inmates out of camp as cooks and dairymen. While no manual laborers seem to have gone to Hampton, Constance Murayama, a graduate of Smith College, was hired as professor of English literature at Hampton and taught there from 1944 to 1946. At the end of World War II, Howard University invited Nisei activist Bob Iki to give a miniseries of four lectures on the subject of "evacuation and relocation."

Fisk University became the most active institution in forming connections with Japanese Americans during these years. In 1942 the Japanese-born sociologist Jitsuichi Masuoka moved to Fisk to serve as chauffeur–personal assistant to the famed sociologist Robert Park, who was a professor there. In early 1943 Masuoka himself was hired as teacher-researcher in the Department of Social Sciences. He became a close collaborator of the distinguished Fisk sociologist Charles S. Johnson. In 1948 Masuoka was promoted to the position of associate professor of sociology. Although Masuoka remained at Fisk for thirty years, his later career there remains somewhat obscure. Meanwhile, a Nisei student, Dorothy Tada, enrolled in sociology at Fisk. The future YMCA director received her master of arts degree there in 1945. In 1946 JACL president Saburo Kido was invited to attend Fisk's famed Race Relations institutes. Kido later related that his experience made him aware of very different points of view: "When I spoke about the costs of the evacuation and what the Federal Government was doing, one of the comments made by Negro leaders was that it may not be a bad thing to have a small evacuation if the government would take an interest in the Negro problem to that degree."

I have been able to find only scattered information on the Nikkei presence at HBCUs in the generation after World War II. In 1955 Peter Igarashi, a graduate of Harvard University, was hired as professor of theology by Virginia Union University. Dr. Osamu Miyamoto graduated Howard's school of dentistry in

1954, as did Dr. Raymond Shoji Murakami in 1960. Setsuko Hirosawa, a student from Hiroshima, attended Hampton Institute. Barbara Takei, a Japanese American from Detroit, attended Howard University in the late 1960s. In 1974 the university's scholarly press published the groundbreaking Asian American literary anthology *Aiiieeeee!* Perhaps more such examples of Japanese Americans at HBCUs will emerge in the years to come.

AFRICAN AMERICAN SCRATCHES ON A NIKKEI CANVAS / BLACK CHARACTERS IN JAPANESE AMERICAN LITERATURE
with Brian Niiya

It is a commonplace that the presence and contributions of racial minorities have been too long and thoroughly erased from the writing of America's history. Yet as the eminent historian Arthur Schlesinger Jr. once observed, if racial conflict has remained excluded from the nation's consciousness, as expressed by the writing of history, then the repressed has returned in its unconscious, as represented by literature—classic American works by Twain, Melville, and others are awash in feelings, fantasies, and fears over racial difference, with nonwhite characters playing crucial roles in these narratives.

At a different level the same split is true of Japanese American society. In the first half of the twentieth century, newspaper editorials and essays in the English-language Nikkei press centered on the struggles of Japanese immigrants and their descendants to adapt to life in white American society. Blacks seldom appeared as subjects of news reports or editorials, and such references as existed were certainly not always positive (see the analysis in this volume of the diverse uses of the N-word in the prewar Nisei press). True, in the postwar years a small circle of progressive activists and intellectuals, led by *Pacific Citizen* editor Larry Tajiri, reminded their readers that anti-Nisei prejudice was but a by-product of the larger discrimination against African Americans and underlined their duty to join intergroup struggles for civil rights. Yet when the first generations of chroniclers, from Bradford Smith and Bill Hosokawa to Yuji Ichioka and Ronald Takaki, came to write the history of Japanese Americans, they failed to discuss the rich history of Black-Nisei connections and downplayed the role of African Americans and anti-Black racism in shaping the group's development as a minority community. Still, if African Americans have been largely absent from the conscious memory of the Nikkei over the last one hundred years, they have remained a powerful presence in community writing.

Indeed, in symbolic terms Nisei literature can be said to have started with African Americans. The very first published novel by an American-born Japanese, Karl S. Nakagawa's 1928 potboiler *The Rendezvous of Mysteries*, opens with the introduction of Jeff Jenkins, an "elongated colored gentleman." Jenkins engages in a conversation with white magnate Lewis Dalton, his seatmate on a train bound for Sacramento. Nakagawa (whose novel did not feature any Japanese characters) presents Jenkins's character as rather comic—a "queer duck," as Dalton refers to him. Nakagawa even uses touches of minstrel humor. For example, Jenkins explains, in crudely rendered dialect, that he was once a "pugilis'" but that he no longer boxed: "Kissin' the canvas had become my habit . . . so I jes' quit the game of fisticuffs." He also proudly states that he eats "at leas' three good meals of po'k chops a day." In an extended scene in the middle of the book, he is staying alone in a haunted house, where he brings a pair of large watermelons to eat but is frightened away by "spooks" (a plot point that anticipates the antics of the "Feets, don't fail me now" school of comically frightened Black servants portrayed by actors such as Stepin Fetchit and Mantan Moreland in 1930s Hollywood).

As it turns out, however, Jenkins is not altogether a stereotype. He soon comes to realize that he has been duped, and at the story's climax he shows bravery and saves a white woman who has been captured by the villains. The book closes with Jenkins, who had previously declared himself to be a "wimmin hatah fo' life," being rewarded by romancing Dinah, a Black housemaid. In view of these developments, a case could perhaps be made that Nakagawa's initial depiction of Jenkins in clichéd fashion was a way to set up his readers for the later surprise.

Another foundational piece of Japanese American literature, *hapa* Nisei writer Kathleen Tamagawa (Eldridge)'s 1932 memoir, *Holy Prayers in a Horse's Ear*, also references African Americans. Unlike Nakagawa, Tamagawa does not include any major Black characters. Rather, her only Black character with a speaking role is "old, fat Nan, the colored wash woman," who works for the family during the author's girlhood in Chicago. When little Kathleen brings together a cat and dog and they quickly attack each other, Nan says, "Maybe cats and dogs don't have no fights in Japan, but they sure do in the U-u-United States." For Tamagawa the phrase becomes a watchword of Americans' cockeyed ideas of Japan and their misidentification of her as Japanese.

Such absurdity comes to a head years later, when the author is in a southern hospital preparing to give birth. She hears an "animal-like cry." The white head nurse is dismissive: "One of those half-n——r girls in the ward. It is her first baby. She has been going on like that for hours. You can hear her all over the place every time the door is opened." Tamagawa asks whether anything can be done for her, and the nurse scoffs: "Oh, she's alright. These n——s make an awful 'to-do' about nothing." The author understands that the nurse's bigotry is outrageous. However, rather than challenge the obviously unfair treatment, she resolves to be silent, even at the cost of great pain: "No-one would ever say, 'It's that Jap girl in room 31, making an awful 'to-do' about nothing.'" Tamagawa is so fixated on being "decent" that she makes no sound at all, leading the nurses to conclude that she has had a *painless* birth, something the nurses claimed was previously known only in the Orient! In sum, the author's reward for letting herself be silenced by racism, even if she considers it absurd, is to be orientalized.

In the decade that followed publication of Tamagawa's book, the young Nisei living in West Coast communities established a prolific literary culture. The English-language Nikkei press ran short stories and poems in Sunday literature pages and holiday editions, while Nisei litterateurs put out a handful of literary journals, including *Reimei*, *Gyo-Sho*, and *Leaves*. James Omura's monthly magazine *Current Life*, established in 1940, published fiction as well. In their essays many Nisei lauded the talent of African American writers who had well expressed the feeling of being a minority and the associated "double consciousness" that they experienced. In a 1937 article, writer Yasuo Sasaki praised such figures as Booker T. Washington, James Weldon Johnson, Countee Cullen, and Langston Hughes. "Will there ever be an Oyama or Koyama to merit mention in the same breath as these men? Will there ever be a Marmaduke Watanabe to blurt out in in fiery print words that come from the very depths of him, words like [those] by James Weldon Johnson, he of *The Autobiography of an Ex-Colored Man*?"

All the same, only a tiny number of short stories in the Nisei press referred to Blacks or had African American characters. Those that did were a mixed bag, both in terms of the depth of their portrayals and their viewpoint. The anonymous sketch "Zip-Biff-Pow," which ran in *New World* in 1933, was the grittiest. It describes an altercation between Black and Nisei youngsters on a San Francisco street corner—the Nisei insults the Black boy by snarling the N-word, whereupon his victim hurls a racist epithet back at him. The two start brawling and attract a crowd. Finally, they are called on to stop by a "colored gentleman," who reprimands them both in the name of interracial solidarity:

"Shame on you two boys. I'm surprised to see you two nationalities fighting like this. The Japanese and the negro races should be dependent on each other. We need each other—we should be like father and son." While it is unclear which race he intends should assume the paternal role and which the filial, his wise diplomacy brings the boys to apologize, shake hands, and separate.

Another African American character is featured in the poignant story "The Chocolate Killer," which appeared in *Nichi Bei Shimbun* in 1936. The sketch was part of a series of sports stories authored by sportswriter-journalist Vincent "Vince" Tajiri. It tells of a Black man, Joe, who shines the narrator's shoes. The narrator notices that Joe has "cauliflower ears" and deduces that he used to be a boxer. He learns that Joe, known as "the Chocolate Killer," was once was a successful fighter and a title contender, until a car accident led to the amputation of his leg and the end of his career. A different kind of story of loss is Kenny Murase's "Resurrection," which ran in *Kashū Mainichi* in June 1939. Murase depicts a Nisei embittered by prejudice who tells his tale of woe to an African American bartender, then is shocked to discover that the bartender was a brilliant scientist who made a great discovery, only to be defrauded by racist whites out of the fortune that it produced.

At the other end of the spectrum lies Ayako Noguchi's "Highway 99," which ran in *Nichi Bei Shimbun* in October 1939. The narrator describes a sedan with three oversized Black women, who stop off at a roadside fruit stand to eat watermelon. The car pulls in, and "for awhile, we couldn't even tell if there was anybody inside it or not. Black car, black occupants . . . whatta plight!" The women's speech is rendered in dialect ("It sho am sweet"), and the author plays up their grotesque size. The whole piece seems to the current-day reader to reflect a storehouse of ugly racial clichés, a sense heightened by the appearance of a blackface illustration by artist Roy Kawamoto alongside the story.

One exceptional story from the 1930s was "Lady in a Bathrobe," which was published under the name Wataru Mori (which may have been a pseudonym for the prolific Nisei writer Joe Oyama) and appeared in two parts in *Rafu Shimpo* in 1937. Told from the point of view of a Nisei boy, it describes his curiosity over the secretive woman in the house next door. "She was neither white nor black. Nor was she brown. Her color was of a creamish tinge that verged on light and dark." The young Nisei is unable to understand why Miss Julie wears a bathrobe all day, why she is continually visited by both Black and white men, and why his mother describes her as a "bad woman." Finally, he accepts an invitation to join Caesar, a neighborhood Black boy, in running errands for her.

When he enters Miss Julie's house, she is friendly to him and pays him well, but he feels unable to return because of his mother's disapproval. The story attracted an unprecedented level of reader comment—not for its portrayal of African Americans but for its morally ambiguous tone and daring sex worker subject. After a half-dozen readers complained, the second half of the story was postponed, only to be reinstated in expurgated form after more readers responded by asking to see the conclusion.

The coming of World War II and the mass confinement of West Coast Japanese Americans under Executive Order 9066 shuttered the community press. Literary activity did continue, to a limited extent, within the WRA camps, where inmates published stories and poems in camp newspapers and in reviews such as *TREK* at the Topaz camp. Except at Poston, which had a handful of Black staffers, and in some areas near the Arkansas camps, confined Japanese Americans had little opportunity to interact with Blacks.

Perhaps as a result, the wartime literary output of the Nisei all but ignored the presence and condition of Blacks. One of the few creative works from camp newspapers to feature African American characters is Frank Hijikata's "Mandy's Dream," which appeared in the *Tulean Dispatch* literary magazine in 1942. In it Mandy Jones, an enslaved woman who is in agony after being beaten and berated by her white master, Arnall Rankin (his name taken from those of liberal Georgia governor Ellis Arnall and race-baiting Mississippi congressman John Rankin), falls asleep. She dreams that she is in Heaven, where she is welcomed by the Lord and the saints and given a large, beautiful house to live in, while Arnall gets a miserable shack. She protests, in broken dialect, "Ah's just a slave, a n——r at dat. Dis can't be mah home." It is explained to her that she is being rewarded for her good deeds on Earth, while Rankin is punished for his misdeeds. While the story did at least point to the horrors of slavery, more than *Gone with the Wind* or other popular writings of the era, this parable of the meek inheriting the (after) Earth offered a flat narrative and had no strongly developed characters. As such, it betrayed the kind of literary weaknesses associated with "protest fiction" such as *Uncle Tom's Cabin* that the young James Baldwin would deplore soon after in his landmark 1948 essay "Everybody's Protest Novel."

Interestingly, Black characters figured strongly in two works published north of the border. The Canadian Nisei newspaper *New Canadian*, which originally began publishing in Vancouver in 1938, had been forced to leave the West Coast in 1942 as part of the mass removal of Japanese Canadians and had set up operations in the confinement site of Kaslo, British Columbia. Its June 30, 1943, issue featured a story entitled "Lost My Baby, Lost Her fo' Good." The author was Hugo Yamamoto, a jazz enthusiast and sometime music critic for the *New Canadian*. The story tells the tale of a man named "Jess" (whose ethnicity is not described) who has been depressed since Jenny, his girlfriend, left him. In order to forget her, he frequents a nightclub with a "colored band" and "ebony dancers." He gets so excited by the dancers and by the voice of the blues singer "Ma" Jordan that he collapses in his chair.

A more pointed and dramatic tale was "Althea and the Negro," which ran in the August 11, 1948, issue of the *New Canadian*. The author was a young Nisei who went by the pseudonym "Jess" (and who nearly fifty years later would publish *Ignomy*, a novel about the Japanese Canadian camps). "Althea and the Negro" tells the story of Ted, an African American in Savannah, Georgia, who meets a white woman, Althea, at a clandestine interracial soirée. The two slowly fall in love. However, as scandalous rumors spread about their upcoming wedding, Althea receives anonymous messages threatening violence if she does not leave her lover. One night Ted and Althea are kidnapped by a group of masked men. Jess starkly describes the ensuing lynching, leaving the reader with a sense of horror and pathos from the violence.

In the years after World War II, Japanese American newspapers resumed operations on the West Coast, and new journals emerged to serve growing communities in cities such as New York and Chicago. The *Pacific Citizen* provided national news coverage. A pair of glossy photo magazines, *Nisei Vue* and *Scene*, boosted positive community images. A handful of Nisei—including S. I. Hayakawa, Setsuko Matsunaga Nishi, Yoné U. Stafford, Ina Sugihara, Larry Tajiri, Hisaye Yamamoto, and Wakako Yamauchi—wrote for the African American and interracial press. Yamamoto later produced the powerful memoir "A Fire in Fontana" (1985) on her experience working as a columnist for the *Los Angeles Tribune* and how an incident of racist terrorism shaped her. Yet amid all this newspaper activity, literature by Nisei all but disappeared from the ethnic Japanese press, which no longer included Sunday literature pages, and editors ceased publishing creative writing and book reviews. Both as a cause and effect of the lack of markets, most prewar poets and story writers stopped producing material or found outside venues for publication.

Within this reduced output, only a few literary works of any kind referenced African Americans. In 1949 Ken Hayashi devoted an installment of his recurring column, In This Corner, in the bilingual New York newspaper *Hokubei Shimpo*, to describing the clients of a set of tawdry bars in Harlem—Hayashi summed them up as "unhappy people haunting Harlem ginmills laughing like hell and fooling everyone but themselves." In the days that followed, there was spirited correspondence in the pages of *Hokubei Shimpo*, both pro and con, over the stereotypical depiction of "Negroes." A Nisei reader slammed Hayashi for dishonesty and abusing the goodwill of the Harlemites. "This kind of indulgence in ginmill elbow-rubbing with other minorities, to imply tolerance and understanding, and then to make back-handed remarks about them, is just as insidious and vicious a racism as the outright racism of the KKK." Hayashi responded that, far from being racist, his intent was to elicit sympathy for a persecuted minority group. Si Spiegel (future husband of Nisei activist Motoko Ikeda-Spiegel) countered in a letter that if Hayashi had indeed meant to convey sympathy, he should not have chosen such a subject: "Here is an article about the Negro that would perpetuate the white supremacist stereotypes of the drunken, shiftless, indolent, lewd and unhappy Negro people."

Another work that featured African American characters was Hisaye Yamamoto's short story "The Brown House," which was published in *Harper's Bazaar* in 1951. The story revolves around Mr. Hattori, an Issei farmer who has developed a gambling addiction. One evening he enters a Chinese gambling club, while his wife and children are obliged to wait for him in a car outside. Soon after, an African American gambler, desperate to evade the police, enters the car and hides inside, with Mrs. Hattori's begrudging consent. After Mr. Hattori returns and they start off, the man asks to get out of the car. Rather pathetically, he expresses his gratitude, which he poses in terms of interracial solidarity. Mr. Hattori, surprised by the appearance of a stranger, expresses anger at his wife for allowing the man to stay in the car with her and the children—he uses *Kurombo*, a derogatory term for Black people. His harsh words reveal the previous gambler's ideas of racial solidarity as naive and absurd. While the African American gambler is more of a device for the author's coruscating irony than a fully realized individual, the man's mix of visible difference and invisibility (in hiding himself among Nikkei) suggests a kinship with the unnamed narrator of Ralph Ellison's classic novel, *Invisible Man*, published the following year.

Another postwar work to bring in African Americans is John Okada's now-classic 1957 novel, *No-No Boy*. In the initial pages of the novel, Ichiro, a Nisei jailed for wartime draft resistance, returns to his old home in Seattle and is harassed when he passes a pool parlor on Jackson Street that has now become a hangout for a raucous crowd of Blacks:

"Jap!"

His pace quickened automatically, but curiosity or fear or indignation of whatever it was made him glance back at the white teeth framed in a leering dark brown face which was almost black.

"Go back to Tokyo, boy." Persecution in the drawl of the persecuted. The white teeth and brown-black leers picked up the cue and jugged to the rhythmical chanting of "Jap-boy, To-ki-yo; Jap-boy, To-ki-yo..."

Ichiro responds with a racist epithet under his breath as he moves on. His former feeling of tolerance is dented by this sad spectacle (as the author terms it) of "persecution in the drawl of the persecuted."

In contrast, Okada relates a story of interracial friendship later in the work. Gary, another Nisei draft resister, tells of Birdie, an African American war veteran who works at a foundry with him. Birdie defends Gary when the other workers are hostile to him. In retaliation, racist foundry workers loosen the lugs of Birdie's car, which flips over at high speed—fortunately, he escapes uninjured. The character of Birdie, though only presented in a secondhand portrait, allows Ichiro (and author Okada) to find "a glimmer of hope" for a happier future.

The first generation of Japanese American writers to integrate African American characters into their work shared some common traits. One was extreme youth: Vincent Tajiri was sixteen years old, Kenny Murase nineteen, and Ayako Noguchi and Frank Hijikata twenty each when their respective pieces appeared. *The Rendezvous of Mysteries* came out on the eve of its author's twenty-second birthday, while Joe Oyama (if he was indeed the author of "Lady in a Bathrobe") was only twenty-four when it was published. The Canadian writers Hugo Yamamoto and "Jess" were each in their midtwenties when their works appeared. The postwar writers, who portrayed more complex and ambivalent interracial encounters, were themselves barely into their thirties. Another common element was the writers' tendency to use African American characters as foils, through whom they talked about the condition of Japanese Americans. (Similarly, while in camp, Murase would produce a series of short sketches featuring "Little Esteban," a Mexican Native American "spirit of Poston" who served as an interlocutor for the narrator.)

The relative dearth of Japanese American literature in general continued through the 1960s and 1970s, and while the civil rights and Black Power movements drew much attention in the Japanese American press, they exerted little discernible influence on the Japanese American literature that appeared during this period. One partial exception can be found in the regular contributions of Joe Ide (also known as "Joseph Patrick Ide" and "Joseph Ide") to the *Rafu Shimpo* holiday editions. Ide lived in south Los Angeles and worked for the All Peoples Christian Church and Community Center from 1951 until his retirement in 1984, becoming executive director in 1977. Throughout that period he contributed annual stories to the *Rafu* holiday edition, most of which were autobiographical pieces or pieces about his family.

Since Ide lived and worked in a multiethnic area that included African Americans, African American characters turn up on occasion in his stories. A particularly interesting example comes from his 1969 contribution, "When I Was 21 . . . Was It a Very Good Year?" Inspired by one of his sons turning twenty-one, Ide reflects on the very different world he and his peers faced when they were twenty-one. He also tells the story of one of his son's classmates, a young African American man named Mack, who had been "quiet, unobtrusive, and never spoke unless spoken to," but after two years of college and involvement with African American student organizations, he had transformed into "an angry activist, a militant among the black students." Ide also uses Mack as a foil to his son, contrasting the former's race-based dilemmas—which he implies are similar to the ones Nisei once faced—to the more universal types of issues of education, occupation, and dating and marriage that his son faced. Many years later one of Ide's sons—who also goes by "Joe Ide"—became the author of a best-selling series of crime novels whose protagonist is African American.

By contrast, a 1960s Nikkei novel with African American characters, Kazuo Miyamoto's *Hawaii: End of the Rainbow*, reads as if such social movements hadn't occurred at all. There is some explanation for this, however: Miyamoto, an older Nisei (born in 1897) who was a physician from Hawaii, began writing his autobiographical novel while incarcerated in various American concentration camps during World War II, with the sections involving African Americans taking place in the 1920s. In the novel Miyamoto's alter ego and protagonist, Minoru Murayama, attends medical school at Washington University in St. Louis, Missouri, from 1924 to 1927. He is one of seventy-five students and the only one who isn't white. Minoru initially enjoys the "the open-heartedness and the geniality of his [new] friends" and notes the "goodwill among all." He also professes to being intrigued by the African American community in the city and to being "a great admirer" of Booker T. Washington. He is thus taken aback when his genial lab partner, Mullinex, expresses overt hostility to African Americans and tells him about having watched a lynching in Columbus, stating that "the only good n——r is a dead one!" While Minoru makes it clear he disapproves of such attitudes, he also explains how it may be understandable, noting that a newly arrived African Americans who migrated to St. Louis from more restrictive southern locales "would become cocky in his exercise of this freedom," thus irritating whites. (Miyamoto makes no mention of the giant anti-Black pogrom in neighboring East St Louis that had occurred less than a decade earlier.) It is an oddly anachronistic passage to appear in a novel published in 1964, particularly since Miyamoto states that one of his goals in writing was so that "America may not repeat the gross mistakes of the past."

That said, during his time in St. Louis, Minoru also has many firsthand encounters with African American patients and medical staff. During a stint in the Negro ward of a local hospital, he encounters "a large mulatto" patient who is initially hostile but whom Minoru wins over in the course of his three-week stay. He describes an encounter with "a very intelligent looking, clean-cut young patient" named Brown, who is a Pullman waiter. Upon finding out that Brown had gone to medical school but had dropped out of the medical profession due to the discrimination he faced, Minoru proceeds to chew him out for "shirking" his duty to his people. Later, in describing obstetrical training, Minoru notes that "all students preferred Negro homes to those of poor white people," since the people in those homes "were more grateful and cooperative" and the homes were cleaner.

After he graduates, Minoru tries to secure an internship and encounters racial discrimination for what he claims is the first time. Here he finds common ground with the African American (and Jewish) doctors who are limited in the number of hospitals they could potentially work for. Along the way he visits a "Negro" hospital in St. Louis and finds that members of its staff "were excellent in any company." Over his four years in St. Louis, Minoru seems to gain a better understanding of the plight of African Americans and, in the end, comes to identify with them to some degree as he, too, faces racial discrimination as a Japanese American.

A later work that shares some characteristics with the sections of *Hawaii: End of the Rainbow* set in St. Louis is Clifford I. Uyeda's memoir *Suspended*, published in 2000. Uyeda describes how he spent the World War II years studying medicine at Tulane University in New Orleans, where he was free of the educational discrimination he faced on the West Coast. While he was accepted as "white," Uyeda remained disturbed by the prevailing racial segregation as unjust and irrational. Uyeda describes a conversation he had with a Black student at his workplace. The student explains that he wishes to teach American history and intends to enroll at a northern university, where he can be free from Jim Crow, even as Uyeda sees the parallel with his own move from the West Coast.

Meanwhile, another novel by a Hawaii Nisei, published eight years after *Hawaii: End of the Rainbow*, parallels Miyamoto's work a different way. Jon Shirota's 1972 novel, *Pineapple White*, is also about a Japanese American from Hawaii who finds himself on the continent, where he encounters racial attitudes that are alien to him. But this time the author largely plays off these encounters as comedy. *Pineapple White* follows its protagonist, Jiro Saiki, a sixty-five-year-old Issei former plantation worker, as he journeys to Los Angeles from Hawaii in 1949 to live out his retirement with his son and daughter-in-law. The story centers on Jiro's bewilderment at big-city life, and much of his puzzlement stems from the racial composition of Los Angeles vis-à-vis what he is used to in Hawaii. On a drive with his son, Mitsuo, when he first arrives, Jiro remarks that there are "so many Kanakas," using a colloquial term for native Hawaiians. His son is amused by this, telling the old man that "they're not Kanakas . . . Negroes." Jiro replies, "They sure look like Moku's children in Waipahu." His confusion about race continues throughout the novel, as he insists that a Latino cabdriver he encounters—along with essentially anyone with darker skin—must be a "Kanaka." When asked by his son's white mother-in-law if there are many African Americans in Hawaii, Jiro replies, "Maybe, maybe not." "Rotsa black boys down Waikiki Beach." When she replies that Native Hawaiians are not the same as African Americans, he replies: "What difference? . . . Some Kanaka more black than Negro, some Japanese more black than Kanaka." The ever amiable Jiro interacts with a number of African American characters in the book and forms a friendship with Sammy, a Black newspaper seller in Little Tokyo. Implicitly embracing Jiro's naive but openhearted acceptance of everyone he encounters, *Pineapple White* conveys the message that African Americans should be accepted like anyone else.

The following year saw the publication of Jeanne Wakatsuki Houston and James Houston's *Farewell to Manzanar*, perhaps the most widely read book on the Japanese American incarceration written by a Japanese American. Told from the perspective of an adult looking back on her childhood spent in part incarcerated at Manzanar, the book has a passage that recalls a neighbor at Manzanar "with light mulatto skin." Young Jeanne played with the woman's adopted daughter in camp and noted that she was "taller than anyone in camp" and "wore an Aunt Jemima scarf around her head." The adult Jeanne comes to the realization that the woman was in fact African American and that the covering of her hair was part of her effort to pass as Japanese so as to be able to stay with her Nikkei husband and child.

For the next twenty years, there was little in the way of Japanese American literature that included any mention of African Americans, even as more Japanese American writers began to be published. One notable exception comes in a trilogy of plays by Velina Hasu Houston that follow the lives of Creed and Setsuko Banks. *Asa Ga Kimashita (Morning Has Broken)* (1981), the first play in the series, is set in Ehime, Japan, in 1945–46. It follows the Shimada family, whose members struggle to adapt to the new realities of a defeated Japan and American occupation. The budding romance between Setsuko, the youngest Shimada daughter, and Creed, an African American GI, brings these issues to the forefront. *American Dreams* (1985) follows the couple to New York City, while *Tea* (1987) takes place in Kansas after Creed's death. The three plays are based on Houston's own family story as the daughter of a Japanese mother and African American father. Several of Houston's other plays also include African American or African Japanese characters. Philip Kan Gotanda's 1999 play *Yohen* also has as its center a Japanese war bride married to an African American GI, examining the couple's relationship after some thirty years of marriage. It should be mentioned that the ethnic Korean author Soon-Tek Oh's groundbreaking 1970 play *Tondemonai . . . Never Happen!* which takes place among Japanese Americans and dramatizes wartime incarceration, also features a Japanese war bride married to an African American GI, though her husband is never shown.

In 1988 Gene Oishi, a journalist best known for his work with the *Baltimore Sun*, published a memoir entitled *In Search of Hiroshi*. Oishi's memoir bears some similarity with the earlier books by Miyamoto and Shirota in that the Nikkei protagonist finds himself thrust into an unfamiliar new world that includes African Americans. In Oishi's case, however, it is the army, with which he is stationed in France in the 1950s. Unlike the characters in the earlier books, Oishi has an advantage in navigating his new world: he is a musician with some talent for playing jazz. Because of this skill, he ends up playing in jazz bands in which many of his fellow musicians, as well as the club audiences they play for, are African American. His nonwhite and non-Black racial status makes him something of a racial mystery. There is also soon a love interest, an African American woman named Yvonne, who is estranged from her soldier husband.

This relationship is frowned upon by those surrounding them, with first the jazz club manager taking him aside and telling him he should end it, then a group of African American soldiers physically preventing him from dancing with her. They subsequently break up. "I decided to hell with her and to hell with black culture," he writes.

Twenty-six years later, in 2014, Oishi published an autobiographical novel, entitled *Fox Drum Bebop*, that depicts the same time period. Once again, his protagonist finds himself in the army in France, playing in jazz bands for largely African American audiences, and once again there is a love interest. But this time the love interest becomes a white prostitute named Suzanne. In both books Oishi writes about the white prostitutes who frequented the Black clubs and who saw only a Black clientele. It was understood by the prostitutes and their customers that they were not see to white clients; if they did, they would no longer be welcomed in the Black clubs. In his memoir Oishi writes that he decided not to approach these women, given his ambiguous racial status. In the novel Suzanne is described as the "girl" of his friend Muncey, a Black trombonist from Harlem. But when a white soldier takes up with her, Muncey attacks and seriously injures him and is subsequently kicked out of the army. Oishi's alter ego subsequently decides to pursue the lonely Suzanne, though she ultimately rejects him. Paradoxically, the pursuit of a white woman in the novel could be read as Oishi identifying more strongly with African Americans than in his memoir, in which he pursued an African American woman.

A final book that includes such "new world" encounters is Stuart David Ikeda's *What the Scarecrow Said* (1996). Ikeda's protagonist is a middle-aged Nisei widower named William Fujita, and his new world is an almost entirely white New England Quaker town in which he has resettled in 1944–45, having experienced great personal tragedy while incarcerated at the Gila River, Arizona, concentration camp. There are two relatively minor characters who are African American. Jim Little is a WRA staffer at Gila who is also an amateur boxer and who trains the son of the protagonist. Described as "a friendly, mild-mannered giant," he is treated as just a gopher by the WRA. Fujita's initial reaction to Jim is stereotypical, but he "soon . . . came to know and become very fond of the giant he'd mistaken for a guard." Little is also a singer and "could talk hepster as if he taught Cab Calloway himself, and he could cuss like nobody's business." Later in the book, while visiting Philadelphia to see his grandchild, Fujita meets Moses, whom he befriends. Their conversations touch on race, with Moses noting commonalities between Asian Americans and African Americans and telling Fujita that "you'll have to decide if you're black or you're white." Both characters—the gentle giant and the wise old man—feel a bit stereotypical and don't serve much of a function in the book other than to illustrate Fujita's tolerance.

While some Japanese Americans leaving the American concentration camps found themselves in small predominantly white communities like Fujita, many others settled in large cities, whether in the East or Midwest or back on the West Coast. In many of these cities, they lived alongside African Americans, as housing restrictions forced "minorities" to settle only in certain parts of these cities. Many younger Nisei and Sansei who came of age after the war grew up alongside African Americans. Daniel I. Okimoto, in his 1971 memoir *American in Disguise*, describes himself as having "lived among blacks" in the postwar years, making him able to sympathize in later years with the emotional fury of militants within Black communities. While Okimoto does not present any individual Black characters, he hints at his interactions with them: "Our Negro friends were always a bit astonished to see us eating raw tuna, dried seaweed, raw eggs, and fermented soy beans—and not with forks and spoons but with chopsticks."

Starting in the mid-1990s, one can begin to see literary works by Sansei that cover the postwar years. While set mostly in Japanese American communities, these novels—and the many plays, novels, and memoirs that followed—organically integrate a variety of African American characters who are friends and enemies, rich and poor, fighters and lovers. Although this trend continues into recent years, for the purposes of this essay, we will discuss only those published up to 2002.

Probably the first of these works to see print was a children's picture book, Sheila Hamanaka's *Be-Bop-a-Do-Walk* (1995). Set in postwar New York City, the story follows Japanese American Emi and her best friend Martha, who is African American, as they accompany Emi's father on his errands that take them across town to Central Park. Along the way they meet a multicultural cast of characters, before making a new friend at the park. The world of the book is a hopeful and idyllic one, in which people of all races, ages, and classes happily get along. Based on the author's childhood memories, the book is dedicated to (Conrad) "Ham" Hamanaka, the author's father, who settled in New York after having been incarcerated in Jerome, Arkansas, and who was a professional actor.

Two further such books, which themselves anticipated many later similar books, were published in 2002–3. Ken Mochizuki's *Beacon Hill Boys* (2002) is an autobiographical coming-of-age novel for young adults set in Seattle in 1972 and centers on Sansei protagonist Dan Inagaki, a junior at the fictional Hoover High (based on Cleveland High, the author's alma mater). In contrast, Perry Miyake's *21st Century Manzanar* (2002) is somewhat of a science fiction novel that imagines another mass removal and incarceration of Japanese Americans in the twenty-first century. It is set in the Venice-Culver Japanese American community in West Los Angeles, another area where Japanese Americans and African Americans lived near each other.

The world of Hoover High School depicted in *Beacon Hill Boys* is one in which the student body is more or less equally divided between African American, white, and Nikkei students. The protagonist, Dan, is something of a long-haired misfit in a seemingly perfect Nisei-Sansei family as the book begins. He journeys through his junior year and ultimately finds himself questioning his and other Japanese American families' fixation on economic status; he also ends up leading a push for ethnic studies on campus. Though most of his friends are also Sansei, there are three African American students who play significant roles in his journey. Davie Miles is a football player who is pursuing Janet Ishino, whom Dan has a crush on. When a young teacher talks about the Japanese American incarceration in social studies class, Greg Moore, who "resembled Nat King Cole, dressed like James Brown, and talked like H. Rap Brown," says that "I think we were right in movin' 'em all out. They could've been a bunch of spies." Though Dan protests, none of the other Asian American students say anything. The only other person to confront Greg is another African American student, Rhonda Du Bois, who later joins Dan in his efforts to bring more books on ethnic American history into the school library and who clearly also likes Dan as more than a friend. Other than Dan's brother's girlfriend, there are no white students who play major roles in the story, suggesting that the white students kept to themselves, while the Sansei and African American students intermingled. But there are also clues about Nikkei racism toward African Americans. Not only is Davie never invited over to any Nikkei homes, but there is a consensus among the Japanese Americans that Janet would only be able to accept Davie's prom invitation on the sly, since her parents wouldn't allow it otherwise. Dan also realizes that he has been stereotyping Davie after he visits Davie's home and is surprised to find that Davie lives in a home just like his and that his elegantly dressed mother is more attentive and doting toward the boys than any of the Nisei mothers.

One of the core characters in the apocalyptic work of *21st Century Manzanar* is Greg Wiley, the close friend of John, protagonist David Takeda's brother. After John is beaten to death by thugs early in the novel, Greg visits David and ends up being part of a small group of friends who drive with him to Manzanar to report for the "ReVac." For his troubles Greg is shot and imprisoned. Later in the book, Greg is part of the multiethnic group that returns to Manzanar to help David escape. Portrayed as loyal and brave—if also hot-tempered and impulsive—Greg shares with the Takedas the "Venice mumble," the speech cadence unique to those who grew up in Venice in that period that make their voices indistinguishable—and indecipherable—to outsiders.

The year 2003 brought the publication of Nina Revoyr's *Southland*, a favorite of both of the present authors and one that continues the trend of books set in postwar communities in which both Japanese Americans and African Americans lived. There are some fascinating genre books as well as some works that insert African Americans into the Japanese American World War II incarceration story to decidedly mixed effect.

As we have seen, depictions of African Americans have been a part of English-language Japanese American literature from its beginnings, and such depictions have continued throughout as part of the ebb and flow of Japanese American literature in general. These literary works have reflected the changing relationships between Japanese Americans and African Americans over time, even as historical works have, until recent decades, largely ignored these relationships. As we have seen, there is much to learn about Nikkei's feelings, fantasies, and fears about African Americans in examining these works.

THE JAPANESE AMERICAN PRESS AND THE HISTORY OF THE N-WORD *with Jonathan van Harmelen*

In the wide world of American racial epithets, one word seems to stand apart as uniquely hateful and wounding: the term euphemized as the *N-word*. Applied to African Americans, it is a corruption of the term *Negro*—a term that has gone through its own complex history. Like the Nazi swastika, the Confederate flag, and the flaming cross, the "N-word" represents such a toxic symbol of prejudice that any use of it, especially by non-Blacks, is taboo. (There are hate words in other societies that have their own special power: Greg Robinson, who spent his early life in an area of the Bronx with many Japanese families, remembers being told to never, ever, use the word *baka* in front of his Japanese playmates, as it was horribly insulting and could spark a fight).

Scholars tend to shy away from dealing with the N- word in academic discussion, whether directly uttered or euphemized, for fear of encouraging its misuse. Still, given the prominent place of the term in American culture and race relations, its past history and the diverse meanings assigned to it certainly merit serious study. In this chapter we will examine the usage of the N-word in the English-language Nikkei press during the years leading up to 1942, with emphasis on the West Coast newspapers. While Hawaiian Japanese American newspapers, like the *Nippu Jiji*, more frequently printed the N-word in their pages, such usage arose primarily in reprints of news articles and syndicated newspaper columns from the mainland and thus represent mainstream attitudes more than specifically Japanese American ones. In any case, given the small presence of African Americans—roughly two to four hundred—in Hawaii and their comparatively high social standing on the islands, the language issue had a different meaning there. As a result, we have largely put aside the press in Hawaii for the purposes of the present discussion.

Uses of the N-word in the prewar Japanese American press can be roughly divided into three different types. The first type is literary pieces. A number of Nisei writers added the N-word to their stories in order to lend them a feeling of grittiness or immediacy. Such blatant uses of the word may have shocked their audiences. As mentioned in the previous chapter, for example, the anonymous sketch "Zip-Biff-Pow," which ran in *New World* in 1933, describes a run-in between two youths on a San Francisco street corner—the Nisei calls a Black teenager the N-word, whereupon the African American shouts an anti-Asian epithet back at him. The two start brawling, until a "colored gentleman" shames them into stopping in the name of nonwhite solidarity. In the story entitled "Resurrection," which appeared in the December 17, 1939, issue of the Los Angeles daily *Kashū Mainichi*, Nisei writer Kenny Murase depicts a scene between a Japanese American, Shiro Katayama, and an African American, Jim Baldwin. Shiro is initially offended by Jim's smiling at him and thinks to himself, "You goddam n——," but then recognizes him as a former college classmate and banishes such hostile thoughts. Their ensuing dialogue reveals their common trouble facing racial discrimination in American society. Jim complains that despite all the economic and political progress of Black Americans, in the eyes of white society, "We're still n——s, and will be indefinitely." Nevertheless he expresses pride in his racial identity. (It should be noted that Murase demonstrates clairvoyance in giving the name Jim Baldwin to his protagonist. Within a decade after the story's publication, a towering African American intellectual named James Baldwin began his real-life career.)

In other cases the N-word appeared in material taken from outside publications (such as syndicated columns). Nisei newspapers, especially in earlier years, ran racist caricatures in comic strips and used racist dialect jokes as filler (they often used dialect variations on the N-word such as *N——ahs*). Reprints of extracts of works from past writers such as Ambrose Bierce retained their original language, including the N-word.

A separate category of writings in the prewar Nikkei press that featured the N-word was that of essays. In them the word generally appears in quotations by other people, or paraphrases of their views, and is clearly deployed in order to illustrate (and deplore) their racism. For instance, during 1940–41 *Kashū Mainichi* printed a series of columns, From Town to Town, in which Nisei journalist Joe Oyama recounted his travels in Mississippi and Alabama, documenting his experiences with the blatant racism of the Jim Crow South. Oyama included the N-word repeatedly in recording the racist language and attitudes of the whites he met. In one column Oyama cited his conversation with a white gas station attendant in Jackson, Mississippi. When asked about a recent lynching, the attendant vividly recalled the incident: "Yea, 'bout two years ago—about fifteen miles south of here in the hills—a couple of n——s got lynched. The mob used torch-blowers on them." Oyama informed another attendant that in Los Angeles "there are n—— policemen," to which he responded, "There don' gonna be plenty of trouble" if one arrested him. Oyama traveled on to Birmingham, Alabama, where he compared the white supremacist mentality to Hitler's Aryanism policy.

In March 1941, following his return to California, Oyama published an article titled "I don't think we should laugh . . ." that underscored the prevalence of racism against African Americans outside the South and the hypocritical attitudes of complacent whites. Oyama cited a case of discrimination that he had witnessed firsthand in Los Angeles. When an African American sat down to eat in a restaurant, a white customer called the police. After the police arrived, an officer told the restaurant owner, "You had no business letting a n—— come in here. There shouldn't be any place in America serving n——s."

Some of these illustrative uses of the N-word were ironic. In an essay published in *Rafu Shimpo* in 1937, Nisei writer Carl Kondo narrated the prejudice facing mixed-race Japanese Americans and presented his commentary from the perspective of an African American: "But it sure is tough to be an *ainoko*, which is Jap for halfbreed. You got no chance with the whites 'cause you're a Jap an' you ain't got no chance with the Japs 'cause you're white—partly. If you're Chink, or n—— or P.I. it's worse."

A third category of writings in the prewar Nisei press was more unconscious, as it involved the use of the N-word as part of common expressions of the time, such as "n—— in the woodpile" (for something unexplained and suspicious), "n—— heaven" (referring to the segregated balcony sections of theaters), the game "n—— baby" (a variant of dodgeball), or in a familiar children's rhyme (later retitled "Ten Little Indians"). In the September 7, 1932, issue of *Kashū Mainichi*, the columnist "Montage" used the phrase "Last one is the n—— baby" to describe the rush by the Soviet Union and other European powers to deal with Manchokuo, the new Japanese-backed (puppet) state in Manchuria.

In a few cases the word appeared as a nickname. For example, *Shin Sekai* reported in 1932 on an ice skating contest and made fun of the skating of a few contestants, who were identified as "Blackie, N——, Jim, Sam, and George." Meanwhile, a number of Hawaiian Nisei athletes, most notably golfer Isami "N——" Higashi, took the name. Higashi's prominence within Hawaii's golf circles meant that his nickname appeared regularly in the sports sections of Hawaiian newspapers. A 1929 article in *Hawaii Hochi* mentioned a football player, "Niger" Shimokawa, but it is not clear how the nickname was pronounced (or if it was a misspelling).

Although the N-word epitomizes anti-Blackness, the derogatory Japanese terms *kurombo* and *kuro-chan* for African Americans also appeared in the pages of Nikkei newspapers. As far back as 1929, *Rafu Shimpo* printed an article calling out Japanese Americans for their widespread use of the phrase *kurombo*, which was not only offensive but hypocritical in view of their own anger over the use in mainstream media of the racist term *Jap*. A decade later Mary Oyama, Joe Oyama's sister, reminded the readers of her *Rafu Shimpo* column Daily Letter, that "we who resent being called 'Jap' should never use the word 'Chink' in reference to the Chinese, or 'n——' or 'kurumbo' for the Colored people. Isn't 'kurombo' the equivalent of 'darky,' which isn't very flattering?" Despite the complaints, such language long remained in popular use. In fact, one actor in a traveling *shibai* (drama group) organized by the Central California Young Men's Buddhist Association used the moniker "Kurombo Joe Louis" Sakaguchi, in homage to the celebrated heavyweight boxing champion.

A survey of the prewar Japanese press is especially illuminating in regard to racial language and hate speech. The writings of the young Nisei, who were immersed in American culture but also themselves subject to racist exclusion, both reflected the influence of mainstream attitudes and critiqued them as they appeared in American society and within the Japanese American community. Understanding the usage of racial language reveals not only the inherent presence of racism, especially anti-Blackness, within American society but also its effect on immigrant communities.

Chapter 4

THE QUEER HERITAGE OF JAPANESE AMERICANS

K. T. TAKAHASHI / TRANSNATIONAL WRITER AND ACTIVIST

During the last years of the nineteenth century, Kazutomo (Kadzu Tomo) Takahashi settled in Montreal, Quebec, where he operated a book and magazine store. Although Takahashi's career in Montreal spanned barely a decade, during that time he managed to establish himself as a pathbreaking Japanese American writer and publicist. He published in mainstream publications in both Canada and the United States on diverse subjects, both Japanese related and otherwise, and went on lecture tours around North America. He won praise both for his English fluency and his powerful arguments.

Yet K. T. Takahashi was more than simply a columnist or essayist—he was also a creative writer. Unique within his output was his 1892 short story "Love in Nippon," which stands as the very first work of English-language fiction published by an ethnic Japanese in North America. Aside from its place in history, what is most fascinating about the story is its queer and gender-bending nature and the feminist attitudes the author expresses.

Kazutomo Takahashi was born in Kawagoe, Japan, in 1862. He traveled to the United States in the early 1880s and attended the University of Michigan, where he graduated with a "bachelor of laws" in 1885. In 1886 he moved to Montreal. During this time he married a Japanese woman, Ute, with whom he raised a son named Masao. (A second son, Kanzo, died in infancy.) The Takahashis were the city's first Japanese residents. After arriving in Montreal, Takahashi was named manager of a branch of the Drysdale bookstores chain. Eventually, he opened his own bookstore in Old Montreal. The *Montreal Handy Directory* for 1894–95 lists "K. T. TAKAHASHI" as offering "the largest Assortment of books and Periodicals in Canada." He was also a stamp dealer, selling used stamps to philatelists. The magazine *Bookseller and Stationer* later reported,

"As a newsdealer Takahashi was well known to all in Montreal, and many a prominent man was to be seen at his counter."

In November 1889 Takahashi contributed an article, "A Japanese Wedding," to the *Montreal Star*. It was an examination of marriage customs in Japan. "[Marriage] is eminently successful in Japan, although divorce is perhaps as easy in Japan as in Chicago. But with us this is in consequence of the original conception of what marriage is, open and honorable, and unlike the shameless maneuverings of lawmongers! Nor have we that legal fiction called a graduated divorce system." After running in the *Star*, the article was picked up by some American journals, including the *Harrisburg (PA) Telegraph*; the *Florida Agriculturist* (DeLand), the *Austin (TX) Statesman*, and the *Dubuque (IA) Times*. It gave Takahashi his first real exposure in the United States.

The next piece of Takahashi's to appear in print was "Love in Nippon," in the September 1892 issue of the popular American magazine *Short Stories*. The story is set in the "Hosokawa Mansion" on the Sumida River, where a group of a dozen Europeans, Americans, and Japanese come together to tell love stories. The last to speak is a middle-aged man of the samurai class, who relates his tale. As a young man at the close of the Tokugawa period, he wooed a maiden, Miyo, but because he was affiliated with modernizers who sought to Westernize Japan, her conservative family would not accept him. Miyo begged him to flee Japan for his own safety and sent along her teenaged brother Taro as his companion. The narrator went together with Taro to the United States and in the process the two fell in love:

> We worked hard and suffered much. When we had mastered English fairly well, we set out on a lecture tour. It was a novelty—novelty always succeeds in America—and we saved enough to enable us to enter a college. Five years sped by as in a dream. All that time Taro and I were like one; we always lived together. When I was ill, he nursed me by day and by night—sweet and gentle, an angel of love to me! When he was sick, I in my turn did for him what brotherly care and tenderness could do, for he grew to be as dear to me as my own life, and more.

After five years they finally get the green light to return home. Takahashi sets the story's climactic scene on the boat to Japan. Taro, with an air of great sadness, asks his lover if he can ever forgive someone who has deceived him, even for a good cause. When he says he could, Taro seems delighted, but the narrator cannot guess why:

> Taro gave me no reply; instead, to my puzzle, he laughed out merrily and said, 'Do you still love my sister?' 'Well—a—yes; but she must be married by this time!' I heaved a deep sigh. 'Oh! no,' returned Taro, pleasantly, and continued, 'But do you love me still?' 'You silly boy, what does all this mean?' I demanded. Taro only smiled and looked at me fondly.

After this exchange the narrator remains in a state of confusion until the pair land in Yokohama: "Taro, now grown to be a tall, robust fellow, in his full, hearty voice, greeted us, just outside the custom-house of Yokohama—not the Taro [who was] my romantic companion of the five eventful years, but Taro the brother of my beloved Miyo. For my Taro was my Miyo in disguise, whom I had loved as her brother." The narrator concludes that he and Miyo were married and that their story shows that pure love is possible in Japan.

Takahashi's tale was well received. A reviewer in the *San Francisco Chronicle* called it "an extremely quaint and interesting story by a Japanese author." One reader wrote to the magazine *Current Literature* to praise the work for its individuality and delicacy. That magazine reported that Takahashi was living in Japan. This was swiftly debunked by a Montreal reader, W. D. Lighthall, who stated that Takahashi was a friend of his, and managed a Montreal bookstore. Lighthall described his friend as "an omnivorous reader of good literature, an original thinker upon social and religious problems, and possessed of a rare degree of that artistic taste for which his race are noted." After praising the story, Lighthall added, "The love-sketch referred to is, without question, not the last that will be heard of Mr. Kadzu Tomo Takahashi."

While in fact it was not the last of Takahashi, it was his last published piece of creative fiction. In the years that followed, Takahashi turned to the task of bridging Japan and Canada. After the Sino-Japanese War of 1894–95 broke out and journalists such as Frederick Villiers denounced Japanese atrocities in China, Takahashi organized his own illustrated lectures in defense of Japan's foreign policy and toured North America. He published articles in periodicals such as the *Week*, the *Canadian Magazine*, and the *Arena* as well as the *New York Herald*.

Meanwhile, Takahashi took Canadian citizenship and campaigned for civil rights for Japanese Canadians. His most celebrated contribution was *The Anti-Japanese Petition: Appeal from a Threatened Persecution*, a pamphlet he produced with the Montreal Gazette Press in 1897. Identifying himself as "K. T.

Takahashi, a Japanese-Canadian," he protested the denial of naturalization rights to Japanese and refuted all the familiar racist arguments about Japanese depressing wages or refusing assimilation. Turning nativist arguments on their heads, he urged Canadians to employ Japanese immigrants, since they intended to stay and build Canadian society, rather than hiring American workers who would take their earnings and return south once finished.

K. T. Takahashi returned to Japan in mid-1897. Because of his unique fluency in English, he was recruited by editor Motosada Zumoto as a staff writer for a new English-language newspaper, *Japan Times*. Soon after Takahashi's arrival, Zumoto left the newspaper, and Takahashi took his place as editor and chief editorial writer. He would remain in that position for nearly two decades, until the newspaper was taken over by J. Russell Kennedy, publisher of the rival *Japan Mail*. Takahashi continued to write occasional features for the *Japan Times* in later years but mostly concentrated his attention elsewhere. He lectured at Keio University for thirty-four years as well as at other universities. He translated such works as Soseki Natsume's novel *Kusamakura* into English. Takahashi died in Japan in 1931.

Is it fair to read "Love in Nippon" as a queer Japanese American story? To be sure, tales of women passing as men and inspiring romantic complications are at least as old as Shakespeare's plays and Beethoven's opera *Fidelio*. Yet such works feature the false "men" loving actual men who have no interest in same-sex affairs, even as they are themselves pursued by women who desire them in their male guise. David Henry Hwang's *M. Butterfly*, conversely, features a white man falling in love with an Asian man in female guise.

In contrast, the plot of a man taking a teenaged male as his "romantic companion" and expressing unapologetic love for him (even platonically, we assume, as he never discovers his lover's true sex) seems unprecedented. By making the narrator a samurai and setting the story thirty-five years in the past, Takahashi evokes the tales of male love among samurai (*danshoku*), described most famously by Ihara Saikaku in early modern Japan. His conscious archaism is underlined in a headnote by the editors: "[Takahashi's] sketch is full of interest, the effect of which is not a little enhanced by the writer's picturesque handling of our language in his description of customs, many of which have already passed away, in his native land."

At the same time, while the unnamed samurai male is the narrator, the principal actor is actually Miyo, who challenges social codes by passing as a man and leaving Japan in her male disguise. Miyo is thereby able to stay with her lover and also to obtain a higher education, something unavailable to Japanese women at the time. However, so far from rejecting his lover for her secret transvestitism and assumption of male privilege, he reveals that the two of them happily married as a result. Thus disguised, Takahashi's story, with its radically feminist messages about gender, higher education for women, as well as the value and purity of same-sex love, could appear in a mainstream forum.

NOT JUST *A SINGLE MAN* / CHRISTOPHER ISHERWOOD'S NISEI CONNECTIONS

Christopher Isherwood's short novel *A Single Man*, which has won increased sales and attention in recent years as a result of Tom Ford's luminous 2009 screen adaptation, stands as a groundbreaking piece of literature. Published in 1964, five years before the Stonewall riots and the birth of the modern LGBTQ+ movement, the book is often referred to as one of the first works of modern queer literature, in that it features a gay protagonist who is "normal" (that is, not evil or self-hating because of his sexuality) and suggests that homosexuals in America represent a minority group whose members face injustice. In fact, a close reading of the text reveals other avant-garde aspects to the work, including discussion of Japanese Americans.

A Single Man traces a day in the life of George, a middle-aged British expatriate in Los Angeles. George is going through mourning for his longtime lover, Jim, who has died in a car accident. Out of a mixture of pride and prudence, he declines the invitation from Jim's family to attend the funeral and hides his loss (as well as the nature of his shattered relationship) from his neighbors and colleagues. Yet George is aware of the burden of concealment and resentful over the prejudice and condescension that gay people face. (In a darkly amusing dream scene, he fantasizes about kidnapping the vice squad policemen and hypocritical ministers who engage in public campaigns against "sex deviates" and humiliating them by forcing them to perform sexual acts with each other while he films them.) Yet his feelings of alienation lead him to develop a sense of solidarity with other minority groups. While en route in his car to the downtown university where he teaches English, he passes by African American and Latino neighborhoods. While he admits to himself that he would not want to live in these areas, if only because of the level of ambient noise, he recognizes that he feels more of a bond with their Black and Mexican residents than with the white middle-class people surrounding him. "These people are not The Enemy. If they would ever accept George, they might even be allies."

George goes on to teach his class, whose diverse student list includes Alexander Mong, a Chinese Hawaiian abstract painter; Estelle Oxford, a bright but hypersensitive African American woman; Sister Maria, a nun; and Mrs. Netta Torres, a middle-aged divorcée. In response to a question about anti-Semitism, George expands the point to hatred of minorities in general (though Isherwood telegraphs that George is speaking in particular about homosexuality) and states that it comes out of irrational fear. Dismissing liberal pieties about how all people are really the same, George points out that minority group members may indeed be different from the majority and have their own faults, but that it is still wrong to persecute them. However, it is wiser for members of the dominant society to admit their prejudice and deal with it than to conceal it. At the same time, he reminds his students that members of minorities are not ennobled by being victimized. "A minority has its own kind of aggression. It absolutely dares the majority to attack it. It hates the majority—not without a cause, I grant you. It even hates the other minorities, because all minorities are in competition: each one proclaims that its sufferings are the worst and its wrongs are the blackest. And the more they all hate, and the more they're all persecuted, the nastier they become!"

George's comments particularly intrigue two students who always sit together in the front rows and whom George assumes to be a couple: Kenny Potter, a lanky blond, and Lois Yamaguchi, a Japanese woman. After class George sees them sitting together on the college lawn and smiles at them, and Lois responds with a "dainty-shamefaced Japanese" laugh. Kenny goes up to George to ask some more pointed questions, explaining that he and Lois consider George to be "cagey" and unwilling to tell all that he knows. George admits that he is reluctant to share what he knows in class, where he might be misunderstood.

That night, however, George runs into Kenny in a bar. After sharing drinks, they head off together for a naked swim and then go on to George's nearby house. There they have a more intimate conversation, in which George feels Kenny flirting with him. In the course of the dialogue, Kenny expresses the wish to live alone, as George does. George is surprised by this and responds with curiosity:

"What I don't quite understand is, if you're so keen on living alone—how does Lois fit in?"

"Lois? What's she got to do with it?"

"Now, look, Kenny—I don't mean to be nosy—but, rightly or wrongly, I got the idea that you and she might be, well, considering—"

"Getting married? No. That's out."

"Oh?"

"She says she won't marry a Caucasian. She says she can't take people in this country seriously. She doesn't feel anything we do here means anything. She wants to go back to Japan and teach."

"She's an American citizen, isn't she?"

"Oh, sure. She's a Nisei. But, just the same, she and her whole family got shipped up to one of those internment camps in the Sierras, right after the war began. Her father had to sell his business for peanuts, give it away, practically, to some sharks who were grabbing all the Japanese property and talking big about avenging Pearl Harbor! Lois was only a small kid, then, but you can't expect anyone to forget a thing like that. She says they were all treated as enemy aliens; no one even gave a damn which side they were on. She says the Negroes were the only ones who acted decently to them. And a few pacifists. Christ, she certainly has the right to hate our guts! Not that she does, actually. She always seems to be able to see the funny side of things."

The exchange is intriguing on several counts. To begin with—apart from African American writer Chester Himes's 1945 novel *If He Hollers, Let Him Go*—this is arguably the first mention of the camps in any mainstream fiction. Isherwood (despite the imprecision of his references to the location and timing of the camps) uses the term *Nisei* and alludes to wartime removal casually enough as to assume that his readers were well aware of it. Revealingly, Isherwood does not give Lois a voice of her own: her narrative and perspective are filtered through a white character's subjectivity. However, Kenny not only recognizes the racism and injustice of wartime removal but accepts that Lois's feelings about the experience would legitimately keep her from marrying him.

Isherwood's inclusion of Lois's story seems to refute George's claims about the impact of prejudice on minorities. Lois seems not to be a nasty person, despite having been persecuted, and her negative feelings are more of disdain than hatred. What is more, the experience does not lead her to fight other minorities. Rather, according to Kenny, she feels that Blacks were the only outsiders to treat the Japanese Americans decently. Such discussion of Black-

Asian solidarity was most unusual in 1964, at a time when Asian Americans generally remained aloof from the African American freedom movement. Indeed, in fall 1964 Proposition 14, a measure to repeal the state's fair housing ordinance, was on the ballot in California. Despite the vocal opposition of the National JACL, many Nisei in California voted to approve the measure and thereby maintain segregation of other minorities.

Readers of *A Single Man* have pointed to important differences between Isherwood's novel and the film adaptation, with regard particularly to plot points and to the invention of new characters. In the film version George's class is not so visibly diverse, and his speech about minorities is shortened and somewhat altered. More importantly, there is no Japanese American presence. Lois (played by Brazilian model Aline Weber) is portrayed as blonde, her ethnicity is never stated, and there is no indication that she has any hesitancy about her relationship with Kenny. Whether this was a simple case of "whitewashing" on the part of the filmmakers or whether they believed that discussion of Japanese Americans would represent a distraction, the exclusion robs *A Single Man* of some of its revolutionary message.

TONDEMONAI / RECOVERING A GROUNDBREAKING ASIAN AMERICAN PLAY

This chapter covers (or recovers) the unknown story of a pioneering theatrical drama, by the name of *Tondemonai—Never Happen!* Premiered in Los Angeles in May 1970, *Tondemonai* was the first commercially produced play to dramatize Japanese American wartime confinement.

Beyond its dramatic and literary merits, *Tondemonai* warrants attention in historical terms for the new ground it breaks, and particularly its engagement with uncomfortable issues within Japanese communities. First, the play takes an unflinching look at the trauma that the camp experience wrought on the inmates, including conflicts between different factions within camp and the targeting of "no-nos" and resisters by loyalists. It likewise explores the complexities of interethnic relations by its dramatic treatment of interracial marriages—a Nisei man who marries a white woman as well as a Black-Japanese couple. Finally, at its heart is a complex love affair between two men: its main character, a middle-aged Kibei Nisei, and a young Chinese American. As astounding as its content is its authorship: the play was written not by a Japanese American but by a young Korean immigrant who was working in his third language.

The story of *Tondemonai* can be said to have begun with the founding of the Asian American theater company the East West Players in Los Angeles in 1965. Established by a group that included Mako, Beulah Quo, James Hong, and others, it was designed to provide a showcase for ethnic Asian actors to play nonstereotypical roles that would draw from their common Asian heritage. This goal gave rise to a central problem for its founders: finding suitable material. To be sure, they could and did produce translations of existing Asian plays—their inaugural production was an acclaimed stage version of the Japanese drama *Rashomon* that featured set designs by Mako's father, the Japan-born artist Taro Yashima. They could also adapt Western plays. For example, in 1968 East West Players performed a version of Gian Carlo Menotti's opera *The Medium*. Still, in order to directly express its group identity, East West Players needed to find plays by and about Asian Americans to perform. While in 1969 the company performed Henry Woon's *Now You See, Now You Don't*, such plays were few and far between, as Asian American authors in those days faced limited opportunities and professional marginalization. In order to encourage submission of original scripts, East West Players announced a new playwrighting competition, with a prize of one thousand dollars (funded in part by a grant from the Ford Foundation).

By good fortune, the company had within its own ranks Soon-Tek Oh (Soon-Taik Oh), an actor who was also a dramatist. Born in Korea during the period of Japanese rule, Oh was educated in both Korean and Japanese. After attending Yonsei University in Seoul, he moved to the United States and studied acting at Stanford Meisner's famed Neighborhood Playhouse. Oh was an MFA student at UCLA in 1965 when he joined East West Players, appearing in the inaugural production of *Rashomon*. (According to Esther Kim Lee's history of Asian American theater, Oh was recruited as a replacement for original member George Takei after he left the group to join the cast of *Star Trek*, but this would appear to be inaccurate.)

Oh rapidly became a central figure in the company. He acted in several of its productions (even as he took outside gigs to help support himself, appearing in episodes of the TV series *I Spy* and others). Meanwhile, he contributed two of his own plays for East West Players' 1967 season. *Martyrs Can't Go Home*, originally written as Oh's MFA thesis at UCLA (where it won the Hurwitz Prize), was a Korean War drama that portrayed the complex lives and loyalties of a North Korean family. *Camels Were Two-Legged in Peking*, set in 1930s Beijing, was adapted from Lao She's novel *Rickshaw Boy*. While neither work dealt with Asian Americans, they were both sufficiently well received that Mako and other members of the company pressed Oh to take on an Asian American subject and compete for the playwriting prize.

Inspired by his colleagues, Oh began work on a new play. He took as his theme the painful human drama of wartime Japanese American confinement. It was a courageous choice. The story of the camps had scarcely ever been dramatized, though Hiroshi Kashiwagi's poignant one-act play *Laughter and False Teeth* had been privately staged in Berkeley and San Francisco in 1954. (The 1960 film *Hell to Eternity* portrayed mass removal and had an interior scene set at "Camp Manzanar," but these details were so sanitized as to be barely recognizable.) By the time that Oh began writing, the issue of confinement, long muted, had regained some currency. In 1969 local activists in Los Angeles organized the first Manzanar Pilgrimage, and in 1970 Edison Uno introduced a resolution in favor of official reparations at the JACL's national convention.

Even so, Oh discovered a considerable amount of shame and repression over the wartime experience within Nikkei communities, especially among older people. (In her searing documentary *When You're Smiling*, Janice Tanaka later attributed the silent epidemics of family violence and drug abuse within Japanese communities in late 1960s Los Angeles to the unmet trauma of the camps.) To dramatize this group denial, Oh gave his work the ironic title *Tondemonai—Never Happen!* (*Tondemonai* is a Japanese phrase meaning "absurd and unbelievable"). Oh later commented that many elder Nikkei did not welcome the idea of a play that would air the community's dirty laundry and expressed bigotry against him as a Korean for writing on the subject. Luckily, he added, Mako was stalwart in his defense of Oh and his text.

Oh submitted his new work for the East West playwriting contest. In early 1970 *Tondemonai* was pronounced a winner, awarded the prize, and set for staging. According to Oh, his thousand-dollar purse was appropriated to finance the production, so there may have been some sleight-of-hand involved in the judging. (That said, the following year Momoko Iko, who was not connected with the company, would win the playwriting contest for her drama *Gold Watch*. Staged by East West Players in 1972, it is often but inaccurately described as the first play to portray the wartime confinement.) Mako was selected as the lead. Beulah Quo and Alberto Isaac, both of whom had previously appeared in *Martyrs Can't Go Home*, were chosen for the main supporting roles.

Other cast members included Shizuko Iwamatsu (Mako's real-life wife), Ernest Harada, and John Mano. (Robert Ito, in the days before he became known for his role in the TV series *Quincy, M.E.*, had a small role.) Oh agreed to serve as director for the production, though he had never before directed a play. He later speculated archly that he might have been selected because he would not charge the company extra money for directing! As it was, Oh was so bereft of funds that he could not afford a living space and spent his nights sleeping on the stage of the company's makeshift theater. Rehearsals took place in a church basement—according to one story, a church deacon was scandalized when he came upon two partly dressed actors preparing a scene. *Tondemonai* opened officially on May 28, 1970, at the Players Lab on Griffith Park Boulevard.

To summarize briefly (with apologies for spoilers), here is the plot. In a bunker-like basement room, Koji Murayama, a Kibei former inmate, is tortured by flashbacks of his past life: his confinement at Manzanar and his marriage to a *hakujin* girl there; the horrors experienced by his parents in camp; the attack he suffered at the hands of superpatriots who targeted him as "disloyal"; his confinement at Tule Lake and his term in prison; and the collapse of his marriage. His traumatic experience has turned him into a cold, unfeeling individual, though he is playful with his landlady, Cherry Williams, a Japanese woman married to a disabled Black American GI. Through a sexual encounter with a young Chinese American man, Fred Chung, with whom he finds himself psychologically (and physically) stripped down, Koji starts to wake up from his numbness and feel strong emotion.

Tondemonai received some hostile reviews in the Japanese American press. Kats Kunitsugu, writing in *Kashū Mainichi* (May 29, 1970), found the dialogue stilted and the camp scenes not credible. Speaking as a Kibei herself, Kunitsugu criticized the insufficient focus on the clash of loyalties that the Kibei faced. Ellen Endo Kayano, reporting in *Rafu Shimpo* (also May 29, 1970), focused rather primly on the nudity in the play, which she deplored as "shock value," and what she called the "sordid" profanity and homosexuality. She did, however, express her pleasure at seeing a play that "for the first time gives an Oriental's version of an Oriental" and at the play's power to transform stereotypes of Asians. Outside the community *Tondemonai* was reviewed in the *Los Angeles Times*, which referred to the play as affecting but confusing, while a notice appeared in the gay magazine the *Advocate*.

After its initial workshop production, *Tondemonai* was not revived, either by East West Players or other theater troupes. Mako continued to serve as actor, director, and teacher to generations of Asian American performers. He died in 2006. Soon Tek-Oh went on to enjoy a distinguished career as a film and TV actor but largely ceased his playwriting. He died in 2018.

Tondemonai is a powerful play. Why has it been forgotten? It was clearly too radical for acceptance by much of its original audience—perhaps it gave voice to a variety of matters that Nikkei, especially older ones, were not ready to discuss. Indeed, looking at the playscript gives the present-day reader an uncanny sense of being in a time warp, as the themes it covers and its approach are both so contemporary. How could people at the time, watching scenes of trauma in camp, have guessed that a movement to demand official reparations for wartime Japanese Americans would triumph in less than twenty years? Seeing two troubled but loving interracial marriages in the play, how could people have predicted that in thirty-eight years Barack Obama, the product of two such interracial couples (first his biological parents, then his mother and Asian stepfather, who raised him) would be elected to the White House? Most of all, in an era when homosexuality was illegal in most states, including California, and mention of it was all but taboo in Asian American communities, the play's portrayal of three-dimensional LGBTQ+ characters was revolutionary. It still seems novel today, in our ostensibly more enlightened era.

As Martha Graham famously said: "The artist is never ahead of his time, the artist is his time. Other people are behind the times." In the four decades after its initial performance, the Manzanar camp and Tule Lake segregation center were declared national landmarks, the heroism of the draft resisters has been publicly celebrated, and Mark Takano, a Sansei from Riverside, became the first open LGBTQ+ Asian American elected to Congress. So perhaps history is truly starting to catch up with Soon-Tek Oh.

RANDY KIKUKAWA AND 1980S ASIAN AMERICAN GAY ACTIVISM

The original appearance of this chapter in 2019 was designed to commemorate a major birthday—the fiftieth anniversary of the Stonewall riots. Set off by a police raid on the Stonewall Inn, a gay bar in New York City, the three-day series of demonstrations by community members that followed has been widely commemorated as the birth of the modern LGBTQ+ movement.

As the movement took shape over the following years, not only did activists win repeal of repressive laws, secure legal protections, and begin to elect openly

Antidiscrimination protest by LGBTQ+ Asian Americans, San Francisco, 1980. Courtesy of RINK Foto.

gay politicians, but queer communities with their own institutions—churches, businesses, medical clinics, and newspapers, among others—began to spring up in New York, San Francisco, Los Angeles, and other cities.

Even before Stonewall, a mainstay of these communities, especially for young men, was the gay bar. The bars served as safe spaces, allowing men places to socialize, meet friends and sexual partners, and be free from harassment. Unfortunately, gay communities were by no means immune from racial discrimination, and for gay Japanese Americans and other people of color, the bars were not always welcoming places. Ironically, it was the climate of harassment at gay bars, ten years after Stonewall, that fueled the rise of activism among gay Asians.

The first triggering incident was that of the Castro Station, a bar with a country-and-western-type atmosphere located on Castro Street, in the center of San Francisco's chief gay ghetto. In July 1980 Randall Kikukawa, a twenty-two-year-old graduate student in linguistics at UC Berkeley who was also codirector of the campus's Gay People's Union, decided to check out Castro Station. To his astonishment, Kikukawa was refused admission to the bar by a bouncer on racial grounds. "I tried to go in and a man stopped me at the door and told me I had to stand in line.... I didn't see a line, so I asked where. He pointed to the left, and so I stood there." Kikukawa later described in interviews. "There was no apparent reason for his directing me to stand in line, and he did not ask anyone else to do so." Kikukawa said that he was ignored and kept waiting while several other men were allowed to enter. "The bar wasn't especially overcrowded, and while I was standing there people were walking in and out. I pointed this out to the guy, but he shook his head and waved me back, and it suddenly occurred to me that I wasn't going to get into the place." Rather than engage in a confrontation, Kikukawa finally left. While this was a particularly distasteful incident, Kikukawa later stated that it was not the first time that he was refused admission—it had happened to him "several times" at various bars, he later stated.

Following the Castro Station incident, Kikukawa met up with his friend Ed Sebesta, who advocated taking action. With leadership from Sebesta and his partner, Jim Jackson (the *hapa* son of an American GI and a Japanese woman), local activists put together a fledgling organization, Gay Asian Information Network (GAIN), which reported on cases of Asian exclusion at gay community institutions. Kikukawa agreed to be the public voice of the campaign.

Together with Sebesta and Gay People's Union members, Kikukawa led a protest. On Saturday November 22, 1980, right before Thanksgiving, a group (described in the media as "about twenty homosexuals" but probably more like thirty, the organizers later recalled) demonstrated in front of Castro Station, alleging racial discrimination against minority gays there and, more broadly, what one demonstrator called "a pattern of discrimination against Third World gays in bars throughout the country." The demonstration drew a large amount of publicity, with articles in newspapers such as the *San Francisco*

Chronicle, the *Oakland Tribune*, and the *Bay Area Guardian*, plus coverage by local radio stations. While Castro Station's owner, Jim Ostrud, categorically denied any discriminatory practices at his bar, he admitted that such an incident was possible. Gerry F. Parker II, president of the Stonewall Gay Democratic Club, pointed to a widespread belief among owners that white patrons spent more than minority ones. Gay bar owners "think it's bad for business to encourage minority gay patrons," he said. Kikukawa later recounted the owner being defensive and justifying exclusion on the grounds that "Your people don't drink."

Despite such bad publicity for the bars, some time later another incident of exclusion occurred. N'Touch was a bar located on Polk Street that was popular among gay Asians. In mid-1981 the management suddenly started asking Asians from their twenties to forties for multiple pieces of identification to enter, even as their white associates entered without even being carded. Activists charged that the cases of exclusion were part of a conscious effort by the owners to shift the bar's clientele. In response, a group of Asians and non-Asians picketed the bar over two nights. Bill Matsumoto, a newcomer to the city from Denver, joined the protest. He later noted: "It was one of the hardest things I had to do in my life. Many Asians actually ran off through fear of letting their families know, or because of potential immigration problems." He also faced pressure from other Asian community members not to make trouble. "In fact, some Asians told me that we might as well go to another bar if they didn't want our business. I would agree to not giving them my business, but I was damned if they were going to stop me from entering their establishment because of my race." Matsumoto was aware that Asian Americans, including Japanese Americans, had been taught not to be assertive. As he stated, "Since World War I and the Asian Exclusion Acts, since the internment camps of World War II, Asians have always been fearful of speaking out and becoming too vocal. Keeping a low political profile kept you safe."

According to protest leaders, while N'Touch's owners, like those at Castro Station, denied engaging in any discrimination, the practices of exclusion were soon abandoned. Following the incident, Matsumoto visited Los Angeles and attended a meeting of a new group, Asian Pacific Lesbians and Gays (founded by the late community activist Tak Yamamoto), and he resolved to help form a similar group in San Francisco. The result was the birth of the Association of Lesbian and Gay Asians (ALGA). Though barely twenty years old, Matsumoto served as its director. ALGA mixed political activism with social and cultural activities. It held regular meetings at the Metropolitan Community Church and published a monthly newsletter. It was active until approximately 1986. ALGA was succeeded two years later by the Gay Asian Pacific Alliance (GAPA), which remains active to this day. GAPA not only held political and social events but produced a regular newsletter, *Lavender Godzilla*, that included literary and artistic productions of high quality.

THE JACL'S SHIFT TO SUPPORT FOR LGBTQ+ EQUALITY

In 1988 the Japanese American Citizens League, the largest Japanese American civil rights group, ratified a new constitution. In that document the organization for the first time adopted a provision prohibiting discrimination on the basis of sexual orientation, and its preamble advocated support for all people "regardless of sexual orientation." (From a current-day perspective, that might seem like quite a time lag, coming some twenty years after the Stonewall rebellion and well after many universities and businesses had created such policies. Yet to put it in perspective, it was only two years after cosmopolitan New York City enacted its first nondiscrimination ordinance, and at the time, Wisconsin had the only statewide antidiscrimination law in the country).

In the years that followed, the JACL's position rapidly evolved. In 1992 the JACL took an official position against Amendment 2, Colorado's constitutional referendum to forbid equal rights for LGBTQ+ residents (the amendment was enacted but was blocked in the courts and ultimately struck down by the US Supreme Court), and the following year the JACL approved a resolution in support of ending discrimination against gays and lesbians in the military and all other such employment discrimination. In 1994 the JACL made history when it became the first national ethnic-based civil rights organization to vote an official policy in support of equal marriage rights for same-sex couples. This action caused a major split within the JACL, provoking the departure of numerous JACL members and officers who opposed the new policy (Allen Kato, the organization's legal counsel, resigned his position on the grounds that as a Christian he considered "homosexual marriage" to be morally wrong).

What made the JACL endorse the cause of gay-lesbian equality, and at such an accelerated rate, after 1988? The historian can point to a variety of causes. First of all, in the wake of redress for wartime confinement, which had long lain at the center of the Japanese community's political agenda and was achieved in 1988 with the enactment of HR 442, many activists understandably sought new horizons in civil rights. By the same token, supporters of these measures favored them in the interests of coalition building. California representative Norman Mineta, the most distinguished spokesman for same-sex marriage rights within the JACL, made clear that part of his motivation was solidarity with Representative Barney Frank, the openly gay Massachusetts congressman who had been an important proponent of redress. The nation's larger political climate also played a role. As the question of LGBTQ+ rights became more visible in the political arena and the media, more Americans turned to supporting the cause. In April 1993 the March on Washington for Lesbian, Gay, and Bi Equal Rights and Liberation drew an estimated one million participants, one of the largest group protests in American history. Among those present were a number of Nikkei from around the country.

One especially important element in the JACL's shift was the activism of LGBTQ+ Japanese Americans and their allies within the organization. To a certain degree, these were people who had long been present in the organization and who now took charge. Tak Yamamoto, a longtime redress activist who was also founding president of the LGBTQ+ group Asian/Pacific Lesbians and Gays in the early 1980s, combined his two roles. In other cases new members took the lead in calling for attention to their issues.

In August 1992 the JACL held its biannual convention in Denver, Colorado. Organizers scheduled a set of workshops on issues addressing the Japanese American community. One of them was a panel on how traditional cultural taboos acted to hinder the progress of personal growth, self-acceptance and the confidence of persons "coming out" and "being out," and the need for acceptance of LGBTQ+ members of the community. The panel participants were Vicki Taniwaki, who also chaired; her mother, Marge Yamada Taniwaki; and Martin Hiraga, a grassroots organizer of support groups for the National Lesbian and Gay Task Force (today known as the National LGBTQ Task Force). The Taniwakis revealed how the traditional Japanese cultural patterns of reticence and fear of bringing shame (*haji*) to the family name worked to limit openness and had made Vicki's own struggle to come out of the closet and speak to her mother extra difficult. (Vicki mentioned that coming out to fathers was even more difficult—despite her mother's support, she hadn't yet felt able to come out to hers.) Martin Hiraga, for his part, commented on the burden LGBTQ+ Asian Americans felt at being a "double minority" and having to deal with racism in the larger society as well as cultural taboos about sexuality within Japanese communities. Hiraga stated that he himself had felt obliged to move three thousand miles from the West Coast to Washington, DC, in order to live his life freely. Hiraga also reflected on the accelerated rates of HIV infection and cases of AIDS among Asian Pacific Islanders in large US cities and spoke of their special needs in terms of support groups.

The veteran YMCA official and community leader Fred Hoshiyama, reporting positively on the workshop, pointed out that ten years earlier, no such discussion would have conceivably been held at a JACL event but that the event showed just how much times had changed. He added, "The openness of Vicki and Martin helped members better understand and perhaps lend support to gays, lesbians and bisexuals."

In November 1994, in the wake of the JACL National Board's landmark vote on same-sex marriage rights, the JACL established a new LGBTQ+ chapter in Southern California to focus on education and advocacy for gay and lesbian issues from an Asian Pacific American perspective. As Tak Yamamoto, the new chapter's first president, stated, "In essence, the formation of this chapter takes the organization to the next step—demonstrating its integrity to secure the civil rights of all people, including gay men and lesbians." Craig Fond, a founder of the new chapter, agreed: "We want to energize the organization with new approaches to new issues and address and advocate for other civil rights issues as well." While the formation of a special LGBTQ+ chapter was not nearly as well publicized (or divisive) for the JACL as the same-sex marriage resolution had been, it likewise pointed the way to a different path and a new set of concerns for the established organization as the twentieth century dew to a close.

Chapter 5
IN GOOD FAITH

LAYING DOWN THE LAW OF LOVE / THE 1936 AMERICAN TOUR OF DR. TOYOHIKO KAGAWA *with Bo Tao*

It was the middle of December 1935. The Nippon Yusen liner *Asama Maru* had just concluded a fourteen-day voyage. After leaving Yokohama and stopping at a port of call in Honolulu, it arrived in San Francisco. As the *Asama Maru* sailed into San Francisco Bay, its eight hundred passengers looked on, no doubt thinking of the ventures and reunions that lay ahead. Among the crowd on deck was a forty-seven-year-old Japanese man whose entry into the United States was unexpectedly halted. He was discovered to have trachoma—an infection of the eye that, if untreated, leads to inflammation and blindness—and was summarily taken off the boat by the Public Health Service and sent to Angel Island for isolation.

Though the passenger may not have been aware of or appreciated the historical irony of his destination, he was headed for the Angel Island immigration station, which had been the main gateway and official detention center for countless Japanese entering the United States over previous decades. What is more, in early-twentieth-century America, trachoma carried a powerful social stigma as an "immigrant disease," associated with impoverished foreigners. Yet the unfortunate man thus detained was neither an immigrant nor from a poor background. Rather, he was Dr. Toyohiko Kagawa, a world-famous Japanese Christian evangelist, writer, and social reformer who had been invited by American supporters to make a six-month lecture tour of the United States and who was scheduled to be guest of honor at a special welcome luncheon organized by the mayor of San Francisco.

It is perhaps difficult for readers in the twenty-first century, when Toyohiko Kagawa's name has faded from notice, to appreciate the level of international celebrity that he enjoyed during his lifetime. Kagawa was often mentioned in the same breath as Gandhi, as a charismatic and even saintly leader who brought his religious faith into politics and social reform but who did not speak as a theologian. Like Gandhi, he was a prominent critic of industrial capitalism. Kagawa's groundbreaking work as labor organizer and founder of the Japanese consumer cooperative movement made him an influential voice for social and economic justice. He also stood out as an advocate of international peace, especially in a period when militarism dominated Japan. A prolific writer, Kagawa published a reported 150 books during his lifetime. He was nominated five times for the Nobel Prize, both for literature and the Nobel Peace Prize.

Born in Kobe in 1888, the son of a shipping merchant and his concubine, Toyohiko Kagawa lost both parents at a young age and endured a lonely childhood. Finding solace in the company of Harry W. Myers and Charles A. Logan, (southern) Presbyterian missionaries from America who ran an English Bible class for Japanese youth, he was baptized by their hands as a teenager. Under their guidance, he attended Meiji Gakuin, a Presbyterian college in Tokyo, then enrolled at Kobe Theological Seminary. It was in 1909, while at the seminary, that he took up residence in a shed in the Shinkawa slums of Kobe and became involved in relief work, aiding thousands of poor residents, a mission dramatized through his 1920 autobiographical novel, *Shisen o koete* (*Across the Death-Line*). (It was during his time in the Kobe slums that Kagawa picked up his aforementioned eye infection.) In the years following World War I, Kagawa took a lead in organizing unions for industrial laborers, founded the Kobe Consumer Co-Operative, and worked for universal suffrage in Japan. In 1921 he and a group of supporters founded the Friends of Jesus, a Franciscan-style Christian fellowship organization whose members strove for spiritual discipline and compassion for the poor. In works such as *The Religion of Jesus* (1931), Kagawa underlined the redemptive love of God and the importance of individual commitment to Jesus Christ.

Kagawa's relationship with the United States dated back to 1914, when he left his humble dwellings in Kobe to study at Princeton Theological Seminary. Kagawa spent three years at Princeton before returning to Japan. He revisited the United States from late 1924 to early 1925 to attend the Pan Pacific Student Convention and conduct a short speaking tour. Japanese American communities in Hawaii and Southern California welcomed his visit and went so far as to establish local branches of the Friends of Jesus. Kagawa made a subsequent tour in 1931. On this trip he was invited to deliver the prestigious Shaffer Lectures at the Yale Divinity School, which described Kagawa as "one of the greatest and most influential of modern Christians." During his absences Kagawa's missionary supporters in the United States, most notably Helen Topping and her family, further cultivated his image as an international Christian and pacifist figure by producing a stream of English-language publications and promotional materials by and about Kagawa, which were distributed to domestic American audiences as well as to mission stations around the world. Several of Kagawa's books, including *The Religion of Jesus*, the novels *Before the Dawn* (1925) and *A Grain of Wheat* (1936), the essay collection *Love: The Law of Life* (1928), and even a volume of poetry, *Songs from the Slums* (1935), appeared in translated editions by American publishers.

Kagawa's arrival in San Francisco in December 1935 and his detention by immigration authorities mobilized his supporters. Stanley A. Hunter, pastor of St. John's Presbyterian Church in Berkeley and one of Kagawa's most ardent collaborators, visited him at Angel Island and explained that "US veteran's associations" and "retailers' unions" were protesting his arrival by sending cables and letters to immigration officials. Convinced that Kagawa was being unfairly targeted for his pacifism and cooperative economic theories, Hunter lodged an appeal on his behalf, which was joined by the members of the coordinating committee responsible for arranging Kagawa's American itinerary. The campaign attracted widespread news coverage. Sympathetic commentators noted the irony that the "Saint Francis of Japan" had been denied entry at the port of "San Francisco" as a direct consequence of his self-sacrificial service for the less fortunate. *Time* magazine called him the "Quarantined Christian." The news coverage, plus a telegram from John R. Mott, international president of the YMCA, caught the attention of President Franklin D. Roosevelt. FDR expressed a "personal interest" in Kagawa's case, leading the immigration board to grant Kagawa admission to the United States on the condition that he be accompanied by a physician or nurse while in the country.

These events, and the president's action, further bolstered public interest in Kagawa and his message, and Americans flocked to hear Kagawa's speeches during his tour. A telling event was his March 4, 1936, appearance in Cleveland, Ohio. The general secretary of the Cleveland YMCA compared Kagawa's visit to the Eucharistic Congress—which had been held recently in the same city—in terms of the scale and excitement generated: "One event was in the nature of a mammoth religious convention [for Roman Catholics] lasting almost a week; the other consisted simply of four meetings on a given day with

Toyohiko Kagawa, frontispiece photo from *Love, the Law of Life* (1928).

overflow audiences in each." The crowd's sole object of interest was a "humble Japanese Christian," he continued, "[who] said nothing very striking" nor revealed any "new or startling truths." Nevertheless, he concluded, the attendees were keenly drawn to the itinerant evangelist's embodiment of a "simple life, absolutely and unconditionally dedicated to the service of humanity in the name and spirit of Jesus Christ." When Kagawa visited Springfield, Illinois, in February 1936, Albert Palmer of the Chicago Church Federation made a Lincoln's birthday radio address explicitly linking the Japanese evangelist to the Great Emancipator. (Palmer's address inspired Helen Topping and other supporters from the Friends of Jesus to compile a pamphlet volume of essays and speeches titled *Kagawa in Lincoln's Land*.)

As before, Kagawa's reception among Japanese American communities on the West Coast was particularly warm. Issei and Nisei were excited to receive a Japanese who was an international celebrity. The English-language press provided widespread coverage of Kagawa's activities. After arriving on May 24 in Los Angeles, where he was greeted by the local Friends of Jesus group, he embarked on a ten-day schedule of lectures in Southern California. His speech to Nisei Christians precipitated a widespread cancellation of regular sporting and recreational events to ensure that all young people could attend.

That the youth were asked to refrain from requesting autographs or shaking hands with Kagawa attested to his star status, while the announcement that transportation would be provided to his lecture venues underscored the community's involvement and investment in his tour.

The timing of the tour, with the United States in the throes of the Great Depression, fostered a ready audience for Kagawa's interpretation of the social gospel. This was apparent in the tour's highlight: his visit in mid-April to the Colgate-Rochester Divinity School in Upstate New York, where he delivered the prestigious Rauschenbusch Lectures (a series named after the Baptist theologian and Social Gospel movement leader Walter Rauschenbusch). Kagawa's lectures drew connections between the spirit of sacrifice as personified by Jesus Christ and the spirit of social solidarity as exemplified by the cooperative system of nonexploitation and mutual aid. The lectures were later adapted into a book, *Brotherhood Economics*, which was subsequently translated into seventeen languages and sold in twenty-five countries.

Kagawa's tour also became a rallying point for advocates of equal rights for Japanese Americans. The Federal Council of Churches (FCC), the official sponsor for Kagawa's tour, saw the event as part of its long-standing opposition to the United States' legal exclusion of Japanese immigrants. Organizations such as the Fellowship of Reconciliation gathered signatures on pledge cards seeking repeal of exclusion. Allan Hunter, the LA-based FOR organizer and younger brother of Stanley Hunter, proudly reported the signing of "several thousand" pledge cards, which leaders presented to Kagawa during the latter's stay in Southern California. The FCC continued to call for the repeal of the "Asian Exclusion Law" after the tour, stating in its 1936 year-end report that the free exchange of ideas represented by the "Christian ambassador" Kagawa should be furthered.

Following Kagawa's departure in June 1936, the pastor of the Community Church in Grant, Michigan, decided to memorialize Kagawa in the form of a stained glass window, thus providing a fitting coda to the Japanese evangelist's celebrated visit. The *Kagawa Memorial Window*, unveiled that December, was installed as the first in a series of seven that paid tribute to "modern major prophets." Its design, inspired by Julian Brazelton's illustrations for *Songs from the Slums*, featured the phrase "Cooperation is love applied to industry," with Japanese characters for the five tenets of the Friends of Jesus—devotion (*keiken*), peace (*heiwa*), purity (*junketsu*), service (*hōshi*), and labor (*rōdō*)—across the top and depictions of Japanese farmers and laborers above the letters KAGAWA on the bottom. The memorial window visually and symbolically encapsulated the sanctification of Kagawa and his teachings among his most ardent American supporters.

Following his return to Japan, Kagawa continued his writing and advocacy of social reform and international peace. In August 1940 he was briefly imprisoned for a public apology he had made six years earlier, on behalf of the Japanese people, for Japan's aggression in China. The next year he revisited the United States, first as a member of the 1941 Japanese Christian Peace Delegation (Nichibei Kirisutokyō heiwa shisetsudan) and then on an independent speaking tour. He was unable to calm US-Japanese tensions, which broke into war three months after his return. He made further tours of the United States during the 1950s and was again warmly greeted by Japanese American audiences. He died in 1960.

Toyohiko Kagawa's social reformism and work with economic cooperatives served as a model for implementing the teachings of the social gospel. His advocacy of labor rights, consumer cooperatives, and universal suffrage mark him as a figure ahead of his time. His cosmopolitan outlook and opposition to war, moreover, made him an appealing advocate for racial reconciliation and world peace.

HISAYE YAMAMOTO AND THE CATHOLIC WORKER MOVEMENT *with Matthieu Langlois*

Hisaye Yamamoto (DeSoto) was a multitalented literary artist and political activist. Though she achieved mainstream renown as a writer of short fiction, notably the widely anthologized story "Seventeen Syllables," her output of stories was small, and most of her stories were written during a period of a few years after World War II. In contrast, Yamamoto worked for many years as a newspaper reporter and columnist and engaged in political activism. These twin activities would come together in the mid-1950s, when Yamamoto joined the Catholic Worker movement and wrote for its newspaper, the *Catholic Worker*.

Hisaye Yamamoto was just fourteen years old when she started work as a community journalist, writing a regular column for *Kashū Mainichi* under the pen name "Napoleon." She continued writing these columns (with differing bylines) through the start of World War II. After being confined with her family at the Poston camp in 1942, Yamamoto was hired by the *Poston Chronicle* and

Hisaye Yamamoto. Courtesy of the family of Hisaye Yamamoto.

started a column called "Small Talk" in its pages. She also produced for the *Chronicle* a serialized mystery story, a potboiler set in camp entitled "Death Rides the Rails to Poston."

In 1944 Yamamoto relocated to Springfield, Massachusetts, to work as a domestic, but found the work so arduous and the town's racial climate so hostile that she ultimately decided to return to camp and help care for family. She adopted a five-month-old Sansei boy, Paul, who had been born into the family, and she raised him as her son.

In 1945, following her return to Los Angeles, Yamamoto was hired as a columnist by the African American newspaper the *Los Angeles Tribune*. The *Tribune*'s editors clearly hoped that Yamamoto would serve as a bridge between the two communities in the former Japanese district of Little Tokyo, which had been transformed into the Black enclave of Bronzeville once the area's Japanese population was forcibly removed. Yamamoto worked as a reporter for the *Tribune* and produced a regular column, again called "Small Talk." Yamamoto found working for the *Tribune* a transformational experience. In addition to her journalism, she became engaged in direct action through the civil rights group the Congress of Racial Equality (CORE), leading nonviolent protests against racial segregation at Bullock's department store and the swimming resort Bimini Baths.

In 1948 Yamamoto published her first short story, "The High Heeled Shoes," in the prestigious New York intellectual journal *Partisan Review*. Encouraged by this success, she withdrew from journalism to devote herself to writing fiction full-time. During this period she produced a half-dozen short stories, most notably "Seventeen Syllables" and "Yoneko's Earthquake," which remain her best-known works.

Even after leaving the *Tribune*, Yamamoto remained interested in pacifism and social justice. Her interest became increasingly centered on the Catholic Worker (CW) movement, a pacifist movement launched in 1933 by the social activist Dorothy Day and her mentor, Peter Maurin. Yamamoto had first been introduced to the *Catholic Worker* in 1945, after she began working for the *Los Angeles Tribune*. As scholar Sarah D. Wald explains, the *Catholic Worker* was one of several newspapers to which she was assigned to read regularly to search for articles of note to reprint.[1] In fact, shortly before Hisaye Yamamoto began working there, the *Tribune* had published "Blueprint for Demoralization," an essay on Japanese Americans that took off from Nisei journalist Eddie Shimano's essay "Blueprint for a Slum," and the *Catholic Worker* had proceeded to run the *Tribune* essay unabridged in its pages. Yamamoto's personal collections included numerous issues of the *Catholic Worker* dating from 1945 to 1948, the period that she worked for the *Tribune*, that were initially addressed to Mrs. Almena Davis, the *Tribune*'s chief editor.[2]

By a strange coincidence, Yamamoto's interest in the Catholic Worker movement was also stimulated by her developing friendship with the Nisei writer Yone U. Stafford, a friend of Dorothy Day and a sympathizer with the Catholic Worker movement.[3] In one of her columns for the *Los Angeles Tribune*, Yamamoto expressed her desire to live according to her pacifist beliefs.[4] This prompted Stafford, who was a committed pacifist, to write Yamamoto to share her own experience and offer advice on how to stay on the path of nonviolence. Stafford also started to send Yamamoto books, newspapers, and magazines about pacifism on a regular basis. Yamamoto later stated that among the literature she received were "books by Jane Addams, Porter Sargent, Sarah Cleghorn, and a magazine called 'Gist.'" Yamamoto, in turn, seems to have connected her new friend with the editors of the *Los Angeles Tribune*. In fact, following Yamamoto's departure from the newspaper, her column was replaced by Stafford's pacifist-themed column, I Go Crying Peace, Peace, which ran off and on in the *Tribune* over the following years. The Catholic Worker movement must have been part of their discussions because years later, while living at the Catholic Worker, Yamamoto would tell Stafford: "You are really the reason I'm here, Yone."

We may wonder why Yamamoto chose to join the Catholic Worker. In one column for the *Los Angeles Tribune*, she identified herself as someone "who [would] tend toward agnosticism, sometimes wallow in atheism."[5] This would seem to stand in open contradiction with the Catholic pacifism of the Catholic Worker, which was based not on political arguments but on religious ones. Indeed, Dorothy Day contended that any act of violence against a human being was an attack on the "Mystical Body of Christ." However, despite her skepticism, Yamamoto was still at least open to the possibility that God existed. As she wrote in one of her columns: "My present pro-peace argument laps over into arguments for a possible God and a possible after-life."[6] Yamamoto's beliefs were thereby closer to those of Day and the Catholic Worker than those of secular pacifist organizations.

All the same, the Catholic Worker was not the only religious organization to champion nonviolence. There were others Yamamoto could have chosen from, such as the Fellowship of Reconciliation. What, then, can explain her special attraction to the Catholic Worker?

The answer to this question may lie in Yamamoto's autobiographical 1960 short story "Epithalamium," which tells the story of a Japanese American woman named Yuki Tsumagari who leaves California to join a Catholic lay community and live within it on a farm on Staten Island.[7] This fictional community had been founded by Marie Chavy, "a carefree Greenwich Village refugee," and a French "scholar-farmer" named René Zualet, with the intent to create a place "where all would live together in Christian love and voluntary poverty, working on the land and studying together, accepting all who came because they had nowhere else to go." In this story Yuki Tsumagari explains that her presence within this community stems from her having read and felt deeply moved by the autobiography of Marie Chavy: "Yuki remembered Madame Marie's published autobiography, the book that had changed her whole life and brought her all the way across the country." In real life Dorothy Day's autobiography, *The Long Loneliness*, was published in 1952, a year before Yamamoto came to live with the Catholic Worker. It seems highly probable that just as with Yuki Tsumagari and Marie Chavy, it was Day's autobiography that inspired Yamamoto to choose the Catholic Worker.

Another important element that can explain Hisaye Yamamoto's choice is her role as adoptive mother to Paul, whom Yamamoto described as "a cradle Catholic." As she later explained to scholar King-Kok Cheung, she intended to respect his faith, "but [she] also wanted him to become the best type of Catholic there was—a Catholic Worker."[8]

Whatever the cause(s) of Yamamoto's decision to join the Catholic Worker, in 1953 she and her adopted son, Paul, moved to Staten Island, New York City, to live and work on the Peter Maurin Farm, a collective farm on Staten Island operated by the CW movement. She was intrigued by the experiment in agricultural collectivism, and she had her own special skills to contribute—unlike many of her new comrades, Yamamoto had wide experience in agriculture, drawn from her work in her youth on family-run farms in California.

Yamamoto's presence at the Peter Maurin Farm gave her a special closeness with Dorothy Day, who made the farm her primary residence during this period.[9] Day, who deeply loved children, often mentioned Paul Yamamoto in her monthly *Catholic Worker* column, On Pilgrimage, and told anecdotes of his life on the farm.[10] Day's comments on Yamamoto herself, while briefer, were laudatory. As Sarah D. Wald has demonstrated, Day perceived Yamamoto as a true disciple of Peter Maurin, someone who was able to combine manual and intellectual work.[11] This was a rare quality among the Catholic Workers, who tended to favor one aspect or the other.

Meanwhile, profiting from her long experience in journalism, Yamamoto began writing articles for the CW monthly newspaper, the *Catholic Worker*, following her arrival. Yamamoto's first article, which appeared in the June 1954 issue, was entitled "Seabrook Farms—20 Years Later." It was a study of labor relations at Seabrook Farms, a giant farming and canning enterprise in central New Jersey. Yamamoto told the story of a worker strike in 1934, during the depths of the Great Depression, then reported on the work of Japanese American resettlers during and after World War II:

> About 3,000 West Coast Japanese were recruited from the several inland "relocation centers" for work in the plants. They began at wages of 50¢ per hour in 1944 paying $8.75 a week for room and board. As their families joined them, they were given free and good government housing. When the housing was later sold to Seabrook, the rent was set at $11 per month.... Mr. Seabrook, who at first welcomed the Japanese for their general industry and reliability, is now said to be cool towards them, ever

since they obeyed union instructions and participated in a "walk-out" a few years ago. This, he reportedly felt, was his thanks for rescuing them from the concentration camps.

The author shrewdly drew parallels between the paternalistic treatment of Nikkei workers at Seabrook and the larger state of labor relations: "Although he has officially retired and sent in one of his sons as replacement, [Mr. Seabrook] is still the real head of Seabrook Farms and the most influential man in the community. What all this calls to mind is feudalism, with Mr. Seabrook as the lord of the castle atop the hill. He surveys a tremendous domain, comprising thousands of acres, thousands of buildings, and thousands of workers representing a goodly section of the races of mankind."

Yamamoto followed up this extended article with a series of chronicles of her work on the Peter Maurin Farm, designed to offer cw donors a taste of the organization's work. In her piece in the December 1954 *Catholic Worker*, Yamamoto stressed their brotherhood: "[It] is still a daily miracle how we, coming from such a wild diversity of backgrounds and thrown together by our common needs, live as one family, struggling to respect one another's personalities. There are about eighteen of us here now, ranging in age from six to seventy, most of us survivors of a virus which knocked us for a loop this past month."

In the February 1955 installment, Yamamoto underlined the diversity of thought that she was exposed to on the farm and how it stimulated her:

> Francisco, who comes out from Chrystie Street each week to help Lee make bread, was up at six o'clock to get the bakery going. He has with him, as always, his favorite book, the Bhagavad-Gita; the New Testament; and the Gospel of Ramakrishna, in one volume, which he had bound together in Chicago when he decided that these books were the ones which held the most meaning for him. It is said that St. Theresa of Lisieux confined herself to the Scriptures and The Imitation of Christ. But most of us here are not so intent on a single track. We do a great deal of reading here, especially these days when we are restricted to inside activity, and our tastes are catholic, including everything from the *Daily News* to *Life of Spirit*.

In her last installment, which appeared in the July 1955 issue of *Catholic Worker*, Yamamoto wrote frankly about the struggles inherent in keeping up the farm and the larger "back-to-the-land" ideology that underlay it:

To begin with, those who join the work because of the rural emphasis are in the minority. Indeed, there are those amongst us who are in favor of dropping the farming idea entirely. Then, although categories are always overlapping or not quite apt, we have encountered those who come as romantic agrarians and find the reality of subsistence-farming a little too grim for comfort, those who are willing and able to cope with the reality but not with the peculiar crosses which seem to burden all our endeavors, and those who will admit the sanity and sanctity of living and working on the land but who will argue that the time is past, that the odds are too overwhelming, that the struggle availeth naught and therefore ought not to be made. And, of course, there are the ones who prefer the conveniences and consolations of the city and who couldn't be persuaded to try to work the land on any basis.

While Yamamoto did not deny the ideological conflicts over the rural experiment, she trumpeted its practical success: "The Farm today is on a self-sustaining basis as far as the animals are concerned, and is furthermore supplying this community of from 20–25 people, plus the flock of summer visitors, with most of its fresh fruits and vegetables."

Despite these brave words, Hisaye Yamamoto herself would soon give up her life on the farm. In late 1955 she married Anthony DeSoto, whom she had met in New York, and returned to Los Angeles. She devoted herself to caring for her husband and raising five children as well as writing occasional pieces for the vernacular Japanese press. While she remained a subscriber to the *Catholic Worker* in later years and produced a handful of pieces for the newspaper, her connection to Dorothy Day's movement rather faded from view. When *Seventeen Syllables*, the signature anthology of her writings, was published by Kitchen Table Press in 1988, it did not discuss her time working with the Catholic Worker movement nor include any selections of her writing for its publication.

Nonetheless, it is clear that Yamamoto's experience with the Catholic Worker was enormously influential on her. In particular, the evidence suggests that she made a shift in her religious views during this period. While as a self-declared non-Christian, Yamamoto was not required to attend or participate in Catholic religious services, Day nonetheless mentioned going with her and Paul to liturgical celebrations and retreats directed by priests. For instance, in the *Catholic Worker* of May 1954, Day wrote that she went for Holy Thursday "to the Franciscan monastery on Todt Hill for Tenebrae which was beautiful indeed. Hisaye and little Paul were with us."¹² A few months later, Day reported that both Hisaye and Paul Yamamoto were present at the annual retreat at Maryfarm in Newburgh led by Father Marion G. Casey.¹³ In a recent book of photos that Vivian Cherry took while she was staying at the Peter Maurin Farm in 1955, we see Hisaye and Paul Yamamoto kneeling and praying with Dorothy Day and other Catholic Workers.¹⁴

This attitude appears to be in total opposition to the beliefs Yamamoto had expressed a few years earlier in the *Los Angeles Tribune*.¹⁵ How do we explain the shift? Even if Yamamoto was guided by an interest in raising her Catholic son properly, it would be false to solely ascribe Yamamoto's participation in religious services simply to her role as a parent. Indeed, in the same interview with Cheung previously cited, Yamamoto stated that she identified herself as a Christian: "I'm a Christian because I believe that Jesus Christ is the Son of God."¹⁶ In view of this evidence, the nature of Yamamoto's encounter with the philosophy of Dorothy Day and with Day herself, as well as the religious exploration she undertook during this period, would seem to merit much further research and discussion.

THE UNDISCOVERED HISTORY OF JAPANESE AMERICANS AND THE CHURCH OF JESUS CHRIST OF LATTER-DAY SAINTS
with Christian Heimburger

A rather unsuspected but significant force in Japanese American life has been the Church of Jesus Christ of Latter-day Saints (LDS), whose members are commonly known as Latter-day Saints, or Mormons (the latter name derives from the Book of Mormon, the church's key scriptural text). Throughout the first half of the twentieth century, LDS congregations and missionaries interacted with Japanese communities in different locations, even as thousands of Japanese Americans subjected to official confinement in Utah and Idaho during World War II came into close contact with LDS Church members. While relatively few Japanese Americans took up the faith during this period, Nisei Mormons ultimately played a disproportionate part in shaping Japanese communities.

To begin with, the LDS Church conducted missionary work in Japan, through which it encountered Japanese people. The first Japanese mission opened in 1901. Among the group of pioneering missionaries was Heber J. Grant, who was later to serve as president of the LDS Church during World War II. The mission closed in 1924, a casualty of growing Japanese nationalism, anti-American sentiment, and lack of interest by Japanese. By that time there were approximately 176 members of the church in Japan.

Meanwhile, as they arrived in North America in the early 1900s, Japanese immigrants came into contact with Mormons. First, a handful of Mormons baptized in Japan settled in the United States. Takeo Fujiwara, who had been baptized by missionaries in his native Hokkaido, Japan, accompanied a missionary returning to Utah and enrolled at the Brigham Young High School and then Brigham Young University, becoming in 1934 the first Japanese to graduate from the university. After graduation Fujiwara returned to Japan to direct missionary efforts. Sadly, he soon contracted tuberculosis, and he died barely one year later. Tsuneko Ishida Nachiye, who had worked for eighteen years as cook and housekeeper at the residence of the LDS mission president in Japan and had joined the church there, traveled to Hawaii in 1923 to see the temple there and began work proselytizing to other Japanese. She remained in Hawaii until her death in 1938.

In the United States numerous Japanese laborers settled in historic Mormon strongholds in Idaho and Utah. For example, according to historian Eric Walz, Japanese laborers came to Sugar City, near Rexburg, Idaho, to work for the Utah and Idaho Sugar Company, of which the Mormon Church was a principal owner. A handful of Issei accepted baptism. For example, Tomizo Katsunuma, who came to the United States in 1889 and settled in Logan, Utah, where he studied veterinary medicine, entered the church in 1895 (and simultaneously was able to naturalize as a US citizen). Katsunuma moved to Hawaii soon after and became a Japanese community leader, immigration inspector, and columnist for the *Nippu Jiji* newspaper. Still, the largest number of the immigrants declined to adopt their neighbors' religion. This refusal may have been as much cultural as theological. While Issei Christians generally set up their own congregations with Japanese-speaking ministers, no separate Japanese Mormon churches were established on the mainland—it is not clear whether this was mostly due to lack of sufficient Nikkei membership or to principled opposition to ethnic congregations among church leaders.

Nonetheless, there was significant interaction between the newcomers and their Mormon neighbors during the prewar generation. Issei in Rexburg used Mormon churches for meetings of the local Japanese Association. Even unaffiliated Issei parents sent their Nisei children to the local Primary Association (a kind of Mormon version of church school). Walz notes that the register of the Honeyville, Utah, Primary lists attendance by Nisei at different times beginning

In Good Faith

in 1927. In 1941 two Nisei children are listed as having donated thirteen cents to the Primary Children's Hospital (a medical center operated by the LDS Church). Mike Ota was invited to speak to the Ogden, Utah, branch of Junior Christian Endeavor in 1937 on "Mormonism as I see it." Outside of the intermountain West, there was more sporadic contact between Nikkei and Mormons, During the 1930s the Church Division of Sacramento's Twilight League featured the Mormon Templars, a club representing the local Latter-day Saints church.

Some Nisei converted as a result of attending Primaries with their Mormon friends. In 1930 thirteen-year-old Wuta Terazara of Sugar City wrote in *Nichi Bei Shimbun* about the fun of attending cooking demonstrations and going on hikes with her friends at the Primary, adding, "I'm a Mormon and I'm proud to be one too." Some years later Frank and Ralph Nishiguchi secured their father's consent to be baptized. Kenji Shiozawa, a teenager in Pocatello, Idaho, in the 1930s, served as Boy Scout leader. He was later elected president of the Japanese Missionary Re-Union Association, comprised of returned LDS missionaries who had served in Japan and Hawaii. Hiroshi Yasukochi, a Nisei Mormon from Murray, Utah, starred on the Salt Lake Nippons baseball team and contributed articles to the West Coast Nisei press.

In Hawaii, where the LDS Church became renowned for its missionary efforts among native Hawaiians, efforts at winning Japanese converts were less concentrated, though there were a handful of Nikkei church members, including Tomizo Katsunuma, as mentioned, and Tokujiro Sato, a Japanese laborer. In 1934 the Kalihi (Honolulu) LDS Church opened a Japanese school. Three years later church officials created a Japanese mission under the direction of Elder Hilton A. Robertson, with forty-two missionaries serving in the various islands. (The Reorganized Church of Jesus Christ of Latter-day Saints [today known as the Community of Christ], a separate LDS Church group, had already opened a Japanese branch in Kalihi in 1929.) When Dr. John Widtsoe, a noted scientist and Mormon leader, arrived in Honolulu in 1938 on a monthlong visit to review church work in Hawaii, he was escorted by Kay Kichitaro Ikegami, manager of the Japanese department of the State Building & Loan Association, who was listed as a local Japanese Mormon leader. In terms of converts, the Hawaii LDS mission proved to be much more fruitful than the 1901–24 mission in Japan. By the end of 1942, there were around three hundred Nikkei members of the church (mostly US-born) in Hawaii. Some of those converted during this time went on to become influential church leaders, including Chieko Okazaki, who became a counselor in the Relief Society General Presidency in 1990.

The most significant connections between the LDS Church and the Nikkei were forged by Dr. Elbert Thomas. In 1907, six years after the LDS Church established its first mission in Japan, Thomas and his wife moved to Japan as Mormon missionaries. Once in Japan, Thomas learned to speak and read the Japanese language so well that in 1911 he wrote a book in Japanese, *Sukai no Michi*. Thomas and his wife named their Japanese-born daughter Chiyo. The Thomases left Japan in the early 1920s (before the mission finally closed in 1924). After returning to the United States, Dr. Thomas served as professor of international law and politics at the University of Utah. He served as a mentor to numerous Nikkei students at Utah, not only because of his command of the Japanese language but also because of his attachment to Japan and its culture. In 1934 he was elected to the US Senate as a liberal Democrat.

One of Thomas's main protégés was Mike Masaru Masaoka. Masaoka, a colorful and controversial figure, was the most famous Nikkei Mormon. However, he clearly separated his religious faith from his public life and did not generally speak publicly about his religion. Born in Fresno, California, Masaoka moved with his family to Salt Lake City as a child. His father died when he was just nine years old, and he was taken up afterward by white sponsors. Sometime during his childhood, Masaoka was baptized as a Mormon and joined a Mormon Boy Scout troop. He attended the University of Utah, where he distinguished himself as a varsity debater and staffer on the campus newspaper. After graduation, he returned to coach the university debating squad, as well as working in the civic field. He was described in newspaper stories of the time as a "priest" in the Mormon Church.

In 1940, at age twenty-four, Masaoka became director of the Utah Conference of Human Relations, an interracial committee. Meanwhile, he served as English editor of the *Utah Nippo* and became active in the Japanese American Citizens League (as we will see, Masaoka's actions in founding new chapters later bore fruit for the organization). For the JACL's biannual convention in 1940, Masaoka penned the "Japanese American Creed," a manifesto that would guide the organization in future years.

Throughout this period Masaoka retained a close relationship with Elbert Thomas. While in college, he volunteered for work on Thomas's successful Senate campaign. Thomas offered support and political contacts to the young Masaoka, which were an invaluable aid in his rise to leadership in the JACL. Notably, as a member of the Senate Education and Labor Committee, Senator Thomas invited Masaoka to a hearing held by the Presidential Commission on

In Good Faith

Equal Employment Opportunities in Los Angeles in fall 1941, which provided him his first nationwide exposure.

As mentioned, throughout the prewar years Japanese Americans, especially those in the intermountain West, developed connections of different kinds with members of the Church of Jesus Christ of Latter-day Saints. To show their appreciation to the Mormon Church for its friendly attitude toward Japan, in April 1941 a group of Salt Lake Japanese Americans, led by Mike Masaoka, presented twenty-five Japanese cherry trees for planting around the Mormon Tabernacle. This relationship would be tested by World War II and by the wartime removal and confinement of Issei and Nisei from the West Coast.

At first church leaders maintained a friendly policy. In the wake of the Pearl Harbor attack and the US Declaration of War on Japan, the First Presidency of the Mormon Church released a public statement deploring the tragedy of war and warning against feelings of hatred. Two days later the *Deseret News*, the church's official organ, ran an editorial: "There is no reason to doubt . . . or to question the loyalty and devotion of the Utah Japanese to this country. The Japanese children in the schools and the Japanese men and women throughout the state should be treated with due respect and tolerance." Such a policy of welcome was not universally applied. In Osgood, near Idaho Falls, Idaho, one Mormon bishop announced, "I don't want any Japs in this congregation." Yet a local Mormon farmer agreed to buy the contraband guns of his Japanese American neighbors for a symbolic one dollar and to hold them during the war—he later returned them, as promised, after the war's end.

After President Franklin Roosevelt signed Executive Order 9066, West Coast Japanese Americans faced mass removal and confinement. The Mormon Church took no official position on the president's order, nor did church leaders send missionaries to assist Japanese Americans. However, Mike Masaoka mobilized his contacts with individual Mormons to win aid for the Nisei. With support from Elbert Thomas and from Salt Lake City mayor Ab Jenkins (a Mormon leader and former race car driver), Masaoka invited the JACL leadership to leave the coast and move to Utah. The JACL not only set up wartime operations in the Beeson Building in Salt Lake City, but JACL leaders sponsored the launching of the *Pacific Citizen* as a regular newspaper and hired the journalists Larry and Guyo Tajiri as editors. According to legend, in mid-1942 Mayor Jenkins traveled to the state's borders to welcome caravans of Nisei from San Francisco personally and escort them into the capital.

It was at this same time that Masaoka's previous efforts bore fruit. In the months before the war, as part of his work with the JACL Intermountain District, Masaoka had gone through Utah and up and down the old Mormon trails, visiting areas such as Rexburg and Idaho Falls, Idaho, to assist local Japanese communities in forming new JACL chapters. With the coming of mass removal and the shuttering of West Coast communities, these JACL chapters were the only ones that remained intact, and National leaders were able to draw from their chapter dues to fund JACL operations. Furthermore, in 1943, using one hundred dollars worth of funds provided by members of these chapters, JACL treasurer Hito Okada started a JACL credit union, which was chartered by the state of Utah. This union would later provide loans for resettlers and in the process helped finance JACL operations. Even after 1952, when the national JACL offices and the *Pacific Citizen* returned to the West Coast, the credit union would remain based in Salt Lake City.

The mass confinement of some twenty thousand Issei and Nisei at the Topaz, Heart Mountain, and Minidoka camps, all of which were located in areas with significant Mormon populations, plus the coming to Utah of waves of resettlers, brought Japanese Americans into large-scale contact with LDS churches and their members. While some Latter-day Saints had previous contact with people of Japanese ancestry in Japan, Hawaii, or California, many Mormons living in the Mountain West first encountered Japanese Americans only after the federal government began releasing detainees from the camps for seasonal agricultural work. From 1942 to 1945 thousands of Nikkei laborers worked in Mormon-dominated communities in Utah, western Wyoming, southern Idaho, and eastern Oregon. The largest percentage of these laborers were recruited by sugar beet companies, such as the LDS-operated Utah and Idaho Sugar Company, to thin, block, and harvest sugar beets. As such, Latter-day Saint attitudes toward the Nikkei were largely shaped or altered by personal interactions in this setting. In turn, many Japanese Americans formed opinions about Mormons as they worked on their farms, in their factories, and in their homes.

Mormon farmers welcomed seasonal laborers with open arms. In 1943 Utah and Idaho Sugar Company man and Latter-day Saint Ford T. Scalley observed: "Some communities, at first prejudiced against the Japanese as a race, warmed up to the situation. Local residents and inmates became mutually better acquainted. At first tolerated as a necessity, thousands of Japanese Americans were later accepted under mutually helpful arrangements as efficient workers." Desperate for laborers, many farmers appreciated the efforts of Japanese

In Good Faith 115

American workers and acknowledged, as Amalgamated Sugar Company district supervisor D. E. Smith did in 1944, that "many acres of sugar beets in the county would have been lost if we had not had this Japanese labor."

For their part, seasonal laborers reported that the Latter-day Saints with whom they interacted generally treated them with respect and even kindness. Reflecting on his experience with residents of the Utah town of Delta, Kinbichi Yoshitomi recalled: "That was my first contact with the Mormons and I found them very delightful. . . . They encouraged us to keep our spirits up, and they gave us a lot of help. Whenever we went into town to do some shopping, why, there was no animosity." In a May 1943 issue of the *Heart Mountain Sentinel*, editor Bill Hosokawa singled out Lovell, Wyoming, as a community willing to "stick out their necks against critics and speak truth as they see it." "One of the reasons attributed to Lovell's friendliness toward us is that it is a strong Mormon community," he observed. "Mormons in all parts of the Mountain states have been unusually charitable toward the evacuees." A number of seasonal workers, such as Dave Tatsuno, also expressed the sentiment that the Latter-day Saints had a "background of being persecuted and so they had a natural sympathy for those of the evacuees who were also being persecuted."

Latter-day Saints, too, were changed by their interactions with Nikkei workers. In an October 1942 letter to journalist Carey McWilliams, one seasonal worker described a conversation he had had with a Utah woman. "She told me of the attitude of the people here toward the coming of Japanese workers. That some were definitely suspicious of us, afraid we might do them harm or that we might be 'spies,'" he wrote. "She said that our coming and living in the same community has dispelled their fears, and now most of them think very highly of us as being well-mannered, friendly, and being perfect gentlemen. . . . She invited us to attend the services at the LDS Church Sunday." In 1943 schoolteachers Rulon and Lucilla Hinckley hired Topaz inmate Gladys Hayashi to care for their young children. The children quickly fell in love with the twenty-one-year-old Nisei, and she was embraced as part of their family. The Hinckleys included Hayashi in their family activities and eventually invited her to attend Latter-day Saint worship services with the family, despite opposition from some other local residents. In time Hayashi embraced the family's faith.

Though Nikkei workers had predominantly positive interactions with members of the Church of Jesus Christ of Latter-day Saints, not every member of the community accepted the outsiders. Latent racism, inflamed by the presence of what some perceived as "dangerous elements," made it difficult for some of the region's residents to overcome their prejudices. While on seasonal work leave, Japanese American laborers faced varying degrees of racial discrimination, and some were even victims of physical violence. In 1943, for example, a group of teenagers fired several gunshots into a labor camp in Provo, Utah, injuring three Nikkei workers. Even in the waning months of the war, some Utahans lobbied to block Japanese Americans from owning land or obtaining business licenses in the state. The acrimonious rhetoric eventually led the LDS Church-owned newspaper *Deseret News* to print an editorial—titled "They Are God's Children Also"—asserting: "Americans who are loyal are good Americans whether their ancestors came from Great Britain or Japan, the Scandinavian countries or Germany. Let us, therefore, endeavor to banish these foolish prejudices from our natures and let us attempt to see that all good and loyal Americans are treated as such."

Ultimately, a number of Japanese Americans in Utah and Idaho did join the LDS Church. For example, Ken Mano, whose family had moved to Utah as part of a "voluntary evacuation," lived in Layton (being housed in a chicken coop), then West Bountiful. He and his siblings were invited to attend the local Primary with all the classmates "because that was the thing to do." Eventually, their house was visited by stake missionaries, and they were baptized. After the war's end, Mano served as an LDS missionary in Japan. By 1944 there was enough of a nucleus that an LDS Study Group, made up of some fifty Nikkei, formed in Salt Lake City and engaged in joint meetings with other Mormon groups. In early 1945 a presidency, made up of three former missionaries to the Japanese mission in Hawaii, was appointed to govern the activities of the study group. A report of a 1947 meeting included speeches by Shigaki Ushio, who spoke of his experiences during the "evacuation"; Priscilla Yasuda, a former Women's Army Corps sergeant in the European theater; and Chi Terazawa, who had served as an LDS missionary in Hawaii during the war years. Another Nisei Mormon social organization was the LDS Fireside Group. In 1947 the group organized to help the Latter-day Saints Welfare Department send Christmas food packages to 116 families of friends and relatives of LDS Church members in Hawaii.

In 1948 the LDS would reopen its mission in Japan (a Nisei, Koji Okauchi, was one of the initial team of missionaries) and attract a new generation of converts. Meanwhile, Nikkei church members in Hawaii and on the continent continued to grow in numbers during the postwar years and to distinguish themselves.

In Good Faith 117

In sum, the rich history of Japanese Americans and the LDS Church remains to be further studied and to be granted its rightful place within the larger group story.

NIKKEI AND THE PEACE CHURCHES / MENNONITES AND BRETHREN *with Zacharie Leclair*

In his 1981 master's thesis, "The Response of the Historic Peace Churches to the Internment of the Japanese Americans during World War II," scholar Charles R. Lord makes a daring comparison between the experience of Japanese Americans confined in government camps during World War II on account of race and ancestry and that of conscientious objectors from peace churches, who were confined in Civilian Public Service (CPS) camps due to their religious beliefs. Remarkably, one individual, George Kiyoshi Yamada, bridged the two groups. In 1941, as a young student of journalism in San Francisco, he registered as a conscientious objector (CO) and was assigned to CPS Camp 21 at Cascade Locks, Oregon. While he no doubt expected to be subjected to anti-Japanese prejudice there, Yamada soon won the friendship of the other camp members. The following year, when Mark Schrock, the CPS camp's director, was ordered to send Yamada to a WRA camp, fifty-four CPS men signed a petition in support of Yamada. The letter's text lamented the infringement on the constitutional rights of those who objected to conscription due to reasons of conscience but also highlighted the fact that the refusal to grant a sincere individual such as Yamada the status of CO and to permit him to remain in the CPS camp had been made solely on account of race. The protest letter, endorsed by camp director Schrock, was sent on to federal authorities. They relented, and Yamada was duly transferred to an inland CPS camp in Colorado Springs, Colorado, outside of the excluded zone, and subsequently to another in Germfask, Michigan.

What is notable is that among the signers of the Cascade Locks petition, half were Mennonites. The petition represented one of the very few statements of opposition to government policy toward Japanese Americans that stemmed from Mennonite and Mennonite Brethren circles during World War II. It might seem astonishing that the Mennonites were so silent, at least in comparison to the Quakers and other communitarian Protestant sects. Lord lists various reasons to explain their reticence about opposing Executive Order 9066. First, Mennonite congregations were concentrated in the eastern United States.

Many Mennonites undoubtedly considered the "Japanese question," concentrated on the West Coast, as distant from them and their concerns (although this certainly does not account for the inaction of Mennonite Brethren in California). Also, the Mennonites, many of whom were of German ancestry and lived in small towns, might have feared a return of the anti-German vigilantism that they had experienced during World War I if they appeared "unpatriotic"—they were already vulnerable as a result of their refusal to serve in the armed forces. Finally, Mennonite congregations might have assumed that the Mennonite Central Committee, a branch of the Mennonite and Mennonite Brethren Churches that had been devoted to international service since its formation in 1920, would organize a group response. However, the committee, which was less drawn to domestic advocacy in that period, failed to act.

Still, there were Mennonites who spoke up in various ways for Japanese Americans. In a June 1942 magazine supplement to the *Gospel Herald*, the official publication of the Mennonites, writer Edward Yoder deplored "the organized and systematic campaign" being whipped up in the country to inculcate hate toward the Axis enemy. As a result of such propaganda, Yoder claimed, people "will freely hate Japanese-Americans, German-speaking Americans, Jews, Negroes, and all who happen to differ from themselves in race, color, opinions, and manner of life."

There were also Mennonites who worked to aid those in the camps, although without directly challenging official policy. According to the May 25, 1943, issue of the *Mennonite*, a children's group in an Eastern District church, the Juniors, made gifts to send to children in the camps. Bluffton College (now Bluffton University) in Ohio was one of the first universities to accept Nisei students under the auspices of the National Japanese American Student Relocation Council. In fall 1942 Robert Kumata and Richard Okada, a pair of transfer students, enrolled at Bluffton. A third Nisei student, Shigeru Matsunaga, joined them the next year. Perhaps the most courageous Mennonite to reach out to the Nikkei was Florence Auernheimer. After being fired from her job as a kindergarten teacher in Reedley, California, in 1942 because she refused to encourage her pupils to buy war bonds, she took a job as a dietitian at the Camino CPS camp, also in California. One year later she was hired as a schoolteacher at the Tule Lake Segregation Center. After one Nisei girl died of pneumonia, amid the fierce winter cold, Auernheimer threatened to quit if the government did not finish the inmates' barrack rooms and was also able to push the government to provide better heating. She remained at Tule Lake until the end of the war.

Astonishingly, among all the peace churches that stemmed from European Anabaptism, the most vigorous response to Executive Order 9066 came from one of its smallest fringe groups, the Church of the Brethren. During spring 1942 Ralph and Mary Blocher Smeltzer, a young couple of Brethren schoolteachers in their midtwenties, took action on behalf of Japanese Americans. First, as Japanese Americans were dispatched to the Assembly Centers, the Smeltzers made and served them free breakfasts. After the Manzanar camp opened, the Smeltzers moved operations and taught there for six months. While in camp, they insisted on living side by side with the inmates, rather than being lodged in staff housing.

In order to assist in resettlement of Japanese Americans confined in camp, in 1943 the Smeltzers joined forces with M. R. Zigler, the head of Brethren Service, to organize the Chicago Brethren Hostel for Japanese American resettlers. The hostel began operations in temporary space at the Bethany Theological Seminary, then ultimately moved into a three-story building. It operated for a year, during which time it sheltered 1,085 resettlers. After it closed, church members founded the Brethren Ministry to resettlers, under the leadership of Dean L. Frantz. In addition to aiding resettlers in finding jobs and housing, the ministry served as a counseling service and fought anti-Asian discrimination. In 1944 the Smeltzers moved to New York to open a new hostel in Brooklyn. There they had to face Mayor Fiorello LaGuardia's public opposition to the project as well as threats of violence from local residents. They refused to back down, and the Brooklyn hostel operated for over a year.

The Church of the Brethren's initiative led by the Smeltzers was a crucial display of courage and critical response toward injustice, but it was also a rather isolated example. The Smeltzers desperately tried to mobilize their counterparts from the peace churches to join them, but with little result. In 1945 editor J. Winfield Fretz of the *Mennonite* bitterly lamented the church's inaction. "But what has happened to the social conscience of the Mennonite Church? . . . If she has spoken out against the great unethical and unjust social practices of our day, I have yet to discover it. Japanese American citizens by the hundred thousands were ruthlessly torn from their homes and families and hoarded into desert concentration camps by the United States Army." No doubt, as Charles R. Lord explained, the reasons for this silence are many-sided.

Whatever the reason, refusing to bear arms was one thing Mennonites already knew; advocating on behalf of vulnerable people was another they yet had to learn. The near-complete policy of inaction by most peace church members during the removal and confinement of Japanese Americans remains a useful subject of reflection and self-criticism for people still used to thinking of themselves as conscientious objectors.

Chapter 6
MIXED-RACE STORIES

KINJIRO MATSUDAIRA / MAYOR OF EDMONSTON, MARYLAND *with Jonathan van Harmelen*

In the pre–World War II years, mainland Japanese Americans were all but absent from electoral office. Whereas in Hawaii there were Nisei representatives in the Territorial Assembly and even a senator, Sanji Abe, those living elsewhere found endemic anti-Japanese prejudice an effective barrier to even running for elected office, though a few West Coast Nisei such as Clarence Arai and Karl Yoneda launched campaigns. After the war, a wave of Japanese American politicians rose to prominence as part of the changing dynamics of politics in the West. James Kanno was elected mayor of Fountain Valley, California, in 1957, while in 1962 Seiji Horiuchi of Colorado became the first Japanese American elected to a state legislature. In 1966 Kiyoto Ken Nakaoka took a seat on the city council of Gardena, California. In 1971 Norman Mineta was elected mayor of San Jose, and the late Eunice Sato was elected mayor of Long Beach, the first Nisei political leaders of large cities. Yet long before the postwar rise of Japanese American politicians, there was Kinjiro Matsudaira. Elected as mayor of the small Washington, DC, suburb of Edmonston, Maryland, in 1927, he was the first identifiably Asian elected official on the North American continent. His political career forms part of a fascinating Matsudaira family saga, which is itself a part of the long history of mixed-race Japanese Americans.

Kinjiro Matsudaira was born on September 13, 1885, in Bradford, Pennsylvania. His father, Tadaatsu (Tada Atsu) Matsudaira, the son of a Japanese noble family, reportedly related to the Tokugawa shoguns, was born in Edo (later known as Tokyo) in 1851. In 1872 Tadaatsu accompanied his brother Tadanari Matsudaira to the United States. While some sources claim that they were part of the so-called Iwakura Mission, a diplomatic mission of statesmen and scholars sent by the newly founded Meiji government, this is contested. In any case, once he arrived, Tadanari enrolled at Rutgers University. Tadaatsu attended Worcester Free Institute (later Worcester Polytechnic) and then Harvard University, where he studied civil engineering. It had been originally planned that the two brothers would return to Japan together following their studies. However, Tadaatsu Matsudaira fell in love with Carrie Sampson, the daughter of a local book and stationery store owner in New Brunswick, and he decided to stay in the United States rather than return to Japan. The couple were married in 1877. In the first years that followed, Tadaatsu worked for the Manhattan Elevated Railroad in New York. Within a few years he took up railroad engineering with the Union Pacific Railroad in Wyoming, then worked at mines in Idaho and Montana. During this period he invented the trigonometer, a surveying tool. In 1884 he was hired as city engineer of Bradford, Pennsylvania. Over these years the Matsudairas had three children, of whom one died in infancy. Shortly after Kinjiro's birth, Tadaatsu Matsudaira was diagnosed with tuberculosis. The Matsudaira family relocated to Denver, Colorado, in hopes that the dry western air would improve his health. There Tadaatsu worked for the Colorado State Engineer's Office, overseeing inspections on mining operations, and as a surveyor. Tadaatsu Matsudaira died of tuberculosis in January 1888.

Kinjiro Matsudaira was only three years old when Tadaatsu died. Interestingly enough, he knew little about his Japanese family until 1925, when Tsuneo Matsudaira arrived in Washington as the new Japanese ambassador and Kinjiro wrote the American embassy in Tokyo to inquire whether he was from the same family. Although the embassy responded that Tsuneo Matsudaira was not related to him, they informed him about his father's family background.

Little documentation about Kinjiro's childhood or education has survived. Following his father's death, Kinjiro was sent to live with his maternal grandparents, William and Rachel Sampson, in Virginia. In the 1900 census the fourteen-year-old Kinjiro is listed as residing with his grandparents in Chesterfield County, Virginia, not attending school, and working as a farm laborer. According to family legend, the Sampsons were unwilling or unable to care for their "Japanese" grandson and placed him in an orphanage they set up. He was so unhappy with his treatment there that he ran away from home and joined the circus. As fanciful as this tale sounds, a business card survives of "Kinjiro Matsudaira," listing him as manager of the Mataleamor trio, a group of three "Novelty Comic Acrobats" that included a "dwarf equilibrist." Various photos reveal Matsudaira both in clown costume and out of makeup.

On September 19, 1909, Kinjiro Matsudaira married Ellen Chisholm, a native of South Carolina (sometimes listed as Georgia) working as a clerk at

Kinjiro Matsudaira in clown costume, early 1900s. Courtesy of the family of Kinjiro Matsudaira.

Goldenberg's store in Washington, DC. The wedding was officiated by Methodist minister Rev. R. L. Wright and was announced in the DC newspaper the *Evening Star*. The wedding announcement characterized Kinjiro Matsudaira as employed by a business firm and as "a thorough American in all but name." (Indeed, despite his Japanese name and ancestry, he would be listed as "white" on all his census returns between 1900 and 1940.)

Matsudaira spent most of his life within the DC area. In the early years of their marriage, he and his wife, Ellen, lived with Ellen's mother and stepfather in Washington, DC. Later they lived in the suburban town of Hyattsville in Prince George's County, Maryland. In the first decade of their marriage, Ellen and Kinjiro Matsudaira had three children, Haru Caroline, Ellen, and Robert Ford Matsudaira. Sometime before 1917, Matsudaira took a job as a clerk and bookkeeper at the Woodward & Lothrop department store in Washington. Matsudaira also worked as an inventor, following in the footsteps of his father. He received a patent in 1914 for a fire detector he invented.

In 1924 Matsudaira helped spearhead a movement to separate the town of Edmonston from Hyattsville, Maryland. The new town was then split between two wards, with Matsudaira becoming city councilman of Ward 2. In July 1926 Kinjiro formally announced his candidacy for mayor of Edmonston, running against fellow councilman D. H. McLeod, of Ward 1. After running on a platform to improve the town's infrastructure, Matsudaira beat McLeod and was sworn into office in 1927. Matsudaira's election as the first Japanese American mayor received significant attention from newspapers across the United States. The *New York Herald Tribune* profiled him as the country's "first Japanese mayor," and nationally syndicated articles featured discussion of Matsudaira and his family connections to Japanese rulers.

In the Japanese American press, Matsudaira's election as mayor of Edmonston was well received. The San Francisco *Nichi Bei Shinbun* headlined its story "Japanese Born in US to Be Elected Mayor of Town in Maryland," although few details were given beyond Matsudaira being no relation to Japanese ambassador Tsuneo Matsudaira. The *Nippu Jiji* of Honolulu described Kinjiro's family history and work as an executive at the Woodward department store. The *Nippu Jiji* also emphasized Kinjiro's physique as a "dark-haired, white complexioned and slender" *hapa* who "resembles a Japanese to be sure, but a good many of his countrymen who have met him could not be quite convinced." The news of Matsudaira's election even reached East Asia, where the election was mentioned in the pages of the *South China Morning Post* in Hong Kong and the *Kaigai Shinbun* in Japan.

Despite the historic nature of his election, the mayoralty seems to have been a part-time and unremunerative position, as Matsudaira kept his day job at Woodward & Lothrop. After his initial term, he did not seek re-election. Sometime during this period, Ellen Matsudaira was appointed as a postmaster. Later she worked at Woodward's. In 1933, in the depths of the Great Depression, Matsudaira ran for the town council and was elected for a two-year term. However, he resigned the next year, for reasons lost to history (his son-in-law Malcolm Dent ran unopposed in a special election to fill his seat). In 1939 he was again a candidate for town council but seems not to have been elected.

Kinjiro Matsudaira retired from Woodward & Lothrop in 1950 and died in October 1963.

Today Kinjiro Matsudaira is chiefly remembered as the sole Asian American to hold political office on the mainland before World War II. Yet if his election represents an anomaly in American political history, his family's presence in the community was not. Even after Kinjiro left office, he remained a resident of Edmonston. When the town was hit by floods in 1933 and 1955, he refused to abandon his home. An *Evening Star* reporter covering the 1955 flood noted that Kinjiro Matsudaira announced his intention to move upstairs until the flood abated, rather than be evacuated. "Why do I want to leave? This is just the way we live." The family remained a fixture in the Edmonston area after the death of its patriarch, and by the late twentieth century, four generations of Matsudairas had made their home there.

BERNARD SPENCER MIYAGUCHI / ICE SKATER EXTRAORDINAIRE

Born on August 6, 1924, in London, England, Bernard Spencer Miyaguchi was the son of Shunjiro Miyaguchi and his British wife, Marguerite (née Spencer) Miyaguchi. The elder Miyaguchi was a representative of the Japanese trading firm Suzuki Shoten. After the Suzuki company went out of business, he found a job with Nissho & Company, an import-export firm built by former employees of Suzuki. Bernard Miyaguchi and his sister, Ranko, three years his senior, grew up in London. Bernard attended Dulwich College.

In 1941, as war loomed, Shunjiro Miyaguchi returned to Japan with his family on the *Fushimi Maru*. Bernard and his sister immediately disliked Japan and made plans to return to England. By the time their required Japanese passports arrived, however, it was two days after the last boats to England had left, and they were stranded in Japan. In the following years, as Japan went through World War II, Bernard was forced into national service. Because he did not speak Japanese, he was placed in a forced labor contingent with Koreans and others and sent to work in a coal mine. In 1944, in the last year of the war, he was conscripted into the Japanese army. In response, he engaged in passive resistance. As he later recalled: "I spent the first four months in uniform pretending I couldn't speak Japanese, and they finally sent me home for a month and a half to learn it. It was a case of learn it, or else!" He returned to his unit and was sent to spend the winter of 1944 serving in Himeji, near Kobe. Although the region had snow piled two feet high, Miyaguchi and his mates had to go through the winter with insufficient clothing. Miyaguchi remained hungry from the poor food that soldiers were offered, which consisted mainly of rice and boiled pumpkin stalks. This diet led him to develop large malnutrition sores on his legs, leaving permanent scars.

When spring 1945 arrived, Miyaguchi was supposed to be sent for service in Thailand. However, Okinawa was undergoing heavy bombing by the Americans, and Japanese ships could not get through. Instead, Miyaguchi was sent to the island of Goto, about sixty miles from Nagasaki, where he was kept busy digging and clearing land for fortifications, as the island was considered a likely invasion target. Whether because of his mixed ancestry and foreign accent or just as part of military culture, he was subjected to rough treatment. He later recalled: "Any man who outranked you could beat you up and you had to take it. I was a first-class private, and anyone from a special-class private on up could do whatever he wanted. I got several beatings, mostly for nothing. Once I was slugged on the head with a boot for some minor infringement of regulations. They gave us an inspection after roll call every evening. My boots were dirty once, and I had to lick them clean then and there." Miyaguchi made himself a further target for harassment when he tried explaining to those around him that Japan was losing the war. His fellow soldiers, who were mostly middle-aged and uneducated, had been subjected to Tokyo's propaganda and refused to believe him, even after the Americans invaded Okinawa.

While serving on Goto, Miyaguchi discovered a group of six American airmen whose B-24 had been shot down and who had been taken prisoner. They faced harsh conditions. As he later recounted: "When I saw them first, they were tied up, stretched out on the ground, and blindfolded.... A friend of mine and I were the only ones on the island who spoke English. We arranged to have the prisoners given the best food available and their position eased a little."

He was still stationed on Goto when word came of the atomic bombings of Nagasaki (which he could not detect). He and his fellow soldiers were warned to move underground quickly whenever they saw an airplane approach. A few days later, while marching, they received word of Japan's surrender. Soon after, Miyaguchi was discharged from the Japanese army.

Following the end of the war, Miyaguchi officially renounced his Japanese citizenship. With assistance from British authorities, he and his sister, Ranko (later known as Marguerite Wilson), were able to leave Japan. The two traveled across the United States, stopping in Seattle en route to speak to journalists.

Once they arrived in England, Bernard expressed the intention of joining the Royal Air Force as a cadet. Instead, he went into professional ice skating, working under the professional name Bernard Spencer (his mother's maiden name). In 1949 he achieved acclaim when he and his partner, Gladys Hogg, entered the British professional ice dance contest. It was the first time that the free dance, previously an amateur event, had been approved on an experimental basis by the International Skating Union for professional competitions. The couple won the competition. The same year, Spencer performed in Hogg's Ice Revue. These achievements helped launch him on a long and successful career, both as a performer and as an accomplished trainer and coach. In 1955, while working as an instructor at Streatham ice rink, he was featured in a TV program, *British Ice Skating*. In 1957 he was featured on the ITV program *Seeing Sport*. During these years he had two children, Julie and Richard.

Through skating, Bernard met Janet Spiker. The two were married in 1972, after which Spencer moved with Janet to Columbus, Ohio. There, together with three ice skating colleagues, he started a restaurant called Buffalo Wild Wings. Bernard Spencer Miyaguchi died in Powell, Ohio, on September 24, 2009, a few months after his wife passed away.

EDITH DEBECKER SEBALD / DIPLOMAT

The heroine of a remarkable love story, Edith deBecker Sebald worked as a specialist for the Office of Strategic Services (OSS) during World War II and later served with her husband, William, in the US embassies in Burma and Australia.

Edith Frances deBecker was born in Japan in 1903 (some sources say Kamakura, others list Yokohama). She was the daughter of Joseph Ernest deBecker, a South African–born British citizen, and a Japanese mother from the powerful Minamoto clan (who claimed to be a direct descendant of Japanese emperor Seiwa). Mr. deBecker practiced international law in Kobe, Japan, was granted Japanese citizenship, and took the Japanese name Kobayashi Beika. Edith was educated in England and later attended a finishing school in Boston, where she became engaged to a British naval officer. When the Prince of Wales (later King Edward VIII) visited Yokohama in 1923, he reportedly praised her as Japan's most beautiful Eurasian girl. After the death of her mother in 1925, she returned to Japan. In 1927 she met William Sebald, a career US naval officer who was working as a language officer attached to the US embassy in Tokyo. After that first meeting, Edith rushed home to tell her father "What do you think—I'm engaged to two men now!" DeBecker was outraged. However, he agreed to meet the young American and was impressed by his fund of knowledge. When asked about his career prospects, Sebald replied: "I might even study law and come back here to practice with you. You said you needed help." Edith's father finally consented to the union, with the expectation that Sebald would ultimately join his law office.

Edith and Sebald decided to marry, although their union meant a sacrifice for both. Sebald's superiors told him that under established rules he couldn't marry until his three-year enlistment was finished and that such a marriage would ruin his career. Even worse for Edith, once married she would lose her Japanese citizenship, while as a woman with 50 percent Asian ancestry, she was racially ineligible to acquire US citizenship through her husband. (It is unclear whether she could have claimed British nationality, since her father had renounced his—two of her brothers did ultimately serve with the British army during World War II, while a sister and her British-born husband were interned by the Japanese at the notorious San Tomas internment camp in the Philippines.)

After marrying at All Saints Church in Kobe, the couple moved to the United States in 1928. For the next two decades, Edith was relegated to the status of a stateless woman. She could only reside in the United States using a temporary residence permit, which had to be renewed every six months. When she returned from a trip abroad, she always feared the consequences if the country refused to admit her. Under pressure from colleagues, William Sebald resigned from the navy, entered the reserves, and was admitted to the University of Maryland to study law. Once Sebald was admitted to the bar in 1933, the couple returned to Japan, and William established the firm of "deBecker and Sebald," specializing in international law. William also wrote a pair of English-language books on Japanese law. During the following years, as American-Japanese tensions grew, Sebald was regularly followed by secret agents and accused of being an American spy.

In 1939, with the clouds of war drawing closer, the Sebalds returned to the United States and settled in Washington, DC. In the wake of Pearl Harbor, both spouses offered their services to the US government. On the afternoon of December 7, William Sebald called Cdr. Arthur McCollum of the Office of Naval Information (ONI) and offered to return to active duty, arguing that his knowledge of Japan and fluency in the Japanese language would be useful to the government. He was initially engaged as a civilian advisor, then activated as a commander in the US Navy. He ultimately rose to the position of chief of the Pacific Section of Navy Combat Intelligence. The Sebalds were initially the target of suspicion because of Edith's status as a (perceived) "enemy alien." In late December 1941 the FBI searched the Sebalds' home and took some items. (After a call from McCollum to the director of ONI, the same agents returned to the house, restored the missing items, and apologized.) While her husband worked overseas, Edith was stationed in Washington, DC, where she was engaged as a consultant in psychological warfare by the Office of Strategic Services. Although her specific assignment remained classified, it presumably also revolved around treatment of Japanese-language materials. Edith later recounted that she was appalled that the OSS people for whom she worked were profoundly ignorant about Japan.

It is not clear how long Mrs. Sebald served in the OSS. However, her service must have been valuable. In 1946, thanks to her wartime efforts, she was "adopted" by the United States and granted permanent residency by means of an Act of Congress sponsored by Senator Millard Tydings of Maryland. When the news arrived that president Harry Truman had signed the law, she stated publicly: "You can't imagine how wonderful it is. I can come and go to America as I please. It's what Billy and I waited for nineteen years. But all that waiting was worthwhile." In April 1953, following passage of the McCarran-Walter immigration act, she would become a US citizen.

Meanwhile, both Sebalds moved to Tokyo, where William Sebald served under US occupation forces as chief of general headquarters of the Supreme Command for Allied Powers (SCAP) and chair of the Allied Council. There he worked closely with Gen. Douglas MacArthur. Edith served as official cohost of many official functions presented by the MacArthurs and became a close associate of Jean MacArthur, the general's wife. (It was Edith Sebald who interrupted an embassy pool party on June 25, 1950, to warn the staff and General MacArthur that North Korea had invaded South Korea—she had heard the news on Japanese radio.)

In 1952 President Harry Truman named William Sebald ambassador to the newly independent nation of Burma (today known as Myanmar). While Burma held to a policy of nonalignment, during his time in Burma, Sebald attended the Manila conference, at which the South East Asian Treaty Organization (SEATO) was formed. Edith ran the embassy in Rangoon (today's Yangon) and collected art. In 1954 William Sebald was named deputy assistant secretary of state for East Asian and Pacific Affairs, charged with advising Secretary of State John

Edith Sebald and her brother, Joseph deBecker, in Tokyo, mid-1950s. Gerald and Rella Warrer Japan Slide Collection, Lafayette College.

Foster Dulles on Japanese issues. The Sebalds thus returned to Washington. In 1957 President Dwight Eisenhower appointed Sebald ambassador to Australia, and he served in Canberra for four years.

After leaving the diplomatic service, in 1961, William Sebald settled in Washington and practiced law and wrote the memoir *With MacArthur in Japan* (1966). For his work in Japan, Sebald would ultimately be awarded the First Class Order of the Rising Sun with Cordon. Mrs. Sebald painted and published a cookbook on Japanese cuisine. In 1966 the Sebalds settled in Naples, Florida. William died in 1980. Edith died of an aneurysm at her home a year later.

THE ENIGMA OF MARION SAKI

A wide selection of Nisei women have made their mark as entertainers, in diverse eras and areas of show business: dance, concert halls, opera, theater, and cinema. Arguably the first female star, and surely the most mysterious, was the multitalented Marion Saki (sometimes known as Marian Saki), a ballerina turned Broadway song and dance star of the 1920s, who reinvented herself as a club and concert singer in the 1930s.

Marion Saki, publicity photo, ca. 1920.

When it comes to Saki's origins and background, nothing is entirely clear. What seems most certain is that her father, George Saki, was born in Japan around 1873 and came to the United States in the 1890s. He married Anna Olson in Brooklyn in 1900 and died in September 1920. The 1910 census lists the Saki family as living in Lakewood, New Jersey, where they were employed as servants in the house of a white family, and having two children, Marion and her younger brother, Archie. A 1915 New Jersey state census lists Marion Saki as having been born in 1903 and living in Lakewood. The 1920 census lists the family (all identified as white) as living in New York City. In the 1930 census, Marion Saki is described as twenty-three years old and living alone with her mother, Annette Olson, a widow of Swedish and Canadian parents. In her European travel declaration in 1926–27, Saki claimed a birthdate of January 27, 1905. When Saki went on a Caribbean cruise in 1938, she claimed to be twenty-five years old. Marion Saki's own statements about her life were as contradictory and questionable as her census forms. In multiple interviews Saki claimed to have been born in Japan as Hatsuyo or Hatsuko Sakakibara, the mixed-race daughter of Japanese dancer Gitsuo Sakakibara, and to have arrived in the United States at four years old.

Whatever her origins, the sources agree that Saki's big break came as a teenager, when she was invited to study ballet at a free dance school organized at New York's Hippodrome by legendary ballerina Anna Pavlova. A newspaper account asserted that Saki, "a little Japanese girl of 605 West 181st Street," was the daughter of a man who had been a famous dancer in Japan and for that reason was the first candidate selected for the school. A feature on Saki in the April 1918 issue of the magazine *Green Book* refers to her as Pavlova's favorite pupil and an important dancer in the ballet *Cheer Up*.

The first record of Saki's dance performance dates from December 1916, when she did a Japanese toe dance at a charity benefit at New York's Biltmore Hotel. A few months later, in April 1917, she danced a "swan song" (her teacher Pavlova's signature dance) at a charity event in Lakewood, New Jersey. In October 1917 she was included in *The Land of Liberty*, a Columbus Day tableau produced by Charles Dillingham at the Hippodrome, with music by legendary band composer John Philip Sousa. The *New York Sun* commented that Saki's inclusion in the tableau "was done in the hope of further convincing the mission from the land of Japan of the friendly attitude of this country toward theirs."

In August 1918 Saki made her smash professional debut at the Hippodrome, when she performed as a Japanese dancer in *Everything* (1918–19). This mammoth musical spectacle, directed by R. H. Burnside, featured music by Sousa and by Irving Berlin, among others, and appearances by such performers as Harry Houdini and DeWolf Hopper. The show ran for ten months. In October 1918 *Billboard* magazine reported that Viscount Kikujiro Ishii, Japanese ambassador to the United States, attended the show with a director of Tokyo's Imperial Theatre, who praised Saki's performance and invited her to dance at his theater.

After *Everything* closed, Saki moved on quickly, joining the Midwest tour of a Victor Herbert musical, *The Velvet Lady*. During early 1920 Saki moved to vaudeville and toured with the Keith-Albee circuit in a "tabloid musical revue," featuring Wellington Cross, in which she performed a high-kicking dance. In mid-1920 Saki secured her first large role, as Peggy in the touring company of the musical *The Sweetheart Shop*. She joined the production in Chicago in summer 1920 and toured with it throughout the West and Midwest over the following year.

In early 1922 Saki got another professional break when she was engaged by the peerless showman George M. Cohan. Cohan put her on tour with the Otto Harbach musical *The O'Brien Girl*, which he produced, then brought her back to Broadway as Marie Langford in the musical *Little Nellie Kelly*, with book, music, and lyrics by Cohan. The musical was a smash success. After the Broadway run, she toured with it over the following year, with performances in Washington, DC, Chicago, and elsewhere.

Through these plays Saki became visible as a performer. The *Daily News* referred to her as a "piquant and talented Japanese-American dancer." The *Brooklyn Times Union* referred to her as "that dainty Dresden china doll who sang and danced her way to popularity." With such popularity, she could secure larger roles. Her next notable turn was as Ruth Kingsley in the 1924 musical *Plain Jane*. When she went to Washington in a tryout tour, *Washington Star* columnist Wood Soanes made a friendly joke on her name: "In the cast of *Plain Jane* there is a girl who is one-fourth Japanese and proud of it. Originally she called herself Marion Saki but now we are informed that she is using her full name Marion Sakytonato [sic]. This will set her lineage definitely as of the samurai and at the same time comply with the Eighteenth Amendment [Prohibition] about moving liquors." *Plain Jane* opened in New York in May 1924. It played on Broadway for several months, then went on the road, touring Chicago and the Midwest during 1924–25. After it folded, Saki returned to vaudeville and played the famous Palace Theater in New York, as part of an act with the team of Nelson Snow and Charles Columbus. She found the rough-and-tumble climate of vaudeville difficult and was temporarily sidelined in July with a broken rib.

In fall 1925 she was featured in a short-lived show, *Some Day*, that played in Brooklyn. Shortly after it closed, Saki was tapped for her first and only starring role on Broadway, in a show called *Sweetheart Time*. It opened in January 1926 and played five months. She then joined a touring production of another musical, *Honey Girl*. Reviewer Wood Soanes complained that her role in *Honey Girl* was too small: "Marion Saki, who can sing, dance and fill the eye, does so not frequently enough."

In late 1926 Saki was recruited to travel to London to star in *Happy Go Lucky*, an adaptation of the 1925 US musical *When You Smile*. Two of the dances Saki did from the show with costar Billy Taylor were recorded on silent film by British Pathé and shown in cinemas. Upon her return to the United States, Saki returned to the Palace Theater for another engagement with the team of Snow and Columbus.

In 1927 Saki achieved her greatest success. She signed as an understudy to Louise Groody, the leading lady in composer Vincent Youmans's musical *Hit the Deck* (which would later be transformed into an MGM screen musical). Youmans quickly put together a North American touring company, with Saki as the headliner. She barnstormed for a year and a half with the show. When the show opened in Winnipeg, Manitoba, Canada, in November 1928, the *Jewish Post* exulted over Saki as "a beautiful young woman who can sing, dance, and act in such a way that she held New York and London captive in this same musical comedy for a year each."

It was around this time, in August 1928, that Saki had a serious career setback. According to newspaper reports, she was engaged to play a supporting role in the Marx Brothers comedy *Animal Crackers*. However, Saki seems to have either left the show during its out-of-town run or been discharged, as she was not among the final Broadway cast. The play would have a long theatrical run before being transformed into a classic film featuring most of the original cast. Instead, Saki was tapped for a supporting role in the short-lived musical *Polly* (1929), which featured future radio comedian Fred Allen (during its out-of-town run, the cast also boasted Archie Leach, none other than the future movie star Cary Grant).

After the demise of *Polly*, Saki faced a career crossroads. With the advent of talking pictures and the Great Depression, vaudeville and the Broadway musical were in decline. Around this time she began studying voice seriously, hoping to move into opera—Saki said she dreamed of singing in *Madama Butterfly*. Saki had a cabaret engagement in 1930 at the International Club, then sang for several weeks in 1930–31 at the Hollywood Cabaret in New York. In 1932 she made a 78 recording of the song "Morning and Evening Comes My Love for You." At the end of 1932, she was engaged to perform the supporting role of Mi in a production of Franz Lehár's "oriental" operetta *The Land of Smiles*, starring Charles Hackett. The production was not a success and never reached Broadway. Nevertheless, Saki received glowing reviews from the *New York Times*, whose critic noted that the audience applauded her because she "brought a light touch and a lively spirit into far too solemn a [group] performance."

In spring 1933, after *The Land of Smiles* closed, Saki was hired to do a weekly singing program on WMCA Radio, which lasted three months. After its demise she lapsed into relative obscurity—her dim prospects underlined by a set of advertisements she placed in a local newspaper for singing or dance pupils. She was seriously injured in a Greyhound bus accident in 1934 and spent time in the hospital. In August 1935 she had a singing engagement in Philadelphia at the Café Marguery. Two years later she performed an engagement at the Hotel Summit in Uniontown, Pennsylvania. The following year she was again listed as singing on radio. In May 1942, at a time of wartime anti-Japanese hostility, Saki performed at a benefit concert in New York under the name "Marion (Saki) Huntington" (a surname previously assumed by her brother, Archer S. Huntington). It was her last recorded public appearance. The rest of her life is unclear.

Marion Saki's intriguing stage career helps complicate our understanding of public images of Japanese Americans in the early twentieth century. Saki got her start as a "Japanese Pavlov," doing "Japanese" ballet, and through her career was identified (and identified herself) as Japanese American. Her Japaneseness formed part of her mystique, and she even claimed (dubiously) to be Japan-born. Yet she was able to play non-Asian parts on the Broadway stage and in nationwide touring companies without controversy, and she was not exoticized the way more "oriental" performers were. It is surprising to find such examples of "color-blind" casting long before the concept was even developed. Still, although Saki assumed her Japanese identity and used her real name, she remained distant from ethnic communities. Her name was hardly ever cited in the West Coast Nisei press and she did not perform within the community (in 1917 a report appeared in the *New York Times* that the Nippon

Club planned to host a dancing exhibition by Saki and famed modern dancer Michio Ito, but it is unknown whether such an event ever took place). It was only when she moved into a concert career, in the forlorn hope of singing the lead role in *Madama Butterfly*, that she was cast in an Asiatic role, in *The Land of Smiles*. It is unknowable whether Saki's Japanese ethnicity prevented her from having a career in Hollywood, but to display her gifts for acting, singing, and dance on the Broadway stage represented a major accomplishment for a woman of that era.

RUTH SATO REINHARDT / FROM CHORUS GIRL TO JAZZ MOMMA

During the 1920s Marion Saki achieved renown in musical shows on Broadway and on road tours, where she played non-Asian roles even as she proclaimed her Japanese identity. Even as Saki left the musical stage, she was succeeded by another *hapa* Nisei performer, Ruth Sato, who billed herself as "the only Japanese chorus girl on Broadway." Sato did not achieve the same level of renown as Saki. Nevertheless, through canny management of publicity, Sato was able to make herself into a public figure. Popular columnists such as Walter Winchell, who lauded her as a "Japanese doll . . . with brains," reported her quips and activities. After spending the World War II years out of the spotlight, she emerged afterward as Ruth Reinhardt, the savvy Chicago jazz club owner and hostess.

Given Sato's flair for embellishing her own life story in interviews, it can be difficult to establish the accuracy of various details. She was born Ruth Satow in New York on December 12, 1904. Her father, Masazo Satow (Sato), born in Japan, moved to the United States in the early 1890s. There he met and married Grace Delia McIntyre, a young woman of Irish ancestry. According to the 1900 census, Masazo worked as a steward. He later became a florist and eventually a dry goods dealer and "importer." Ruth was the couple's second child (Masazo also had a daughter, Stella, by a previous relationship). She spent her first years in New York City—she later claimed to have lived in a "boardinghouse" in Brooklyn that was actually a brothel! For some years in the 1910s, the family lived in suburban Rye, New York, where they were the only Japanese family. Sato later commented dryly about the experience: "I learned to be hated at an early age. But my father always told me we were special." By 1920 they were again living in New York City.

Mixed-Race Stories

The *Pacific Citizen* would later claim that Sato attended Barnard College at her father's insistence, preparing for a teaching career, and that he permitted her to study with famed modern dancer Michio Ito. She then decided to enter show business once her father died. In fact, by the end of her teen years—at which point her father was very much alive—the young Satow had already worked up an act under the name Ruth Sato (she may have decided to spell her name *Sato* in tribute to an earlier song and dance performer, Ruth E. Sato). In early 1923, having just turned eighteen, she went on the road, touring in *Take a Chance*, a musical comedy by Harold Orlob. She then worked small towns on the B. F. Keith vaudeville circuit, in an act starring Leslie F. Caulfield (called variously "Dance Gambol" and "Love Steps").

In mid-1924 Sato achieved her first publicity coup. Gracie Gould, one of a pair of performers playing in a "midget" act, announced that she was suing her partner, Tommy Kennan, for fifty thousand dollars for breach of promise, alleging that Keenan had forsaken her for Ruth Sato, a chorus girl in the same show. Sato denied that she and Keenan were in love. "He is nice, but Gracie needn't be afraid of me carrying him off under my arm." The piece, with accompanying photographs, ran in a variety of newspapers.

At the tail end of 1925, Sato made her Broadway debut as a dancer in *Song of the Flame*, an operetta (billed as a "romantic opera") about the Russian Revolution that featured lyrics by Otto Harbach and Oscar Hammerstein II and music by George Gershwin and Herbert Stothart. The company had a Russian ballet and an American ballet—Sato was in the American one. It played for 219 performances. That fall she joined the ensemble of another operetta with libretto by Harbach and Hammerstein, Rudolf Friml's *The Wild Rose*, but it ran for only sixty-one performances, and then she appeared in another unsuccessful show, *Lady Do*.

Sato's next project, which she later claimed was her real debut, was in the chorus of George and Ira Gershwin's 1927 musical, *Funny Face*, starring Fred and Adele Astaire. Sato claimed that she used dark makeup and painted her eyes rather than whitening her face, like the other chorus girls. The result was that all audience eyes were on her. Her reputation became solidly established with her next project, the 1928 musical *Hold Everything!* The show, with songs by the team of Buddy De Sylva, Lew Brown, and Ray Henderson, featured actors Victor Moore and Bert Lahr.

Even though Sato was only a chorus girl in *Hold Everything!* she appeared in newspaper photographs even before the show opened, and even appeared

"GIRLS DRIVE MEN CRAZY," SAYS MIDGET, SUED FOR $50,000

Ruth Sato, newspaper photo, *Bartlesville (OK) Morning Examiner*, ca. 1924.

in newspaper advertisements for Tru-Lax laxative. She scored a further media coup when she announced that she had secured the Japanese rights to the show and intended to use her experience in the show's chorus to mount a production in Tokyo. "There is no reason why my native Japanese should not like musical comedy done in the American manner." Sato insisted dubiously that the lyrics of the show's hit song, "You Are the Cream in My Coffee," would have to be changed—they would not be understood in Japan, where coffee was not drunk! In the end Sato never mounted any production in her "native land" of Japan. Nevertheless, the newspaper interviews and publicity photos (showing her in both kimono and revealing theatrical costume) earned her jealous hostility from the other "chorines," Sato later related: "The girls hated me, so my only friends were the boys, and they were all gay. Some life!"

Mixed-Race Stories

In 1929, after *Hold Everything!* Sato performed in the original Broadway cast of *Heads Up* by Richard Rodgers and Lorenz Hart—one of that famed duo's less successful shows. In the following years, she was signed as a dancer by showman Billy Rose. Sato performed on Broadway and in tours of Rose's revues *Sweet and Low* and *Crazy Quilt*, both starring his wife, the legendary performer Fanny Brice.

In October 1934 Sato opened in the *Casino de Paree Revue*, where she worked opposite Milton Berle, the show's star. Sato later claimed that she toured with Berle as his comedy partner, under the name Ming Toy Goldberg. After leaving New York, the show played Philadelphia and Boston. Around this time Sato separated from her husband and settled in Boston. She appeared in a stage show, *Round the Word Cruise*, at the Metropolitan Theater, in which she performed a specialty dance—her first solo onstage. She also performed in a musical comedy called *The Penthouse* in June 1936.

In 1931 Sato married her first husband, Gus X. Basco, but the two divorced in 1936. For the next two years, while Sato awaited payment of her divorce settlement (which was ultimately reported as thirty-five thousand dollars), she paused her stage career and worked as a journalist. According to contemporary sources, she was engaged as secretary to *Boston Record* columnist George C. MacKinnon—in March 1939 columnists reported that MacKinnon wished to marry her but could not secure a divorce. By Sato's own account, she worked under the table as a "legman" for local columnist Walter Howey and collected hush money he charged to keep items out of his column. Whatever the case, she yearned to return to the stage. In summer 1938 the Intercollegiate League, an intervarsity student social group, sponsored her as a dancer for work in nightclubs and colleges. The league plugged her bookings as both educational and entertaining.

In November 1939, a year after her father's death, Sato returned to New York and took up residence in Greenwich Village. She was engaged to dance in the *Evening in Paris* floor show at Leon & Eddie's nightclub. It was her first overtly "oriental" role. A critic in *Variety* described the act: "Ruth Sato is an Oriental-looking femme who does a Chinese dance as before and after 'the coming of the Marines.' First, in a long mandarin coat, is in classic style, while the coat is shedded for the latter portion for a shim-sham in g-string and bra." Sato later recalled that she had been hired as "an exotic FAAAN dancer . . . imported from JAPAAAN" who was supposedly unable to speak English. As a result, she did not interact with customers. Nevertheless, her performance brought her the best reviews of her career. Columnist George Ross said, "The female sensation of the revue seems to be a Eurasian charmer named Ruth Sato, who is thus advertised as America's Most Beautiful Eurasian, and if there are any challengers, let them speak up now." *Billboard* magazine added, "Miss Sato demonstrates excellent tassel showmanship and should be a good item in any café's layout." Writing in *Women's Wear Daily*, Ben Schneider praised the outstanding beauty of the "exotic Eurasian." A critic in the *New York Times* dissented, slamming the show as "honky tonk" and dismissing Sato for "displaying an unblemished epidermis in a manner not unique."

After her stint at Leon & Eddie's, Sato was engaged for a part in a legitimate stage production, as the Chinese princess Tsoi Tsing in a revival of Sigmund Romberg's operetta *East Wind*. It opened at St. Louis's well-known Municipal Theater in August 1940. It would be her only stage speaking part. She soon returned to New York and was featured in an "all-Oriental revue" at Ching's Waikiki Club, a newly opened Asian nightclub on Fifty-Second Street. Sato served as hostess, introducing the acts, and was praised by Sam Honigberg in *Billboard* for her "cleverly phrased speeches [and] quiet, charming and sophisticated manner." Despite Honigberg's endorsement, the show was unsuccessful. Sato and her colleagues were forced to sue owner Ching for four weeks' unpaid wages—they eventually were awarded five hundred dollars in court. In April 1941 Sato served as master of ceremonies and comedienne at the opening show of a New York branch of San Francisco's Asian nightclub Forbidden City, located in a former Swedish restaurant on Fifty-Eighth Street. (The opening night featured benefit performances for the Chinese Women's Relief Association.)

Throughout the prewar years, Ruth Sato was extolled by journalists as a "Eurasian beauty," and her photographs appeared frequently in the press. For her part she played up her unique presence as "the only Japanese chorus girl on Broadway." She claimed at times to be named Keiku Sato and to have lived in Japan (which she likely never even visited) and agreed to give an "oriental view" to journalists. For example, in 1936 she told an interviewer that her eventual goal was to move to Japan and open a dancing school, and she shared her thoughts on Japanese women: "Women there are just beginning to have a taste of freedom. . . . But even so, they have a long way to go before they have the same rights and opportunities as American girls." In 1941 she declared that American audiences were easier to please than those in "her native land" because they appreciated beauty and charm, while audiences in the Orient favored technique—all their great stars were men who did female impersonation.

That said, she had always had artistic and intellectual interests. During the 1930s she dated writer John O'Hara, with whom she discussed literature. *DownBeat* magazine reported in 1939 that Sato was a "hep chick" and jazz enthusiast, who had a major record collection and knew all the members of the major swing bands. In September 1939 Sato published an odd "open letter" in *DownBeat*, unjustly taking to task a fellow letter writer for anti-Black bias, in which she pointed to the social barriers that she experienced as a "half-Japanese and half-Irish" and the positive role of jazz in breaking them down. "As for prejudice, jazz is a common means for eliminating any so-called bugaboo." During 1941 Sato wrote a gossip column, Could Be, for the jazz magazine *Swing*. During this period she began dating William "Bill" Reinhardt, a jazz clarinetist four years her junior.

With the coming of World War II, Ruth Sato shifted from showgirl to more serious pursuits. She later recalled being unemployed following the Pearl Harbor attack: not only was demand for Japanese exotic dancers way down, she asserted, but she was followed by the FBI because of her late father's role as a community leader, and she dyed her hair blonde in order to escape notice. Even her name was a liability. In January 1942 popular columnist Walter Winchell, who had previously been a leading publicist for Sato, noted facetiously that "the Eurasian entertainer (half Jap, half Yankee Doodle) will change her name to Pearl Haba." She demanded a retraction, under threat of lawsuit. Winchell published her denial, but with little grace, and never again mentioned her in his column.

In response to the pressure, she left New York—columnist Danton Walker proclaimed that she had disappeared from Broadway—and moved to Virginia to be with Bill Reinhardt, who was stationed there. On June 6, 1942, the two were married in Norfolk. Ruth Reinhardt (as she was henceforth known) gave differing versions of her life during the years that followed, while her new husband was overseas. In a 1948 profile she claimed that she had spent the war years restoring a seven-room farmhouse in Williamsburg, Virginia, while Bill was stationed at Peary Naval Training Station. In a later interview she revealed that she had taken over a small farm on Florida's Gulf Coast, where she passed her time killing snakes. "I would zap 'em with Lysol. Nobody ever taught me how to use a gun. I was from New York, where anything suspicious got it with Lysol right away." Reinhardt contributed a series of columns to *DownBeat* magazine that displayed her talents as music critic and comedic writer. For example, Reinhardt's piece "Saxes Should Be Played Not Tossed for a Goal," in the December 15, 1943, issue, features the author's outspoken criticism of the "pseudo showmanship" of the saxophone players who wrestled furiously with their instruments in playing: "One man looked like a huge mastiff tugging at a large, brass bone." These columns hint at a New York connection. Not only did "Saxes" bear a New York dateline, but the September 15, 1944, issue also featured Reinhardt's "Random Ramblings from Rhythm Row," a column with gossip about the New York jazz scene whose items strongly suggested that the author had been spending time in the city.

Whatever the case, once Bill Reinhardt secured his discharge from the navy, the spouses faced the decision of where to settle and what to do. Ruth Reinhardt later stated that she had considered taking over a sponge fishing business in Tarpon Springs. In the end the couple moved to Bill's hometown of Chicago and decided to make a living out of music by opening a jazz club.

Reinhardt recalled that the couple were so naive that they placed a newspaper advertisement offering a one thousand–dollar reward for information regarding a suitable establishment, but received no responses. Instead, Bill Reinhardt went out walking one day and found a basement space that seemed ideal. The property was located at 11 East Grand Avenue on the near North Side—the main center of Japanese American resettlement in Chicago. The couple settled on Jazz, Ltd. as the name of their club (their lawyer had vetoed the original name, Jazz, Inc.).

Jazz, Ltd. opened in June 1947. It offered New Orleans- and Chicago-style Dixieland music. The music was entirely instrumental: to avoid an extra 20 percent nightclub tax, the Reinhardts did not permit singing in the club. Bill led the house band, a five-piece ensemble with four regulars (Doc Evans among them) plus a special guest star. Ruth acted as hostess and greeted all customers personally. She also took up the role of manager and administrator, bringing to the task a hardheaded business skill and capacity for hard work: she was present in the club every night, six days a week, from 7:00 p.m. to 4:00 a.m. She also took up the unpleasant task of asking undesirables to leave. As she remarked in a column in *DownBeat*: "I guess I have become quite a character. One drunk told me that that I should be a schoolmarm rather than a saloonkeeper. My shell is thick, and after all we are not selling me—we are selling jazz." *Chicago Tribune* columnist Savage described Ruth as the club's guiding hand, "a combination of modified Texas Guinan [a famed speakeasy operator in 1920s New York] and implacable house dick."

The club offered its patrons a unique experience. For one thing, it was the first jazz club outside the African American district of Bronzeville without a color bar, and from the beginning its audiences were integrated. Conversely, the Reinhardts imposed strict rules to underline the club's status as a respectable institution (and discourage prostitution): reservations were encouraged; patrons had to wait behind a velvet rope until seated; gentlemen were required to wear jackets; unaccompanied women were not admitted; and no women were served at the bar under any circumstances. The serving staff was all male. In order to stay "clean" of racketeers, the Reinhardts refused to install jukeboxes or cigarette vending machines. Ruth Reinhardt also relied on her flair for publicity. Rather than run expensive newspaper or radio advertising, she maintained an extensive mailing list and made use of columnists such as disc jockey (and future TV host) Dave Garroway to spread the word. The Reinhardts shrewdly began the practice of making live recordings from the club and selling them onsite, in the process gaining both money and publicity.

Jazz, Ltd. was immediately popular. It became even more so in its second season, when the Reinhardts signed legendary New Orleans jazzman Sidney Bechet to an exclusive contract and he began a residency at the club. With encouragement from Ruth Reinhardt, newspapermen began discussing Bechet in news stories and gossip items, providing extra publicity for the club. Unfortunately, the Reinhardts' relationship with the musician proved contentious. In May 1949 Bechet left for Europe without alerting the club owners, leaving them to scramble to fill his place. When he returned in November of that year, he pledged to return to Jazz, Ltd. However, he played an outside gig in Chicago, violating his exclusive agreement with the club, whereupon Ruth Reinhardt successfully sued him for breach of contact.

Even after Bechet's departure, Jazz, Ltd. continued to prosper. It attracted notable patrons such as writer Nelson Algren. While the club moved to a larger location in the 1960s, the Reinhardts continued to manage it closely. By the time it closed its doors, in February 1972, a casualty of declining public interest in jazz, it had been open nearly twenty-five years and claimed to be the oldest traditional jazz club in the world. Following the demise of her club, Ruth Sato Reinhardt went into retirement. She died on December 9, 1992.

Ruth Sato Reinhardt once described herself as "tone-deaf" and stated that her main interest in her club was in making money. All the same, she made an important contribution to Chicago's music scene and provided a space for interracial contact. Her newspaper writings, though limited in number, reveal both her real passion for music and her talent as a prose stylist.

Chapter 7
MUSIC

YOICHI HIRAOKA / ISSEI XYLOPHONE VIRTUOSO
with Jonathan van Harmelen

Yoichi Hiraoka was an internationally renowned xylophone virtuoso, one who helped popularize the xylophone as an instrument for both classical and popular music. Through daily radio performances and live concerts, he became the most celebrated Nikkei musician in the United States during the 1930s. However, even his fame and connections did not save him from being targeted as a Japanese alien after the United States entered World War II.

Yoichi Hiraoka, born in Hyogo Prefecture on August 16, 1907, grew up near Osaka. He studied the piano as a child but gave it up when his tiny hands proved too small to span even an octave. He switched to the *mokkin*, a miniature Japanese-style xylophone. After he heard some Western xylophone recordings, he decided to study the instrument. Though there were hardly any such instruments in Japan in that period, he bought a secondhand xylophone and began playing on his own. While at Keio University, where he studied economics, he joined a jazz band as a xylophonist. After breaking his first instrument while rehearsing, in 1928 he persuaded his family to sell a treasured ancient oriental flute to finance the purchase of a better instrument from the United States, which he then proceeded to use for the next several years.

In 1930 Hiraoka played a series of five xylophone recitals in Tokyo. Pleased by this success, his father offered him a trip to the United States. In mid-1930, the depths of the Great Depression, Yoichi Hiraoka traveled to New York. Though he arrived without contacts, within weeks he found work performing on the radio for the National Broadcasting Company. That October he began appearing on a daily fifteen-minute morning show for NBC's New York–area radio station WEAF. In 1933 he switched to WJZ. In the ten years that followed his debut, he performed an estimated four thousand solo spots on NBC radio programs. In addition to his daily performances, he also performed interludes between news bulletins in times of international crisis.

In December 1936 Hiraoka made his live New York debut with a solo recital at Town Hall, under the sponsorship of the NBC Artists Service. Included in the program were transcriptions, mostly made by Hiraoka himself, of pieces by Haydn, Bach, Beethoven, Mozart, Yamada, and others. The concert was warmly received. The *World-Telegram*'s critic praised not only his tone but his "footwork and exuberant gesturing." The *Sun* lauded his "considerable skill." Unfortunately, he chose the night of the Metropolitan Opera season's premiere for his recital, so it was less well-attended and did not attract major critics. In November 1937 he played a second Town Hall recital, this time with selections from Handel, Rameau, and Beethoven, plus his own transcriptions of pieces by composers such as Haydn and Mozart and a traditional Japanese minstrel song, "Echigo-Jishi." A critic marveled: "He knows how to realize compositions in a lofty vein as well as a music that is earthbound. He can play with humor and with dignity."

He went on to other notable performances. In January 1937 he performed on the Town Hall radio program hosted by popular comedian Fred Allen. He also performed that year before a visiting Japanese Economic Mission and then at the Japan Day festivities at the New York World's Fair in June 1939. In March 1939 he performed with the New York Philharmonic under the baton of Ernest Schelling in a Young People's Concert at Carnegie Hall. Hiraoka played two movement's from Mozart's serenade "Eine kleine Nachtmusik." Two years later he performed at a second Young People's Concert, this time under the baton of Rudolph Ganz. In this concert Hiraoka performed a solo xylophone arrangement of Georges Enescu's "Romanian Rhapsody" that had been transcribed especially for him by Leo Russatto, then joined the orchestra in the Trepak from Tchaikovsky's *Nutcracker Suite*. It was reported that the great conductor Arturo Toscanini personally asked Hiraoka to play for him, but it is unclear whether he ever did.

Hiraoka also became known though his recordings. In May and June 1940 he made a set of recordings for Decca, with piano accompaniment by Vladimir Brenner. His selections included Western classical works such as Saint-Saëns's "The Swan" and pieces by Mozart and Bach, plus a set of traditional Japanese compositions such as the folk song "Sakura Sakura." Eight of the classical pieces were released the following year on the album *A Xylophone Recital of Classical Music*.

Although Hiraoka remained based in New York City, during the 1930s West Coast Japanese American communities followed him closely. Numerous articles from the *Rafu Shimpo* and the *Nichi Bei Shimbun* extolled Hiraoka as both a musician and symbol of Japanese American success. In its 1938 Christmas issue, the *Rafu Shimpo* boldly declared, "Yoichi Hiraoka Hailed World's No. 1 Xylophonist." The Nikkei press also covered his 1937 marriage to Shizuko Yamaguchi, a New York–born Nisei.

While Hiraoka rose to stardom in America, his fame could not protect him from the influence of world events. On December 7, 1941, Hiraoka was preparing to play on his NBC program when news of the Japanese bombing of Pearl Harbor was announced. Because of Hiraoka's Japanese citizenship, the network canceled his appearance and ordered him banned from its program. Hiraoka's friends pointed out vainly that he was a friend of democracy. Columnist H. E. Spencer, sarcastically referring to Hiraoka as the war's first enemy casualty, added, "Somebody owes NBC a medal" for its craven attitude. New York mayor Fiorello LaGuardia publicly invited Hiraoka to appear on a local radio program with him. Hiraoka performed a series of patriotic songs, including "The Marine's Hymn." After the broadcast, LaGuardia told the *New York Herald Tribune*, "I thought that I could in no better way testify to my confidence, as mayor of this city, in Mr. Hiraoka than to have him on the program with me." Nonetheless, NBC refused to rehire Hiraoka, claiming that as an enemy alien, he was unacceptable. Fearing for his life and livelihood, in June 1942 Hiraoka decided to move to Japan with his family and sailed on the exchange ship *Gripsholm*.

Hiraoka soon became a star performer in Japan. During the postwar years he played some eighty concerts a year, plus radio appearances. He performed for the US occupation forces and General Headquarters (GHQ) radio. In April 1949 he was featured in an all-star program presented by the Special Services Section of GHQ at the Stilwell Theatre in Tokyo. In 1955 he played sets at the Latin Quarter, a Tokyo nightclub, and by 1957 was listed as having his own show on NHK. In November 1961 he made a concert tour of Okinawa (then under occupation by US forces).

Throughout this period Hiraoka dreamed of returning to the United States. In 1951 he visited Los Angeles to play a set of concerts at the Wilshire-Ebell Theater and in Little Tokyo. Nevertheless, he remained based in Japan until 1961, when the New York Philharmonic arrived on tour. Hiraoka renewed friendships with his old colleagues, who encouraged him to return and helped make concert bookings for him. On November 27, 1962, Hiraoka appeared at Carnegie Recital Hall, his first concert in New York since the attack on Pearl Harbor, accompanied by the Philharmonic-Symphony String Quartet (made up of members of the New York Philharmonic), a pianist, and percussionist.

The concert was enthusiastically reviewed, and it relaunched Hiraoka's American career. He moved to New York and undertook a recital tour around the country. His career took a further turn when American composer Alan Hovhaness produced his "Fantasy on Japanese Woodprints for Xylophone and Orchestra," a piece commissioned by conductor Andre Kostelanetz and dedicated to Hiraoka. In July 1965 Hiraoka performed its world premiere at the Ravinia Festival, with the Chicago Philharmonic Orchestra under the baton of Seiji Ozawa. In March 1966 he performed the piece with Andre Kostelanetz and the New York Philharmonic, then recorded it with Kostelanetz in 1967. In the following years, Hiraoka performed the Hovhaness "Fantasy" with the St. Louis Symphony, Kansas City Symphony, and Hollywood Bowl Orchestra. He did an encore performance of the piece with Kostelanetz and the New York Philharmonic in 1972, shortly before his retirement from the concert scene. Hiraoka died in 1981.

The legacy of Hiraoka's story is twofold. First, he helped establish the importance of the xylophone and other mallet percussion instruments for classical ensembles. According to musicologist Akiko Goto, the xylophone was never truly accepted as a solo instrument until individuals like Hiraoka demonstrated its potential. In his preface to the 1941 book *Xylophone Album*, Hiraoka lamented that "there is a widespread prejudice against the xylophone, even among music lovers and players themselves . . . because of the belief that the xylophone is an instrument that cannot sing." Over the course of fifty years, Hiraoka showed that in the hands of a true artist, the xylophone could be made an instrument of delicate expression. His staunch support helped to move the instrument from the back of the orchestra to front and center stage.

The other is his legacy for Japanese American communities. At a time when Asians were generally barred from performing on the national stage in music and film, and classical ensembles were largely staffed by white performers, Hiraoka demonstrated through his impressive talents that Japanese Americans artists were capable of shining. Hiraoka's dream that when "instrumentalists know how to play beautiful music on the xylophone, the prejudice will disappear" spoke not only about the instruments but the artists themselves. For musicians and historians alike, Hiraoka's story is well worth telling.

CLASSICAL MUSIC IN THE WRA CAMPS
with Jonathan van Harmelen

In the tragic and difficult conditions faced by Japanese Americans confined in the WRA camps during World War II, one imposing arena of achievement for them was the arts. In recent years a number of books and exhibits have highlighted not only the extraordinary skill and craftsmanship of inmate painters, illustrators, and producers of decorative art but the important role that production of arts and crafts played in the everyday lives of those confined. As Delphine Hirasuna has revealed through her book and exhibit *The Art of Gaman*, art offered inmates of all ages, but particularly the Issei, a powerful means of overcoming the rigors of the camp experience and documenting hidden injustices.

At the same time, chroniclers of the camps have noted how music, whether performing or listening, provided a source of enjoyment and sense of achievement to Japanese Americans. In recent years there have been stories about such figures as Mary Kageyama Nomura, the "Songbird of Manzanar," who performed at talent shows and dances. Also celebrated has been the youthful music director Lou Frizzell, who mentored and aided inmate performers at Manzanar (and was later invited to play himself in the 1970s TV-film version of Jeanne Wakatsuki Houston's memoir *Farewell to Manzanar*). The most comprehensive work on music in camp, George Yoshida's monograph *Reminiscing in Swingtime*, documents the popularity of big band music among Nisei in camp as well as taking up Yoshida's own experience as a leader of a jazz quartet in the Topaz camp. A contrasting approach is taken in Minako Waseda's article in the *Densho Encyclopedia* on music in the camps. Waseda provides a cogent discussion of the place of both traditional Japanese music and American jazz and popular music in camp and the tension that these represented between preservation of a traditional Japanese cultural identity and forces of Westernization.

Yet while the lives of Japanese Americans were saturated by Western classical music, for some reason it is rarely mentioned in discussions of camp life. As in the case of the musical genres discussed by Yoshida and Waseda, the performance and appreciation of classical music functioned for Japanese Americans as a means of gaining acceptance within mainstream American society. What is more, the organization of string quartets, choirs, and even full-fledged orchestras represented a different example of *gaman* by the inmates.

The musical activities of Japanese Americans in camp were built on a broad foundation. As Mari Yoshihara reminds us in *Musicians from a Different Shore*, there is a long-standing tradition of people of Asian ancestry playing Western classical music. Certainly, during the prewar period, masses of Nisei took music lessons and played in school orchestras and local ensembles. (As we find in this volume, a series of outstanding Nisei opera singers were products of prewar West Coast communities.)

In camp, classical music was presented in a number of different ways, including concerts of recorded music, recitals by soloists, and performances by organized ensembles such as chamber music groups, choirs, and orchestras. Concerts of record albums were the earliest medium of classical performance because of their simplicity and the lack of available instruments. These concerts became sources of joy and solace amid the boredom and suffering of camp. Most of these phonograph recordings were provided by the inmates themselves and represented some of the few prized possessions taken along by families at the time of the incarceration. As a result, concert organizers produced a census of record holdings by different inmate families.

Among the first such concerts took place in the Fresno Assembly Center, where former music student Kazue Sekiya organized "listenings" in recreation halls and ran advertisements in camp newspapers for upcoming concerts.[1] Sekiya's concerts included selections from George Gershwin's 1935 African American "folk opera," *Porgy and Bess*; Beethoven symphonies; and Tchaikovsky ballets. Similarly, on Sunday, November 8, 1942, community members at Tule Lake congregated for a concert of Georges Bizet's opera *Carmen*, played on a phonograph in the center of the mess hall. A sign was hung outside the hall to notify guests to wait and enter between pieces. At the end of the session, inmates were asked whether the concerts should continue. One respondent from Block 24 wrote: "What else would I have to look forward to on Sundays? Especially in view of the fact that there are no other avenues open for Sunday evening enjoyments (theater) I think they should be continued—after all, we do have a large audience each Sunday evening."[2]

Meanwhile, as Japanese Americans moved from the Assembly Centers to the ten WRA camps, officials began to officially request musical instruments

Snare drum section, Rohwer camp student band, Rohwer, Arkansas. Photo by Tom McGehee. War Relocation Authority Photographs of Japanese-Style Evacuation and Resettlement, UC Berkeley, Bancroft Library.

with which to hold music classes. In an interview many years later, Mae Hara, who worked with education, explained that the music program began with no budget, relying mostly on donations of pianos by local churches.[3] WRA officials reached out to local schools to donate instruments to the camp as part of the school curriculum. Once instruments became readily available, choirs, pianists, and string groups could organize as part of school classes and provide a new outlet for both children and adults.

Interestingly enough, the quality of music programs varied along the lines of state educational standards operating in each camp. Thus, while Manzanar had a vast curriculum on music education available, funded by the state of California, Rohwer and Jerome in Arkansas could offer less funding for music appreciation. (Interestingly, when Jerome closed its doors in 1944, the camp instruments were forwarded to the Topaz camp in Utah.)

Performances of classical music, while less prominent than that of the big bands that provided music for social events, were common in camp. For

152 *Chapter 7*

example, either piano or violin soloists were featured at countless graduation ceremonies. Edward Elgar's "Pomp and Circumstance" remained a commencement staple in camp schools. The Manzanar High School band even played excerpts of Prokofiev's *Peter and the Wolf*, then only a few years old, for their Christmas ceremony in December 1943. By the later years of camp, full orchestra concerts appeared. The *Manzanar Free Press* on February 21, 1945, reported a concert by the Manzanar Symphony Orchestra, featuring selections of Wagner's *Tannhäuser Overture*, Grieg's *Peer Gynt Suite*, excerpts of works by Johann Strauss, and a composition by inmate Harry Tashima.[4]

In the postwar years a number of Japanese Americans rose to prominence within symphonic circles. Helen Matsunaga Shaw, who was confined at Santa Anita before relocating to Rockford College, became a renowned violinist and performed with the National Symphony Chamber Orchestra. Violin prodigy Kazuko Tajitsu (Kawamoto) shined as a soloist and opened up a studio in the New York area. The percussionist Tom Tsuji, who started as a jazz drummer in Topaz camp and played alongside George Yoshida, went off to become the principal tympanist of the New Orleans Symphony and the Minnesota Symphony Orchestra, and stands as the first Japanese American regular member of a national orchestra. Kazue Sekiya, who started listening classes at the Fresno Assembly Center, served as a choir pianist in the Fresno area after the war and would receive an honorary music degree from California State University, Fresno, sixty-eight years after her forced departure in 1942.

Overall, what this story illustrates is the importance of music for those who endured the camp experience and attests to a continuing tradition of Japanese Americans as successful classical musicians to this day. Indeed, Kent Nagano, former conductor of the Montreal Symphony Orchestra and likely the most eminent Japanese American musician, has traced his own interest in classical music in part back to the experiences of his parents in camp. Nagano lists his mother, Ruth Okamoto, as a major influence on him.

AKIRA KIKUKAWA AND THE JAPANESE AMERICAN ORCHESTRA *with Jonathan van Harmelen*

Some time ago, while my collaborator Jonathan van Harmelen and I were studying the life and career of the pioneering Japanese xylophonist Yoichi Hiraoka, we found that in 1970 Hiraoka had performed a concert in Southern California with an orchestra of which neither of us had ever heard, the Japanese

Philharmonic Orchestra of Los Angeles. Intrigued by the name, we resolved to check further into the history of this ensemble. What we discovered is that the story of the orchestra is very much that of its founder and longtime director, Akira Kikukawa.

Born in Osaka, Japan, in 1932, Akira Kikukawa studied cello at the Tokyo Music Academy, earning his bachelor's degree in music in 1954 and a master's in music in 1955. Over the three years that followed, Kikukawa joined the classical music circuit in Japan, performing as a cellist on television and NHK Radio and in various concert halls throughout the country. During his 1958 tour, Kikukawa met the celebrated Hungarian cellist Gabor Rejto, then chair of the Music Department at the University of Southern California (USC). Rejto encouraged the young Kikukawa to continue his musical education at USC. In early 1960 Kikukawa arrived in the United States and enrolled at USC, studying cello under Rejto and conducting under professor Ingolf Dahl. That fall he also joined the Los Angeles Music and Art School as an instructor.

After arriving in the United States, Kikukawa was approached by Katsuma Mukaeda, founder of the Nisei Week Festival and the Japanese American Cultural and Community Center, who asked him about organizing a Japanese American classical ensemble in Los Angeles. With encouragement from the Japan American Society of Southern California and the Los Angeles Japanese Chamber of Commerce, in spring 1961 Kikukawa founded the Japanese Philharmonic Orchestra of Los Angeles (also known as the Japanese Orchestra of Little Tokyo). The mission of the orchestra was to foster classical music among Japanese Americans and promote young Japanese composers in the United States. At the time classical compositions by Asian composers were all but unknown in the West. What is more, professional symphony orchestras in America were largely white male clubs, and few hired Nikkei musicians. (Even as Kikukawa organized his orchestra, the Japanese conductor Seiji Ozawa, a few years his junior, attracted widespread attention when he was appointed assistant conductor of the New York Philharmonic by music director Leonard Bernstein for the fall 1961 season.) Kikukawa led the orchestra in its premier concert on August 17, 1961, during that year's Nisei Week Festival, with performances of pieces by Mozart, Bizet, and Nicolai.

At first all of the new orchestra's performers were Nikkei—a testimony to the level of interest in classical music among the West Coast Japanese communities. To meet its goal of fostering classical music, Kikukawa included young students, or "Little Angels," as part of the ensemble. Kikukawa encouraged young musicians to join, arguing that musical talent was fostered rather than instilled at birth. Kikukawa also continued the tradition of including the orchestra in Nisei Week performances. For the 1963 Nisei Week, he commissioned his friend, Japanese composer Setsuo Tsukahara, to compose a piece titled "Gardens of Pasadena." In addition to catering to admirers of classical music, Kikukawa made efforts to offer concerts to the Los Angeles–area Japanese American community. In 1971, for example, Kikukawa led the orchestra in a concert in Long Beach to celebrate the sister city agreement between Long Beach and Yokkaichi, Japan.

From the beginning the Japanese Philharmonic Orchestra ventured beyond the traditional Western repertoire to include both traditional Japanese folk music and classical compositions by young Japanese composers. In a 1972 concert, for example, the orchestra premiered Akira Miyoshi's violin concerto from 1965, paired with tenth-century Japanese court music, a performance lauded by *Los Angeles Times* reviewer Melody Peterson. Outside groups such as UCLA's Gagaku ensemble regularly collaborated with the orchestra to provide traditional Japanese music. Kazue Kudo, a Japanese-born Koto virtuoso, was a frequent soloist with the orchestra. In 1987 the orchestra performed a program at the Los Angeles Music Center that included sutra chanting by priests of the Los Angeles Buddhist Church Federation, Japanese composer Toshiro Mayuzumi's "Mandala" Symphony, "Haru no umi" (a work for koto and orchestra), and Tchaikovsky's Fifth Symphony as the finale. Kikukawa boldly declared that "our motto is to perform Japanese music at each concert, except when we do Beethoven's Ninth. That is a whole evening." Yet even his performance of Beethoven diverged from established norms. At one memorable concert of the Ninth Symphony that took place in 1982, the orchestra was joined by the Angel Choir, Chinese Choral Society of LA, the LA Seoul Choral, and the Santa Barbara Choral Society.

As the years went by, the orchestra shifted from an all-Nikkei group to one composed half of Japanese Americans and the other half from diverse backgrounds. The group likewise recruited more professional musicians in order to perform the works of more avant-garde composers such as Strauss and Stravinsky. It attracted some important soloists. As mentioned, Yoichi Hiraoka performed as a xylophone soloist with the orchestra in 1970. Two years later the orchestra played a concert with Akio Tashiro as piano soloist. The orchestra was renowned not just for its skillful playing of both Eastern and Western music but for its discipline. In 1980, at the orchestra's debut concert in Orange County, Kikukawa lost his place in the score during one piece. The entire orchestra stopped and waited for him to recover—like "the routine ending of a movement," stated critic Clint Erney—and then continued as if nothing was amiss.

During his first years in the United States, Kikukawa continued to perform on cello. In June 1961 he played cello in a piano trio program at Union Church in Los Angeles. In March 1962 Kikukawa played a recital at the Berkeley College Women's Club. He was accompanied by the pianist Anni Victorius, a professor at Kobe College. Once he took up the direction of the orchestra, however, Kikukawa largely abandoned his career as a soloist, though he occasionally played with his orchestra.

Tragically, Kikukawa died suddenly of a heart ailment on October 12, 1989, at age fifty-seven, just days before a scheduled performance of his orchestra at the Orange County Performing Arts Center. On October 17 the Japanese Philharmonic Orchestra of Los Angeles performed a modified concert in his honor, with guest conductor (and former concertmaster) Frederic Balazs. A *Los Angeles Times* review noted that the orchestra struggled following the sudden loss of their conductor, though the reviewer commended the ensemble for performing at all under the circumstances. James Chute, critic for the *Santa Ana Orange County Register*, posed the question of the ensemble's future. Even if the need for an ethnic orchestra had receded, as mainstream symphonies were more open to Asian musicians and recordings of world music became more widely available, Chute affirmed nonetheless that "Kikukawa's dedication to bridging musical and cultural gaps was reason enough for the orchestra's existence."

In the years after Kikukawa's death, the Japanese Philharmonic of Los Angeles struggled to remake its identity. It changed its name to the Japan America Symphony and boasted conductors such as LA Philharmonic violinist Heiichiro Ohyama. Today the orchestra exists as the Asia America Symphony, renamed to acknowledge the growing diversity of Los Angeles's Asian American communities. Its director, David Benoit, is a former student of Ohyama. The orchestra's programs continue to foster the tradition of an "East and West" repertoire. Its mission has expanded since its founding, but it remains true to Kikukawa's vision. If, as Ralph Waldo Emerson reminds us, "an institution is the lengthened shadow of one man," Kikukawa continues to tower over the orchestra, which in turn underscores the rich musical legacy of Japanese America.

JUILLIARD-TRAINED SONGBIRD MARIKO MUKAI ANDO DEFIED EXPECTATIONS *with Jonathan van Harmelen*

After getting her start in Japanese community circles in Seattle, operatic and concert singer Mariko Mukai Ando moved to New York, where she shined as one of the first Japanese American students at the renowned Juilliard School of Music. While her professional career was cut short by her marriage and wish to raise a family, she served as a symbol both of Nisei achievement and the union of art and progressive politics.

Born in Seattle, Washington, in 1919 to Seizaburo and Sawayo Mukai, a Japanese immigrant couple, Mariko Mukai was the firstborn of five children. As a young girl, she and her siblings, Frank, George, Lily, and Henry, helped their father to operate a series of movie theaters as well as a bait and tackle shop located in Seattle's Chinatown. Mariko was recognized as a talented vocalist from an early age. She performed her first public concert at the age of ten and continued training throughout her adolescence. She graduated from Garfield High School in 1937 (serving as salutatorian at commencement) and then enrolled as a music major at the University of Washington. In November 1937 she sang a recital at Seattle's Century Theatre, mixing opera arias and lieder. The next year, while still at UW, Mariko appeared as Abigail in a Seattle Lyric Opera production of Karl Goldmark's *The Queen of Sheba*, becoming the first Nisei to sing grand opera in Seattle. Two years later she took her first lead roles, as Susanna in Mozart's *The Marriage of Figaro* at UW's Lyric Theatre and as Rosina in the Aeolian Society production of Rossini's *The Barber of Seville*.

Mukai gained significant local attention as a result of these performances. On the basis of her excellence as a singer, the local newspaper *Taihoku Nippō* nominated Mukai for the national "Nisei of the Year" contest. Interestingly, in her recitals and operatic appearances, Mukai did not perform Puccini's *Madama Butterfly*, the bread-and-butter role for Japanese American singers. In August 1941, after she traveled to Los Angeles and sang in a Nisei Festival Week program, a critic in *Kashū Mainichi* suggested that Mukai's coloratura voice was more suited to the "gay, light arias of Mozart and Verdi" than to Puccini's heroine.

In 1941, following her graduation from UW, Mukai was awarded a four-year scholarship to the Juilliard School of Music in New York. This represented a considerable endorsement of her talents. She moved to New York to begin her

Mariko Mukai Ando, professional portrait, ca. 1945. Courtesy of the family of Mariko Mukai Endo.

studies. However, within a few months, her life was turned upside down by the Japanese attack on Pearl Harbor. Following the attack, Seizaburo Mukai was arrested by the FBI and ultimately was interned at a camp in Santa Fe, New Mexico, for the duration of the war. The rest of the family was displaced from Seattle.

Although spared mass confinement during the war years, Mariko Mukai faced racial bias and housing discrimination in New York. It was during her time in New York that Mukai was interviewed by Japanese American sociologist Charles Kikuchi for the Japanese Evacuation Research Survey project. (Kikuchi was impressed by Mukai—while at first he described her as having an "Am I Good" attitude, he ultimately found her "delightful, nice looking, personable and intelligent.") Kikuchi recorded in his notes that Mukai confessed her anxieties over choosing between marriage and a career. Even with her connection to Juilliard, she stated, it was difficult for her as a Japanese American to find gigs as a singer.

Despite the obstacles, Mukai persevered in her studies and performance. Her appearance as "Blonde" in a Juilliard production of Mozart's opera *The*

Abduction from the Seraglio in 1944 received a standing ovation from a packed house. Meanwhile, she began making appearances outside. Most notably, in December 1943 and January 1944 she performed a pair of joint recitals with instrumentalists at New York's Barbizon Hotel. She became a regular choir member and soloist at Sunday services at the Community Baptist Church in nearby Scarsdale, New York.

Throughout this period Mukai combined her artistry with political commitment. She associated herself with the antifascist Nisei activist group Japanese American Committee for Democracy, performing in June 1943 alongside Nisei violinist Kazuko Tajitsu, a fellow Juilliard student, at a "Resettlement Benefit entertainment" for new arrivals from the camps. In November 1944 she performed with African American tenor Pruth McFarlin at an interracial concert in Flushing, New York, sponsored by the local branch of the NAACP. In January 1946 she performed in a playlet, *How Do You Spell Democracy?* at the JACD's Rally for a Democratic Japan. That May she performed at a joint concert with Kazuko Tajitsu at Carnegie Chamber Music Hall sponsored by the JACD. Also that year, she made her radio debut in a non-singing role as a Japanese American in Philip A. Young's antiracist play *Nine September*, alongside Fredi Washington, Canada Lee, and Gene Kelly.

In April 1947 Mukai achieved a peak in her career when she made her formal New York debut, in a recital before a packed house of fourteen hundred spectators at Town Hall. Accompanied by pianist Brooks Smith, she put together a program of songs and arias that included selections by Mozart, Richard Strauss, Gustav Mahler, and the modern American composer Paul Bowles. A *New York Times* review extolled her "exceptional charm, skill and intelligence," as both a coloratura and lyric soprano, and the "graceful ease" with which she moved from one operatic style to another.

In September 1947 Mukai married Tomomi Ando, a Texas-born Nisei World War II veteran. In the years that followed, she was forced to balance her professional career against an intense set of domestic demands, as the wife of a career army officer and mother of four children. After relocating to Denver, Colorado, with her family in 1955, Mariko Ando performed in Denver's Tabor Grand Opera House as Gilda in Verdi's *Rigoletto*. Later that year she sang for President Dwight D. Eisenhower and Mamie Eisenhower and was congratulated by the president for an "enjoyable" performance. Over the years she lived on several military bases in Baltimore and Seattle, before ultimately settling in Alexandria, Virginia, with her family. In September 1962 she starred as Rosina in a production of Rossini's *The Barber of Seville* that was presented by the Arlington Music Theater. In later years the sang in chapel choirs at Fort Myer, Virginia. She died on March 10, 2017, of respiratory failure and pneumonia.

Mukai's story is unique among the Nisei songbirds of her generation who embarked on musical careers. She trained at the renowned Juilliard School in an era when nonwhite students were exceptional there (trombonist Ferdinand Lewis Alcindor Sr., father of future basketball legend Kareem Abdul-Jabbar, and singer Carol Brice were among the few others). Furthermore, Mukai defied expectations by going beyond typical Japanese American roles such as Madame Butterfly and refusing to sing Japanese songs. In her few appearances on the opera stage, she performed a variety of roles—in part because of her unique voice, which proved well suited for both lyric and coloratura roles—and proved her versatility as well as her talent.

NISEI SINGER AND CIVIL RIGHTS ACTIVIST
RUBY HIDEKO YOSHINO *with Jonathan van Harmelen*

Along with classical instrumentalists, quite a number of Japanese American operatic and concert singers, mostly women, began their careers on the West Coast during the 1930s. Of all these prewar singers, perhaps the most successful was Ruby Yoshino (Schaar), who became notable in later years for civil rights activism as well as performing.

Ruby Hideko Yoshino was born in Alameda, California, in 1913, one of five children of Yoshimatsu and Mitsuye Yoshino. John Y. Yoshino, her eldest brother, would become a JACL youth leader and ultimately a longtime equal employment opportunity specialist for the federal government. Ruby Yoshino started out as a singer while at Alameda High School. Her music teacher, Hazel Hunter, introduced her to David Carlyes, a representative of the Pacific Coast Opera Company. She would later be accepted as a pupil by San Francisco voice teacher Lona Carol Nicholson.

With help from an introduction by her father, she played her first major concert in 1931, aged eighteen, before an audience of two thousand at the California Teachers Institute in Oakland. The concert helped jump-start Yoshino's local career as a singer and led to a variety of appearances, often with patronage from women's clubs or organizations. For example, in 1933 she performed before the Alameda Business and Professional Women's Club and the Glenview Women's Club. The following year she played a free lobby concert at the Oakland YWCA,

Ruby Yoshino, photo from *Current Life* magazine, 1940–41.

sang at an "International Concert Tea" at the Hotel Leamington produced by Matinee Musical Society, and appeared at a benefit tea for the Piedmont Children's Hospital. In 1935 Yoshino appeared in a concert before an audience of four hundred at the UC Berkeley International House, presenting an aria from Puccini's opera *Tosca*. In a review of the concert, the *Nichi Bei Shimbun* praised her as a "nisei songbird."

In January 1936 Yoshino received an invitation to sing on radio for local CBS affiliates in San Francisco. The success of her performance led to the recording being broadcast nationwide. That summer she reached the semifinals of the Oakland Tribune–California State Fair amateur contest. In September 1936 Yoshino sang at the Northern Democratic Conference's Oakland picnic as part of a fundraiser for President Roosevelt's reelection campaign. It was followed by an invitation to appear at the Hotel Oakland in January 1937 at one of the "Birthday Balls" organized under Roosevelt's aegis by the March of Dimes as a fundraiser for polio research. In her performance at the ball, Yoshino was accompanied by the great musician Duke Ellington, whose band was headlining the event.

In addition to her concert repertoire, Yoshino distinguished herself as an "inspirational singer" performing at churches such as the Berkeley United Japanese Church and in tours under the auspices of the Epworth League.

Beginning in 1936, Yoshino was engaged on an approximately monthly basis to sing at church services at the Unity Wayside Center in Oakland—a rare mainstream gig for a Nisei singer in the prewar era.

In September 1938 Yoshino enrolled as an undergraduate at UC Berkeley. A few months later, in January 1939, she traveled to New York. According to one source, she intended to audition for the famed Juilliard School. Either she decided in the end not to audition or was not accepted. While in New York, she appeared on the nationally broadcast radio program *Major Bowes Amateur Hour*. Yoshino sang "Una voce poco fa" from Rossini's *The Barber of Seville* and was warmly praised by the host. She studied for a time with Charles Hackett, former tenor at the Metropolitan Opera.

In part as a result of her successful radio appearance, Yoshino grew more active on the West Coast. In December 1939 she made her San Francisco debut, performing at the War Memorial Veterans Auditorium. Two months later, in February, she undertook a spring recital tour with performances at Fresno, Berkeley, and Palo Alto. That August she sang at the Greek Theater at UC Berkeley before an estimated audience of five hundred. In January 1941 she gave a recital at Berkeley Music Center. That year she launched a goodwill recital tour of eight California cities, under the auspices of the Methodist Board of Missions. In November 1941 she sang the "Alleluia" from Mozart's "Exsultate, Jubilate" at Stanford University's Memorial Church.

Like other Nisei artists, Yoshino was forced to deal with being exoticized as Japanese. One the one hand, Yoshino often appeared onstage in a kimono and agreed to perform as part of "international night" events. Her programs included songs by modern Japanese composers, notably Kōsaku Yamada and Kishi Yasuichi. Nonetheless, her repertoire consisted mostly of selections from classical European composers, including operatic arias by Rossini, Verdi, and others plus lieder. (She emphasized songs by living composers such as Sergei Rachmaninoff, Richard Strauss, and Rudolph Ganz.) Unlike other Nikkei sopranos, for whom Cio-Cio-San in Puccini's "Japanese" opera *Madama Butterfly* was their "bread-and-butter" role, Yoshino never sang the role onstage, though she occasionally performed the aria "un bel di" in costume, such as at a "Professional Tryout Night" in Oakland in January 1936. She seems not to have auditioned to perform in the annual West Coast touring productions of *Madama Butterfly*, starring soprano Hizi Koyke, that the San Carlo Opera Company put on during these years.

While Yoshino's career was slowly rising, world events halted her performances. On December 7, 1941, she sang at an international fellowship at Oakland's First Methodist Church. It would be her last West Coast appearance. Shortly after, following Executive Order 9066, Yoshino's family was sent to Tanforan, before ending up in the Topaz camp in Utah. Ruby escaped incarceration by moving to Denver, where she worked in a cleaning establishment—a photo of her working in the shop was used by the WRA as part of its resettlement program. She sang occasionally before church and club groups. In July 1944 she traveled to the Amache camp and performed a concert for the inmates in the camp high school building.

In August 1944 Ruby Yoshino was offered the opportunity to make an East Coast publicity tour for the JACL to promote understanding of Japanese Americans and build support for resettlement from camp. Accompanied by speaker Dr. Thomas T. Yatabe of the Chicago JACL, Yoshino presented concerts in areas along the East Coast. On one occasion Yoshino sang before wounded soldiers at Walter Reed Army Hospital, and a photo of her performance appeared in a JACL pamphlet on the Nisei contributions to the war effort. In January 1945 Yoshino returned to New York to sing for a fundraiser for the new Japanese American Committee of New York.

After the end of the war, Ruby Yoshino settled in New York City and resumed her singing career. In 1948 Yoshino helped form the One World Ensemble, an interracial "quartette" dedicated to showing that music "is beyond racial and nationality barriers." Napoleon Reed, an African American tenor, was a member of the ensemble. As with Yoshino's previous solo repertoire, the quartet sang operatic arias from composers such as Mozart, along with songs from Japan and other countries. The group toured in New York and Chicago for a year.

She soon married pianist Rudolf Schaar, performing alongside him at recitals. In December 1950 she made her formal New York concert debut at Times Hall. She sang a number of Japanese songs as well as a Beethoven aria and a group of songs by contemporary American composers. A *New York Times* critic remarked: "Miss Yoshino sang everything loudly and in a metallic tone that soon palled. There were a few relaxed notes which gave an inkling of her true beauty of voice, however." Shortly afterward, she played a sold-out concert at Kimball Hall in Chicago. In September 1951 she sang at the Brooklyn Museum of Art, a concert broadcast over radio station WNYC. In May 1953 she sang a recital at the Community Church of New York. She also began work as a vocal instructor for celebrities, counseling famed actors such as Anne Bancroft, Joan Crawford, and Don Ameche.

In addition to her singing career, Ruby Yoshino also established herself as a JACL leader. During the early 1950s, she lobbied for the right of Japanese immigrants to naturalize, which was established by the McCarran-Walter Act of 1952. Yoshino ultimately served as president of the New York JACL chapter in the 1970s, and as a board member of the JACL newspaper *Pacific Citizen* from 1974 until 1980. In 1986 the New York Chapter of the Japanese American Citizens League honored Ruby Yoshino Schaar for her public advocacy with the creation of the Ruby Yoshino Schaar Biennium Playwright Award. On August 26, 1987, following a yearlong battle with cancer, she died.

Before there was Mary Kageyama, the "songbird of Manzanar," there was Ruby Yoshino. By her graceful appearance and singing, she was able to transcend racial categorization and communicate with people of different backgrounds.

Chapter 8
LITERATURE AND JOURNALISM

T. JOHN FUJII / COLLABORATOR OR COSMOPOLITAN?

The story of Tatsuki John Fujii, a journeyman writer and journalist who was one of the earliest Nisei book authors, offers a rich illustration of the international connections (and complications) of Japanese Americans.

Tatsuki Fujii was born in 1914 in Aichi-Ken, Japan, the son of Jiryu "Jirie" Fujii and Toshi Fujii. He was still an infant when his family moved to California in 1915. Jiryu Fujii had been a Tendai Buddhist priest in Japan, but he converted to Christianity and became a Methodist minister. The family lived in Merced and later Alameda and Walnut Grove. During these years two more children, Grace and Henry, were born. The eldest child took the name John but was also known as "Johnny," "Piggy," or "Jofu." Despite his Japanese birth, he considered himself a Nisei. Like many minister's sons, Fujii was active in church affairs and served as president of the Junior Epworth League and the Alameda High School League. Conversely, as his future friend Bill Hosokawa described him, "Like many a preacher's son he spent much of his youth violating the 'thou shalt nots.'" For much of his life he would remain a heavy drinker and bon vivant.

After graduating from Alameda High School, Fujii moved to Los Angeles, where he enrolled first at Pomona Junior College (later Mt. San Antonio College), then at Pomona College. While at Pomona, Fujii took an interest in journalism. He was engaged as a sports editor of the college daily, the *Student Life*, and worked as assistant to managing editor Joe Shinoda. Fujii soon began writing for the Los Angeles newspapers *Rafu Shimpo* and *Kashū Mainichi*. He also performed in a play with the Little Tokyo Players, through which he met journalist Larry Tajiri. Although Tajiri was still in his teens, like Fujii, he was already English section editor of *Kashū Mainichi*. The two became warm friends.

In 1933 Fujii left Pomona and returned to the Bay Area. There he was hired by Tamotsu Murayama as English editor of *Hokubei Asahi Daily* (a breakaway publication founded by striking staffers from the *Nichi Bei Shimbun*). In addition to editing, he wrote a column called "Hodge-Podge." After the *Hokubei* folded, he was unable to find work.

During the next years, amid the Great Depression, the young Fujii drifted. He relocated to Los Angeles, returned to Pomona, and went to work for the local Nisei press. In February 1934 a daily sports column, Potpourri, published under the name T. John Fujii, debuted in *Rafu Shimpo*. It lasted just three months. Fujii left Pomona and toured Texas and the Southwest. He enrolled at Southern Methodist University in Dallas but did not remain for long. He ultimately returned to California, spent some time as an itinerant farm laborer, then took up work as editor of *New World Sun*, assisting James Omura. (Omura later recalled that Fujii had physically attacked him over a trivial difference of opinion and was fired on the spot by the newspaper's Japanese editor.) Fujii soon moved to writing for *Nichi Bei Shimbun*, edited by his pal Larry Tajiri. In addition to sports columns and features, he penned a pair of short stories, "Drinks Don't Mix" and "Scandal Song." When Tajiri took a leave in early 1936 to tour Japan and East Asia, Fujii briefly took over his Vagaries column.

In fall 1936 Fujii moved to New York. He enrolled at Drew University, a Methodist college in New Jersey, and joined the editorial board of a student weekly, *Drew Acorn*, rising to the rank of associate editor in 1937. However, he spent much of his time in Manhattan attending shows and visiting nightclubs. He contributed to the West Coast press and wrote a column, A Nisei in Manhattan, which reported on New York events, especially show business. Fujii left Drew in mid-1938 and returned to Oakland. Having failed at three different colleges and with job prospects limited by anti-Japanese discrimination and the lack of a diploma, the future may have seemed dim. In August 1938 he published a newspaper piece counseling West Coast Nisei against settling in the Big Apple and sounded a bitter note. "At the end of the Rainbow, I found a pot not of gold but of excrements. I shook the dust of California only to grovel anew in the muck of New York. But I, I who went, found a land for the rich and the dead, return to the land of the poor but the living."

At this juncture, fate intervened. In September Fujii found work in the New York bureau of the Tokyo and Osaka *Asahi Shimbun* newspaper. His work clearly reached an appreciative audience, as in February 1939 he was recruited by a Japanese consular official in New York to join the staff of the *Singapore Herald*, a new English-language newspaper to be published in Singapore. Thus, in late March 1939 Fujii crossed the Pacific. Following stops in Tokyo, Shanghai, and Saigon, he arrived in Singapore. At the *Herald* Fujii served as assistant to editor Bill Hosokawa, a Nisei from Seattle. In May 1940 Hosokawa moved on to Japanese-occupied Shanghai, and Fujii was named managing editor of the *Herald*. In keeping with his own background with the Nisei press, he emphasized sports coverage—notably by offering racetrack results on the front page. Otherwise, he reprinted dispatches from the Japanese official news agency Domei and other sources, plus sensational crime stories from the local police blotter.

On December 8, 1941, the Pacific War broke out. The *Singapore Herald* was closed down. Fujii was rounded up by the British and jailed in Changi Prison in Singapore, then shipped for internment at the Purana Qila fort outside New Delhi, India. There he became the liaison between the Japanese internees and the British authorities. In August 1942 Fujii was one of a group of internees exchanged for British prisoners at Laurenco Marques (today's Maputo) in Mozambique and "repatriated" to Japan. He soon returned to Singapore, by then under Japanese military occupation. He worked for Domei, Japan's official news agency, and for the Information Section of the Imperial Japanese Army.

Even as John Fujii was interned in Asia, his family in the United States was confined at Tanforan and Topaz. In August 1942 diarist Charles Kikuchi wrote in a letter from Tanforan: "John Fujii's family lives next door, and his sister Grace, and brother Henry are here living with their parents. John is supposed to be in camp in Singapore someplace, and his folks are very much concerned about his welfare. They received a letter he wrote around Christmas just recently, so what has happened since then, they do not know." In 1946, shortly after the end of the war, Henry Fujii enlisted in the US Army.

In 1943, writing under the name "Tatsuki Fujii," Fujii produced a memoir, *Singapore Assignment*. The text first appeared in three installments over May and June 1943 in the Tokyo-based English-language newspaper *Nippon Times* (the long-established *Japan Times*, which had adopted a more nationalistic name during the war). Soon after, it was released in book form by the Nippon Times Press. (Takabundo Press in Tokyo put out a Japanese-language edition.) Though just 122 pages in all, *Singapore Assignment* is arguably the first full-length book by a West Coast Japanese American to be published by a mainstream press. It is a highly colored (and colorful) account of his experience working with the *Singapore Herald* in prewar Singapore and the life he found in the British colony, followed by a discussion of the hardships he and his comrades experienced at the hands of the British authorities during his internment.

In June 1943 Fujii made a trip to Tokyo, which may have been connected with publication of his book. He was en route back to Singapore when his ship was unexpectedly rerouted to the Philippines, due to the threat of American submarines. Fujii spent one month there. His description of Manila, written shortly after the war and later published by historian Grant K. Goodman, offers an illuminating account of life under the Japanese occupation. During his stay in Manila, Fujii visited the Santo Tomas internment camp, which would later become notorious for the oppression of the prisoners confined there. In his postwar manuscript, Fujii defended the Japanese governors. "Their internment camp, it appeared to me then, compared very favorably with the treatment I had received from the British at the Purana Qila camp in New Delhi, India."

In the latter stages of the Japanese occupation of Singapore, Fujii prospered. He found work as a liaison between Japanese civilian officials and the general population. He also got married. Once World War II ended and Australian troops came to occupy Singapore, Fujii found employment as a liaison between the Australians and the defeated Japanese. At length he decided to settle in Japan with his wife—the couple separated not long after.

Once in Tokyo, Fujii was hired as a correspondent by the International News Service (owned, ironically enough, by anti-Japanese newspaper baron William Randolph Hearst), and his pieces started to appear occasionally in the mainstream US press. As a result, he was well paid by the miserable standards of devastated postwar Japan. He also contributed occasional pieces to the Nisei press. For example, in 1946 he published an article in the newly founded *Nichi Bei Times* on jazz bands in Japan. He noted sardonically, "Although there are several good musicians in Japan, most of the present-day bands are run-of-the-mill 'not good but loud' types." He produced a second memoir of his wartime experiences, which he dubbed "Postscript to Surrender," but it remained unpublished.

Around the end of the occupation, Fujii was hired as a foreign correspondent by the Associated Press. In October 1952, the second full year of fighting in the Korean War, he was sent by the AP to Korea as a war correspondent. His dispatches appeared regularly in the American press. Historian Monica Kim cited the manuscript of a censored article that Fujii wrote after he followed an interrogation team of the Military Intelligence Service (MIS) onto the battlefields. "There is a babel of tongues on this much fought over ridge—a babel of Chinese dialects, Korean, Japanese and one soft Louisiana drawl," he began his article. (According to legend, Fujii was fired from the AP after he was left alone to staff the office on Christmas Eve. Angry at missing the holiday, he pulled the plug on the Tokyo AP's electronic connections, thereby severing for several hours its contact with the rest of the world.) During this same period, he served as editor of the *Yomiuri Japan News*, an English-language offshoot of *Yomiuri Shimbun*, and wrote a regular column for it, The Last Word. In 1954 he founded and edited *Orient Digest*, a monthly entertainment magazine.

In 1955 Fujii published a new book, *Tears on the Tatami*, with the Japanese publisher Phoenix Books. In his author's note Fujii referred to himself archly as "the only illiterate journalist in Japan, John Fujii." His friend Larry Tajiri described the book as "something of a guidebook for foreigners, a pertinent and often impertinent guide to living in post-Occupation Japan." Subjects included Japanese mothers-in-law, the problems of buying a house in Japan, and information for foreign visitors such as eating and drinking on the Ginza. The book was accompanied by illustrations by renowned Nisei cartoonist Jack Matsuoka. Two of Fujii's essays from the book later appeared in Jay Gluck's 1965 anthology, *Ukiyo: Stories of the "Floating World" of Postwar Japan*.

In later years Fujii worked for Fairchild Publications (he spent fourteen years as Tokyo correspondent for *Women's Wear Daily*) and wrote for various British newspapers. He died in Tokyo on August 18, 1996. In a sign of Fujii's journalistic renown, his memorial service in Tokyo was attended by two former Associated Press bureau chiefs, Tom Dygard and Henry Hartzenbusch, as well as former NBC correspondent Jack Reynolds.

T. John Fujii's career in wartime Singapore, as discussed in his book *Singapore Assignment*,[1] offers a stark lesson in the ambiguity of Nisei responses to the conflict of loyalties between the United States and Japan in the era of the Pacific War. During these years a whole cadre of educated Nisei, who had been excluded on racial grounds from employment with mainstream American businesses and had accepted positions with Japanese firms in North America and in Japan's growing empire in Asia, were caught in the middle of the growing Japanese-US conflict. They were forced to maneuver and negotiate between loyalty to their native land, their economic prospects, and their responsibility to their employers.

For Fujii the issue of loyalty and identity was even keener because of the circumstances of his birth. In fall 1985 he attended a conference at UCLA, "Coming of Age in the 1930s," on prewar Nisei writers and journalists. At the conference Fujii described himself as a "Kibei in reverse": whereas the Kibei were Nisei born in the United States who were sent to Japan for their education and then came back to America, Fujii was born in Japan, came to the United States as a baby and was educated entirely in the United States, and settled in Japan after World War II. Despite his long residence in the land of his birth, he never learned to read or speak Japanese and always considered himself a Nisei.

So, why did Fujii accept a position with the *Singapore Herald* in 1939? The *Herald*'s creation as a propaganda organ for Tokyo, as part of a worldwide push, was an open secret. (The Japanese government denied that it financed the newspaper, but the Japanese foreign ministry did in fact offer a subsidy, one that enabled its editors to reduce the price to three cents a copy, thereby undercutting other Singapore dailies that charged five cents.) Fujii was clearly aware that the position was a form of apprenticeship for future propaganda work. "The Nisei future is in the Far East with Japan's destiny in Asia," he told an unnamed interviewer (likely Larry Tajiri) in March 1939, while en route to Asia. "I expect to stay in Singapore for two or three years, and later return to Tokyo, to work with the Foreign Office in propaganda work. Japan is in need of trained men and more Nisei should take advantage."

In Tajiri's sympathetic view, expressed in the early postwar years, the fact that Fujii was everywhere an alien, unlike his American-born Nisei counterparts, was decisive for him: "He could not vote. He could not own property in the state of California. Many jobs and most professions were closed to him. His status influenced his political opinions, or lack of them. His status, or lack of it, made him opportunistic." According to Tajiri, the liberal activist, Fujii held to the position that a journalist should confine himself to objective reporting and not advocate for any position, either through journalism or outside actions. Ironically, such a stance of political detachment bred opportunism. Since Fujii was excluded on racial grounds from working on mainstream American newspapers, he would look to the Far East for opportunities.

Tajiri's position is illuminating. In 1940 he himself took over the job as New York correspondent of the *Asahi* newspapers that Fujii had left behind and remained in that position until Pearl Harbor. Tajiri did his best to balance objective reporting against the pressures of the job and surely felt some discomfort. Yet in speaking about Fujii's opportunism, he may have been protesting too much. Tajiri further stated, moreover, that once he was in New York, Fujii invited him to come work with him on the *Singapore Herald* and promised him not only passage on an ocean liner for himself and his wife but a vacation trip to Bali. Tajiri insisted that he turned down the invitation, mostly for ideological reasons.

Yet if the *Singapore Herald* was so ideologically objectionable, more so than the *Asahi*, what are we to make of the fact that its first editor was Bill Hosokawa? As his future career showed, Hosokawa was a patriotic American, not a simple-minded shill or Japanese propagandist. All the same, the *Herald* under Hosokawa's editorship expressed from the outset a certain pro-Japanese bias. The newspaper supported Japan's position in international affairs and criticized what it called the "Chungking faction" (the official Chinese government that had moved to Chungking to escape the Japanese occupation). True, once Hosokawa left the editorship, the *Herald* under Fujii took a more openly critical stand against the colonial government of Singapore. According to later accounts, however, even Fujii was convinced that Japan and the Western powers could find some accommodation, and he played down the possibility of war.

Fujii's is more open to charges of opportunism and pro-Japanese propaganda for his 1943 book *Singapore Assignment*. In it Fujii presents himself as adjusting psychologically from an American to a Japanese point of view and offers fulsome praise for Japan and for Tokyo's "mission of Greater East Asia." Yet even publishing amid Japanese wartime censorship, he speaks positively of the Americans he met in prewar Singapore, who had a measure of "tolerant understanding." In contrast, Fujii devotes his most powerful passages to attacking the smug and pretentious British in Singapore and their economic exploitation of the Malay and Chinese populations. He draws a strong parallel between the attitude of the British in the Straits, who treated the native population as inferiors, and racial discrimination in the United States. "The more I saw of British life, the more I learned to hate their smug arrogance. The Americans that I had known in my childhood were narrow-minded and prejudiced but the British in Singapore were ten times worse."

There is also an intermittent nasty tone of anti-Semitism in the book, one that had appeared sporadically in Fujii's writings in the prewar Nisei press. For example, Fujii dismisses a rival publication, the *Malaya Tribune*, as a tool of its Chinese and Jewish capitalist owners. "[It] was the Chinese capital that remained, coupled with Jewish greed, that made the *Malaya Tribune* prostitute itself to Chungking propaganda. On the whole the *Malaya Tribune* was a poorly edited newspaper. In its endeavor to please both its Jewish management and Chungking support, the *Tribune* was at best a cheap, sensational journal."

John Fujii's writings in the prewar *Singapore Herald* made him a controversial figure. During World War II two books were published that commented on him. In his 1943 book, *Suez to Singapore*, CBS radio correspondent Cecil Brown

Literature and Journalism 171

called him "Johnny Fuji, the Japanese spy." According to Brown, Fujii was a Japanese agent who had been stationed in Singapore in the months before Pearl Harbor to entertain visiting American dignitaries, newsmen, and others at bars and at dinners and lure them into offering confidential information. Fujii's Nisei friends such as Larry Tajiri, who were aware of his fondness for going out on the town, responded by accusing Brown of having mistaken such friendliness for an officially-inspired effort to get information. Rather, they claimed rather poignantly, these were the actions of a homesick American who desperately wanted to talk with someone from his home country. Mark J. Gayn, an authority on Far Eastern affairs who had attended school with Fujii at Pomona College, likewise took a more generous view in his 1944 memoir, *Journey from the East*, seeing Fujii primarily as a victim of circumstances.

Even once the war ended, Fujii remained controversial. In 1946 the Singapore newspaper *Morning Tribune* reported the shocking information that "Johnny Fuji," the man about town and former Japanese agent, was now at large in town, making money by interpreting for the Australian occupiers and tooling around in a jeep wearing a white suit and a solar topee. Its article presented on page 1 a set of anti-British quotations from *Singapore Assignment*, which it referred to as a "notorious, news-distorted book." Shortly afterward, columnist Leonard Lyons reported with shock that Fujii had returned to Japan, where he been screened by US occupation authorities and approved for a job with an American news agency, the International News Service.

What was Fujii's own attitude toward his identity and his wartime actions? One useful clue might be a review he did in the *Yomiuri English News* of the first edition of John Okada's epochal 1957 novel, *No-No Boy*. Fujii started his review by giving a curious version of the history of Executive Order 9066 and Japanese Americans: "The outbreak of World War II threw them all into American-style concentration camps out of which the majority either volunteered or were drafted into the US armed services. The nisei fought heroically as the 442nd Regimental Combat Team to prove that they were 'good Americans.' But after the war, many found that the battle had just been joined." (It is unknown whether the experience of Fujii's brother, Henry, who was confined in camp and later enlisted in the US Army, played a role in this all-male and militarist conception of the Nisei generation.)

Fujii went on to describe Nisei unflatteringly as searching for their identity within a country that only partially accepted them, as with other "hyphenated

Americans," and being "filled with such bitterness." In contrast, those (like himself) who had embraced Japan were at peace with themselves.

> Many nisei who sought an identity, gave up the land of their birth, and returned to Japan before the war. They had their tribulations, their period of adjustment during the war as they tried to fit themselves into a society that was ruled by kempeis [Kempeitai, Japanese military secret police] and the brutal sergeants. But these Japanese-Americans, who dropped the second half of their hyphenated nomenclature, served in Japanese intelligence corps, as front-line combat reporters, as voice interceptors in submarines and as staff interpreters during the surrender ceremonies. Few of these individuals will admit any regrets, if they have any, at this late stage.

Fujii's brave words about resolving his identity crisis and adopting a unitary Japanese identity are belied by the record. Fujii never became fluent in Japanese, and he jumped at the chance to connect with other Nisei. When wartime JACL president Saburo Kido visited Japan in the late 1950s, Fujii was eager to meet him. In 1974 Fujii called for the founding of a JACL chapter in Tokyo and took steps toward organizing it. In 1983 he organized a reunion dinner of the staff of the *Singapore Herald* and invited his old boss Bill Hosokawa to attend. After Fujii died, in 1996, Hosokawa would include a reminiscence of his old friend in his Frying Pan column in *Pacific Citizen*.

BUNJI OMURA / NEW YORK JAPANESE ANTIFASCIST WRITER AND PUBLICIST *with Jonathan van Harmelen*

Although the saga of the Issei generation has been written by any number of historians, our understanding of the views of Issei writers and thinkers on Japan is still incomplete. While the work of Eiichiro Azuma delves into the connections of the Issei to Japanese expansionism and the rise of militaristic nationalism, few have examined their counterparts who spoke out publicly against Japan's move toward fascism and who defended democracy. One such voice was that of Bunji Omura.

Bunji Omura was born in 1896 in Takakura, Fukuoka, Japan. Although his parents were farmers, his family belonged to a long line of samurai dating back to the fourteenth century. After moving to Tokyo to study law, and then

Bunji Omura and his family, New York, ca. 1970. Courtesy of the family of Bunji Omura.

railroad engineering, Omura left Japan and migrated to the United States in 1919, at age twenty-three. Initially, he entered as a seaman but then jumped ship and remained in the United States as a farm laborer in California, where he attended night school to learn English. In 1928 he returned to Japan for a few months, then reentered the United States on a student visa. Omura enrolled at the College of the Pacific (now known as University of the Pacific) in Stockton, California, where he completed his bachelor's in political science in 1929. During his senior year he was president of the Japanese club. After graduation he left California for New York, with the idea of pursuing a master's degree in public law at Columbia University. His master's thesis, produced the following year, was on "Local Government in Japan."

While at Columbia, Omura became fascinated with the early Meiji period. His desire to understand the period led him to undertake a doctoral program in political science. Although he completed coursework for his doctorate, in the end he did not obtain his degree (according to family lore, he was not able to arrange publication of his thesis, which was required for graduation). Instead, he remained in New York as a freelance writer and instructor. During this period Omura worked with International House, located at Columbia

University. Through his activities there, Omura met a white woman, Martha Pilger, who was a specialist in German with degrees from Ripon College and the University of Wisconsin. The two were wed in 1934 and remained together until Martha's death forty-five years later. The couple had two children, June and George. George Omura would later become a distinguished physician, while June Omura Goldberg was a journalist and editor.

During the 1930s Omura watched anxiously as Japanese society slowly turned toward fascism. Following the Japanese incursion and occupation of Manchuria in 1931, Omura rose to prominence as an expert on Japanese foreign policy. That October he debated Chinese community leader Chih Meng at Columbia University over the justice of the Japanese invasion of Manchuria. Omura denied that Tokyo intended to annex Manchuria and insisted that Japan had entered Manchuria out of "absolute economic and strategic necessity," given its growing population and lack of natural resources. Similarly, in 1932, after Japan had established the puppet state of Manchukuo, Omura and Chinese scholar Daniel Chang presented a discussion at Columbia University, with Omura arguing that Tokyo's intervention was driven by its justified attempt to protect its nationals from rising anti-Japanese sentiment. Nonetheless, Omura agreed that a third-party intervention was needed to evaluate the situation fully.

Despite this hedged support for Japan's occupation of Manchuria, Omura soon grew concerned over the assassinations of Japanese political leaders by the militaristic right, and he gradually became more openly critical of Japan. In an article, "Dagger and Pistol in the Hand of the Japanese Superpatriot," published in *Asia* magazine in 1932, he warned that the recent wave of assassinations was the sign of a larger national crisis, one that revealed the dangerous state of unconscious feeling among the larger population. In early 1934 Omura told an audience of students at Long Island University that the fascist movement was rapidly developing into a potent force in Japan. Soon after, he penned the article "Fascism Lures Japan" for the journal *Current History*. It described the rise of fascism in Japan as the exploitation of working-class woes by military elites and warned that ultranationalistic and non-parliamentary political forces were spreading rapidly throughout the nation.

Over the following years, in a series of articles, Omura critically examined different aspects of Japanese policy. For example, in the 1935 *Asia* article "What Profit Manchuria?" Omura questioned whether the Japanese occupation was worth the cost. Following the military's failed February 26 coup in 1936, Omura produced a syndicated article for the United Press on the coup and the fascist message it sent, with the army ensuring that Communist and leftist groups were "effectively wiped out so that fascism would be the only hope" for Japan. In his 1940 *Asia* article "No Party Rule for Japan," Omura denounced the Japanese army and its allies as composed of extremists blocking democratic rule. "These extremists have no intention of returning to the two-party system which Japan followed for a brief period in the Nineteen-Twenties. On the contrary, they intend to introduce in Japan the pattern of a totalitarian political set-up, similar to the Fascist, Nazi and Communist parties." Meanwhile, Omura assisted author Edwin A. Falk with research for Falk's 1936 book, *Togo and the Rise of Sea Power in Japan*, which warned of the danger of Japanese naval power in the Pacific.

The rising tide of Japanese militarism also led Omura to transform his abandoned dissertation into a novel. The work, *The Last Genro: The Statesman Who Westernized Japan*, is a fictionalized version of the life of Prince Saionji Kinmochi, a leading Japanese liberal statesman who was twice prime minister of Japan and who helped select a dozen others. Presenting the prince's life in gritty detail, Omura's study narrates Kinmochi's career from his youth in Paris to his rise in Meiji-era politics. Yet *The Last Genro* was more than just a biographical novel; rather, Omura used Kinmochi's life as a basis for a broader discussion of Japan's diverse political forces. Kinmochi embodied the antithesis of fascism; as a young man, he had studied at the University of Paris, and he embraced a cosmopolitan worldview over the decades that followed. He remained a pro-Western liberal and opposed military supremacy. For Omura such an alternative narrative was needed not only in Japan but in the United States, where anti-Japanese publicists used Japanese militarism as a means of scapegoating the Japanese living there.

Omura's novel was published in mid-1938, under the imprint of the distinguished Philadelphia publisher Lippincott. A British edition was put out at the same time by the publisher Harrap. Harrap was pointed in its advertising about the book's theme: "Written by Bunji Omura, Japanese democrat, this book gets behind the bristling front of Japanese militarism." The work was widely publicized and reviewed in the United States, though not always positively. In the *San Francisco Examiner* Isaac Don Levine called it a "charming and quaint work" and lauded the author as a "sincere democrat by conviction." However, *New York Times* reviewer Katherine Woods slammed the book: "Developed in a strikingly colloquial style which lacks verisimilitude in just so far as it falls short of natural dignity and is run through with several threads of romance, *The Last Genro* is not wholly satisfactory either as biography or as a novel."

Not all of Omura's works on Japan during the late 1930s were equally weighty. On a lighter note, during this period Omura produced a pair of articles, "Japan's Happiest Village," for the tourist magazine *Travel*, and "Japan Speeds Up," for *Esquire*. He also published book reviews in the *Nation* and the *New Republic*. In a 1939 article Omura was cited as stating that he was working on a second book, a study of the Japanese statesman Prince Ito. Omura was listed in the 1940 census as working as a writer and translator for a project of the New Deal agency the Works Progress Administration (WPA)—presumably he was employed by the Federal Writers' Project. During 1940–41 he penned a brief history of the Japanese American press and other articles for the pro-Tokyo New York newspaper *Japanese American Review*.

Omura's life, like that of other Issei, was strongly touched by the coming of the Pacific War. In a June 1941 article in the Seattle *Taihoku Nippō*, Omura called upon Japanese residents to support the United States in the event of war, expressing optimism that law-abiding Japanese would not be subjected to persecution. In the wake of the Japanese attack on Pearl Harbor, however, he became an enemy alien, with restricted movements. During the war years Omura enlisted in the war effort. He first offered his services as a Japanese teacher at the Naval Government School at Columbia University. Omura likewise produced for the navy a dictionary of Japanese legal terms. He later offered his skills to the US Army as a Japanese translator, working at the Military Government Translation Center in New York. Omura translated the first reports of the atomic bombing of Nagasaki. Outside of government work, Omura also worked for *Fortune* magazine, preparing articles for its special issue on Japan.

In 1945 the federal government instituted deportation proceedings against Omura as an illegal alien and called him in for questioning. However, because of his outstanding wartime record and the potential damage to his family that would result from his expulsion, his deportation was suspended, and he was permitted to stay in the United States. During the same period he transferred to teach Japanese at the University of Michigan's School of Military Government, then from 1946 to 1947 headed the Japanese translation section at Wright-Patterson Air Force Base in Dayton, Ohio. His status nonetheless remained precarious until he was admitted to US citizenship in 1953, following the McCarran-Walter Immigration Act.

During the postwar era, Omura briefly worked for Voice of America, the US government's international news network, and ran a translation service. He continued to speak publicly as an expert on Japan. In a 1954 letter to the *New York Times*, Omura argued that anti-Americanism and militarism remained present, though dormant, in Japan despite the occupation. Citing the lack of a formal police force and the instability of the Japanese economy, Omura argued that Americans should be wary of extremism in Japan and the potential rise of militarism. In 1969 he was awarded the Order of the Sacred Treasure, sixth rank, for promoting Japanese culture in the United States—a sign of Japan's changing views on Omura's vocal antifascism. In 1970 he debated union organizer Karl Yoneda in the pages of the *New York Nichibei* over alleged gaps in Bill Hosokawa's book *Nisei: The Quiet Americans*.

By the time Bunji Omura died, in September 1988, his earlier work had been all but forgotten. Still, Omura's writings are important both for understanding the diverse views of the Japanese community toward militaristic Japan and the presence of Issei immigrants in American intellectual life. Likewise, Omura's productive writing career for mainstream publications such as the *Nation* and *Fortune* underscores the continuing importance of Issei who could offer expertise on Japan. While most anti-Japanese propagandists portrayed Japan as inherently servile to fascism, Omura stood out as a voice of reasoned analysis. Although his career in journalism was relatively brief and *The Last Genro* remains his only published book, Omura nonetheless deserves further attention as an influential public intellectual and supporter of Japanese democracy in the years before the Second World War.

IWAO KAWAKAMI'S INTRIGUING ELEGY FOR TOPAZ

One of the people who enriched my life was the journalist and educator Guyo (Marion) Tajiri, whom I was fortunate to get to know near the end of her long life. I was further blessed to receive an additional gift from her years after her passing.

I first met Guyo in 2003. She agreed to let me interview her about the years during and after World War II, when she served with her husband, Larry Tajiri, as columnist and coeditor for the *Pacific Citizen* newspaper. (I subsequently described this visit in the afterword to *Pacific Citizens*, my anthology of the Tajiris' writings.) That first encounter with Guyo led to several further meetings, and a warm friendship blossomed between us. In 2007, shortly after I began writing for the *Nichi Bei Times* (as it was then), I learned from a mutual friend that Guyo had been hospitalized and had not long to live. I devoted one of my first "Great Unknown" columns to revealing her career and accomplishments and immediately sent the manuscript on to her family members to share with her in her last days.

Following Guyo's passing, I kept in sporadic touch with different family members, such as her niece Karen Okagaki and her nephews Gregg Nakanishi and Jon Funabiki. They kindly offered me documents and granted me assistance with family photos and rights for *Pacific Citizens*. In early 2016 I received a message from another of Guyo's nephews, Alan Okagaki. Alan told me that he and his wife, Donna, would be traveling from Seattle to Montreal for a vacation, and we agreed to meet for coffee. I was glad for a chance to get together with one of my old friend's relatives. During our chat Alan mentioned that he had a box of material from Guyo's house that he had inherited after her passing, and asked whether I could give him guidance as to its scholarly value.

Thus it was that when I visited Seattle in 2016, Alan came to see me at my hotel and carried over Guyo's box. It turned out to contain books on diverse subjects, including a volume on gardening and an album of protest songs by the famed folksinger Woody Guthrie (who had once written columns for the *Pacific Citizen*).

One of the books in the collection was a slim volume of poetry, *The Parents and Other Poems* by Iwao Kawakami. I had never seen the book and knew nothing of it. (I later learned that two copies were housed in public collections—at Smith College and the University of Minnesota.) I saw that it had been published in 1947, right after the end of the war, by the newly founded *Nichi Bei Times*—the very newspaper for which I had subsequently written my own columns. While Kawakami was primarily known as a journalist and columnist (and onetime husband of the better-known poet Toyo Suyemoto), I knew that he had written poetry as well, as I recalled seeing his work in numerous anthologies of Asian American writing.

Even before opening the book, I was intrigued, as it represented a rare work of Nisei literature from the early years after the war. Whereas before Pearl Harbor the young Nisei on the West Coast and elsewhere had produced a dizzying amount of poetry and short fiction, they had largely ceased publishing afterward, when the mass of previous writers struggled to make a living and recover from the trauma of their camp experience. Even among such works as they produced, the camp experience remained all but untouched.

Indeed, as I started reading through the poems, I was a bit disappointed that none of them seemed to reference the wartime confinement, despite the fact that Kawakami had been confined at Topaz and had edited the weekly *Topaz Times*. Then I came upon "The Paper." This poem was an intriguing elegy for Topaz (which the author compares to Nineveh and Virginia City as ruins of abandoned cities lying bare in the desert). It centered on a horrid act of injustice—the shooting of a man who violated regulations by straying too close to the barbed wire fence surrounding camp. I realized that the work was inspired by the 1943 shooting of Issei inmate James Wakasa. I had seen artworks by Miné Okubo and Chiura Obata that depicted the events of the shooting and Wakasa's funeral, but this was the first literary treatment of it that I had found. By citing regulations in bloodless parentheses, Kawakami conveyed through understatement the horrible inhumanity of life behind barbed wire and the waste of people's time and lives that it entailed.

I told Alan that I was excited to learn more about the Kawakami book. Upon seeing my enthusiasm, Alan generously offered to give me the book and any others from the box I wanted, saying that he knew that Guyo would approve and that I would make good use of whatever I had. In the end I took a selection of books that I thought would be helpful or good additions to my library.

Since receiving *The Parents*, I have tried to find further information on its writing and publication but without much success. Kawakami died in 1976 and seemingly left no archives, so the sources of "The Paper" and its eloquent protest over confinement, so rare in the postwar years, remain unclear. I am nonetheless grateful to Guyo's family for bringing me the volume, which serves as a final echo of the generosity my friend showed me during her lifetime.

IWAO KAWAKAMI, THE PAPER

(the desert wind blows and sand covers the barbed wire posts—here was
    once a city a mile square: Topaz, "Jewel of the desert"—a city of ten
    thousand people, aliens and citizens bound by barbed wire)
reconstruct now the first days of Topaz—
In the grayness following a sunset an old man shuffles along the road
    near the barbed wire fence
focus the lens of imagination upon an unshaven face
beneath a shapeless straw hat—
the face of a Japanese seventy years old

a blue working shirt—patched denim trousers—brown boots
that rise and fall, leaving small craters in the dusty road
(this is the beginning of a Utah night and a wind springs up)
Two pieces of paper start to flutter in the hands of the old man—
His lips are moving
(what are you reading, sir? Even if it is the camp's mimeographed news-
    paper it cannot be as absorbing as the sight of purple mountains rest-
    ing on white sands of the desert)
this is a man who once had a celery ranch near San Diego—
He remembers the wet green stalks on frosty mornings
The Mexicans who said "La Golondrina" as they slashed at the
roots with long knives
the imperturbable young Japanese American truck drivers
the fat Italian commission merchants who kidded him in a market
    jammed with vegetables
(war has forced an evacuation—harrows and discs begin to rust)
a sheet of paper flies out of the old man's hands
the wind carries it along like a white lifeboat bobbing in the
middle of an ocean
a few yards beyond the fence the paper swerves to rest upon
the sand
(regulation of the War Relocation Authority: all residents of
the center are hereby warned not to go near the fence)
The old man stops, looks at the watch tower some distance away—
surely guards would not mind if he went after a piece of paper
slowly he walks toward the fence, bends down to go through
The wires
a buzzard circles lazily above him—swings away in alarm
as a shot shatters the silence of approaching night
dust rises in a cloud as the old man falls sideways in the road
The body twitches—grows still—blood seeps through the hole
in the back of the heart
(order of the Military Police: fire if necessary if any resident
is seen going through the fence)
a GI with a Garand runs down the stops of the watch tower
"Christ, was he trying to escape?"
he sees a mimeographed paper clutched in the dead man's hand

but does not notice the wind beginning to push another
piece of paper beyond the fence
(Topaz is now with Virginia City and Nineveh—the paper,
buffeted by the rain and wind, has crumbled into dust—
only the mountains and the desert remain)

EDDIE SHIMANO AND GERALD CHAN SIEG *with James Sun*

One little-known but vital aspect of the history of New Deal agencies such as the Works Progress Administration was their knack for hiring talented Asian Americans in diverse fields. Writer Pardee Lowe worked for the WPA investigating San Francisco Chinatown. Nisei researcher May Matsumoto canvassed homes in Japanese districts to obtain information on family employment. A pair of Chinese American authors, Steven C. Moy and Boqi Zhu (Peter Chu), helped produce a two-volume theater history, *Chinese Theatres in America*. Actor Goro Suzuki, who later achieved fame under the name Jack Soo, made his theatrical debut in a Federal Theatre Project play, *These Few Ashes*.

The Federal Writers' Project was an important locus of WPA activity by and about Asian Americans. Employees collected Asian folklore and performed sociological studies of Chinese and Japanese communities for their New York and San Francisco city guidebooks. Researchers produced statistical reports on Filipino agricultural labor in California and interviewed members of the famed flower-growing Sawada family in Mobile, Alabama. The FWP hired several Asian American social scientists. Thomas Chow produced research reports on Manhattan Chinatown. Jon Y. Lee collected Chinese American narratives in Oakland. Jo Morisue researched Japanese communities in San Francisco. Mary Fujii, a graduate anthropology student at the University of Chicago, assisted Katherine Dunham in investigating Chicago's African American religious cults and storefront churches.

The outstanding Asian American staffer on the FWP was Eddie Takato Shimano. Shimano was born in Seattle on May 28, 1911, one of five children of a baker. After graduating from Franklin High School, he made a six-month trip to Japan with his family, returning to Washington in mid-1932. In the months that followed, Shimano toured forty US states, before ending in Boston.

In 1932 Shimano enrolled at the University of Washington as a journalism major and joined the Japanese Students Club. In the fall of 1934, he transferred to Ellensburg Normal School (now Central Washington University) and was named associate editor of the student newspaper, the *Campus Crier*. He gained attention when his editorial "Wolf, Wolf" was reprinted in the weekly *Commonwealth Builder*. However, when the paper's faculty advisor told him that his editorials would be subject to censorship, he resigned in protest and moved to the University of Iowa.

In 1936 Shimano received a scholarship from Cornell College in Mount Vernon, Iowa. There he joined the English club and so impressed his classmates with his tales of talented Nisei writers that they agreed to produce a Japanese American literary magazine as a club project. Shimano contacted writer Mary Oyama Mittwer, who directed a Los Angeles Nisei literary club, the Writers of Southern California. She agreed to recruit contributors. Henry Tatsumi, a lecturer at the University of Washington, provided a title for the magazine.

Gyo-Sho appeared in May 1936, in a handsome twenty-four-page edition, handbound with handset type, containing stories and poems. As Shimano explained in his foreword, "GYO-SHO, literally Dawn-Bell, means 'the peal of the gong at the break of day.' In Japan, the temple bell is struck at the first glimmerings of the break of dawn to announce to the inhabitants that a new day awaits. And so we think of this magazine as the bell which we strike to announce to the world a new day, symbolizing the awakening of the Nisei."

Shimano left Cornell in June 1936 and relocated to San Francisco, where he was hailed as a leading literary light. The Nisei newspaper *New World Sun Daily* (*Shin Sekai*) employed him as a writer and as editor of its Monday magazine. He wrote several short stories and poems, some under the pen name "s. takato," including sections of a planned Nisei novel, "Futility Is Our Cry." In December 1936 he left the paper, a departure likely prompted by political differences with its largely Republican editorship.

In the summer of 1937 the Japanese army invaded China. Shimano bravely took a public stand against the Japanese occupation and the atrocities in Nanking. He helped raise funds for American Friends of the Chinese People, joined that group's board of directors, and called for boycotts of Japanese goods. He told the press: "I may be ostracized by my own people. I may be called a renegade, but I am working for China in this war and will continue to follow the dictates of my own conscience." In early 1938 he participated in anti-Japanese demonstrations on San Francisco's waterfront. As he predicted, he was ostracized by Japanese community leaders—even the progressive intellectuals of the

Nisei Democrats did not dare to publicly challenge the Japanese war machine in China. In the end, although he retained many Nisei friends, Shimano's writings disappeared from Japanese ethnic publications.

It was at this time that FWP hired Shimao. His first assignment was in 1937 as a "rewrite man" with the WPA-funded California Art Research Project, a massive collection of over twenty volumes of artists' biographies. Shimano worked on a study of famed painter Chiura Obata. The volume was credited to Gene Hailey, but Shimano likely helped draft and reshape the essay. Shimano also worked with the FWP's History of San Francisco Journalism Project, contributing material for the three-page section on ethnic Japanese press.

Shimano's principal assignment was as monograph author for the California Theatre Project (CTP). Between 1938 and 1942, under the direction of Lawrence Estevan, litterateur and editor of the journal *Coast*, the San Francisco office of the CTP produced twenty monographs on diverse aspects of the history of theater in San Francisco, including little theaters; minstrelsy; the French, German, and Italian theaters; the Chinese theater; opera performances; the history of theater buildings; and biographical studies of theater folk. Eddie Shimano was the principal author of monographs on actor John McCullough, theater managers Dr. David G. "Yankee" Robinson and M. B. Leavitt, and circus manager Joseph A. Rowe. Additionally, the volume on theater buildings, authored by Lawrence Estevan, credits Shimano for "preliminary writing."

By September 1939 Shimano had ceased most public activities because of his failing health. He spent much of 1940 and 1941 in a tuberculosis sanitarium, during which he wrote a short novel, "Bread." Although it was hailed by friends, he was unable to find a publisher.

After he recovered, Shimano reconnected with West Coast Japanese communities in the weeks after the outbreak of the Pacific War in December 1941. He expressed solidarity with Nisei targeted by racial hostility and accusations of disloyal activities. (Shimano told the story of a drunk and bigoted white who snarled at him, "Jap . . . Why don'tch go back where you came from?" to which he responded by falling back in mock terror and saying, "No, no . . . Anything but Iowa!"). Shimano joined journalist Larry Tajiri and sculptor Isamu Noguchi to form an antifascist political group, the Nisei Writers and Artists Mobilization for Democracy. The NWAMD sponsored petitions, commissioned studies of Japanese American contributions to agriculture and commerce, and contacted sympathetic government agents. In March 1942, on behalf of the NWAMD, Shimano wrote a set of columns for *Nichi Bei Shimbun*—his first writings in the Nisei press since 1936.

Despite the group's efforts, the US Army rounded up and confined the entire Japanese community following President Franklin Roosevelt's Executive Order 9066. Eddie Shimano was separated from his new fiancée, Katherine Morton, and sent to the Santa Anita Assembly Center. There he was named editor of the center newsletter, the *Pacemaker*. He explained that he chose the title—paying tribute to Santa Anita's prewar fame as a racetrack—to help "set the pace" for Nisei and encourage them to overcome their difficulties. The newspaper was subject to strict government censorship, and Shimano complained privately that it was mainly a mouthpiece for the camp administration. Still, his pithy editorials and column, Win, Place, and Show, were popular with readers, and the Office of War Information awarded Shimano and the *Pacemaker* an official commendation.

In October 1942, after several months at Santa Anita, he was moved to the Jerome Camp in Arkansas and named editor of its newspaper, the *Denson Communiqué*. In a sign of his popularity, Shimano's residence block also elected him to the camp's Community Council. As at Santa Anita, he chafed over restrictions on freedom of the press in camp. He told Isamu Noguchi: "I knew beforehand that the Negro problem was untouchable and I am told now that anything to do with workers' organizing or protesting is also taboo. The mess hall workers here got together and demanded a minimum of $16 per month and when I wrote it up for the COMMUNIQUÉ, the camp bulletin, the reports officer here just about blew up." Nonetheless, Shimano found ways to express his views. The December 1, 1942, issue of the *Denson Communiqué* featured an open letter by Shimano, deploring rumors of luxurious camp conditions and commenting on the shooting of a Nisei soldier in nearby Dermott, Arkansas. Referring to the Nazi anthem, Shimano stated, "The future of America will be dismal indeed if we substitute the 'Horst Wessel' song of racial-superiority for the glorious refrain of the 'land of the free.'"

Soon after he arrived in Arkansas, Shimano was recruited by the Common Council for American Unity, a New York–based group that defended immigrants and minorities. Though still without a definite job offer, Shimano left camp in February 1943 and moved to New York, where he reunited with Katherine. In March 1943 the council hired Shimano as director of public relations. Ecstatic, he wrote (semi-facetiously) to his old colleagues, "To be out in the world again after almost a year of the restricted subnormal and morbid life of the centers makes me, to use a good old American phrase, 'feel like a white man again.'"

Once installed at the Common Council, Shimano organized a public forum on Japanese Americans, which attracted some two hundred people, and worked with Common Ground's editor, M. Margaret Anderson, on a special journal issue, entitled "Get the Evacuees Out!" Shimano contributed the essay "Blueprint for a Slum," which remains his signature work. It described in harsh—and arguably exaggerated—terms the psychological toll of mass incarceration on Nisei in the camps and claimed that confinement would lead to the social dysfunction common among other ghettoized minorities. He advocated for the full integration of Nisei into larger society: "The hope is in resettlement.... Such dispersal resettlement, I am convinced, will go far to effect speedily and drastically, with surgical thoroughness and surgical disregard for sentiment, the integration of the Japanese into American life."

Shimano's piece was a sensation. Even before it was published, *Pacific Citizen* editor Larry Tajiri wrote Anderson enthusiastically, "Eddie's 'Blueprint for a Slum' is probably the most interesting and comprehensive article so far on the problems inside the camps." The African American journal *Los Angeles Tribune* published an extended (and largely positive) analysis of the essay, comparing its descriptions of Nisei to the plight of African Americans. The *Tribune*'s piece was in turn reprinted in the *Catholic Worker*.

Ironically, though Shimano's employment with the Common Council enabled him to leave camp, he remained with the cash-strapped organization for only about one year. In 1946 he was selected as editor of a community newspaper, the *Nisei Weekender*, that was an offshoot of the New York–based political group the Japanese American Committee for Democracy. It folded after a year, and the JACD disbanded soon after.

In the following years, Shimano worked with the New York State Committee on Discrimination in Housing and prepared letters to media outlets in support of an open housing bill. He served as a freelance journalist and ghostwriter. By the late 1950s he took a position as a research scientist at the Nathan S. Kline Institute at Rockland State Hospital. There he helped invent a device for continuous tracking of the circadian rhythms of blood sugar, electrolytes, hormones, and other components in plasma. He died in 1986.

Another notable Asian American writer who worked for the FWP is Gerald Chan Sieg. She was born Geraldine Chan in 1909, the first daughter and third of six children of Cecile Ann Lee and Chung Tai-pan (Annie and Robert Chan Chung). Chung Tai-pan left his native village in Guangdong Province, China, and came to America in 1888, eventually arriving in Savannah on April 6, 1889. Although he was not the first Chinese immigrant to live in Georgia, he was the first to settle and raise a family there, along with his California-born wife. Chung Tai-pan ardently supported Sun Yat-sen's revolution to overthrow the Manchu Dynasty and build democracy in China. His daughter seems to have inherited her father's revolutionary spirit; as a child, she shortened her name to Gerald, affirming that she "knew early on that boys were considered better than girls, so if [she] couldn't be a boy, [she'd] at least have a boy's name."

In her 1970 book, *The Chinese Christmas Box*, Gerald Chan Sieg fondly reminisced about her childhood, when her father would play traditional Chinese music, recount tales of Chinese history, and recite Chinese poetry. Chung Tai-pan was a skilled poet; in his last year in China, he won his village's annual poetry contest. Through his stories Gerald Chan Sieg grew to love her father's birth country and her ancestral culture—especially its poetry.

She also experienced anti-Asian prejudice, though she did not speak publicly about it until long afterward. In a 1992 interview, Sieg recalled: "We did not play with other children. My father thought it was best for us to stay to ourselves. There were feelings about Asian people at that time. Our father didn't want us to be hurt." The discrimination she faced likely had a strong effect on her. As one chronicler noted, "In the fifth grade, she wrote her first poem, about a lonely and sad girl"—presumably, a reflection of her own life. Because of segregation laws and anti-Chinese sentiment, Chinese children in Savannah could not attend white schools. Consequently, her family hired private teachers. The local school board ultimately changed its policy, and Chan attended public junior high and high schools.

Although Chan began writing poetry as a young girl, her writing career formally began in 1927, when she was attending Savannah High School. Lowry Axley, head of the school's English Department and president of the Poetry Society of Georgia, encouraged her to enter a competition sponsored by the society. She submitted a poem entitled "The Sad Lady," which won first prize. A year later she was invited to join the society. Sieg remained a lifetime member and served the Poetry Society of Georgia in many positions: secretary, committee chair, vice president, and eventually president.

It was also in high school that Gerald Chan met Edward Sieg, a young white man of part-Cuban ancestry, who became her closest friend. The two faced family opposition and Georgia's anti-miscegenation law. In July 1928 Gerald Chan eloped with Edward Sieg to South Carolina, where the two were married. A few months later, on November 8, she gave birth to a son, Edward Chan Sieg. Their daughter, Geraldine—later known as Jerry Dillon—followed soon after. After her marriage, Gerald Chan Sieg cared for her family and wrote more poetry. She later commented bluntly, "With the Depression, two children, and a husband, as well as my job, there was just no time [for college]."

During the mid-1930s Sieg began publishing her poems outside the orbit of the Poetry Society of Georgia. Her first poems to appear in a major magazine were published in fall 1936 in *Asia*, a monthly journal of Asian affairs. Then, in the months following September 1937, the *Atlantic Monthly*, *New York Herald Tribune*, and the *New York Times* featured her verse. Beginning in 1941, she contributed several poems to the *Washington Post*—she even published four poems in the pulp magazine *Weird Tales*. It is remarkable that Sieg, a young woman of color, managed to gain such an outstanding national platform. Apart from the biracial Canadian authors Edith Maude Eaton (Sui Sin Far) and Winnifred Eaton (Onoto Watanna), there had been hardly any published literature by ethnic Chinese women before 1937—and none by US-born Chinese. Sieg expressed pride in her Chinese identity—she was identified in *Write* magazine as "America's only Chinese poet writing in English"—and her powerful championing of China found a receptive audience in the period following Japan's invasion in July 1937. For example, in "Mo-Tze," published in *Asia* in 1938, Sieg alludes to Mo-tze (Mozi), the famous Chinese philosopher who espoused the radical idea of universal love (兼愛) and opposed war. In two central stanzas, centering on references to "flags of conquest" and "futility," the author expresses sorrow and frustration over militarism and the Japanese occupation of China:

> All are deep in darkness
> And futility,
> Suchow and Peking,
> Honan and Shensi.

It was at this juncture—having made a name for herself as a "Chinese" poet in mainstream publications—that Sieg was hired for work on the Federal Writers' Project by southern director William T. Couch and assigned to conduct oral history interviews with older Chinese in the American South (a project assignment that followed in the wake of other FWP oral history projects, most famously that with formerly enslaved African Americans). In early

1939 she submitted "Laundryman," her most notable work for the FWP. The text of "Laundryman" is in the form of a dialogue between an unnamed Chinese American narrator and a new acquaintance, the prosperous, progressive laundryman Chung Tai-pan (Sieg's own father, a point concealed in the text). The dialogue takes place in Chung Tai-pan's house, which is decorated with a mixture of Chinese artifacts and Western curios. Chung expresses both his devotion to his Chinese heritage and assimilation to white American norms—he even supports his children's marriages to white Americans.

The purpose of Sieg's narrative, though unstated, is clear: to humanize Chinese immigrants and depict them as good people and good neighbors, thereby challenging stereotypes of them as "perpetual foreigners." What is remarkable by its absence is any discussion in the text of anti-Asian discrimination, despite the author's own experience. Neither the narrator nor Chung alludes to the fact that his children were initially barred from public school or that their marriages with white Americans were illegal in Georgia. Indeed, the author even has Chung claim American citizenship, though she and her father were both surely aware that they remained barred from naturalization on racial grounds: "I takee out citizenship papers, for I know I will be here long time before revolution come. Some of them takes out papers follow me."

Gerald Chan Sieg's work on "Laundryman" for the FWP served as an inflection point in her writing career. In many of her writings after 1939, she worked to valorize Chinese culture and humanize Chinese people. For example, her children's story "Mee-Mee's Lost Mother," which Sieg first published in *Scholastic* magazine around 1940, presents many Chinese people helping a lost boy. Sieg delivered a lecture, "China, the Oldest Democracy in the World," before the Savannah chapter of the Daughters of the American Revolution in 1943.

In the years after World War II, Gerald Chan Sieg worked at Fine's Department Store in Savannah as an advertising copywriter. However, in the 1960s, she returned to journalism, publishing articles in the *Atlanta Journal-Constitution* on Georgia's history, with a focus on local Chinese. Her most notable column was a Christmas story, "The Wonderous Box from China," which she later adapted into the children's book *The Chinese Christmas Box*. In it she described how her devoutly Christian family would celebrate Christmas by ordering a large box of wares from China and sharing the contents with people in their community.

Many of Sieg's later writings openly criticized discrimination. For instance, in a 1953 poem, "The Hunter's Children," she critiqued settler-colonialist policies and norms that strip Indigenous tribes of their land and voices. In the title poem of a 1982 chapbook, *A Gull Speaks*, she protested the harmful impact of industrialization. In a 1997 poem, "Eve," she retold the story of Adam and Eve from Eve's point of view, scolding Adam for "let[ting her] take all the blame."

The writings of Eddie Shimano and Gerald Chan Sieg deserve rediscovery. In particular, their FWP work reveals a largely passed-over aspect of the New Deal: its outreach to Asian American writers and artists. While the two seem not to have met, they shared multiple qualities: both were in their mid-twenties, cosmopolitan in their friends and interests, and outspoken antifascist supporters of China against Japanese aggression. In Shimano's case the experience and contacts he made through the FWP may have been decisive in his recruitment by the Common Council, which allowed him to leave camp and find a community of progressive Nisei in New York.

FLORENCE CRANNELL MEANS / THE WOMAN BEHIND *THE MOVED-OUTERS*

In the face of the tragic events of official confinement and loss that Japanese Americans experienced during World War II, there were numerous non-Japanese who found ways to help Issei and Nisei or who protested their official treatment. Some years ago the Kansha project was founded to commemorate these individuals, whom one might call the "righteous gentiles" of Japanese America. Writer and activist Shizue Seigel wrote the intriguing book *In Good Conscience*, which told some of their stories. The historian and curator Eric Saul has established a website with a list of individuals and their contributions.[1] While I pride myself on my knowledge of Japanese American history, I learned a lot that I didn't know from reading Saul's entries.

To be sure, there will always be quibbles—occupational disease of historians!—about those missing from the list. One candidate for inclusion whom I would consider especially worthy is Florence Crannell Means. In the years surrounding World War II, as part of her larger project of writing children's books that dramatized the lives of members of minority groups, Means produced works that examined the plight of the Nikkei sympathetically. Thanks to the able research efforts of my cousin Corwin Meichtry, I was able to discover important information about this remarkable woman in the Means archives at University of Colorado.

Florence Crannell was born in 1891 in Baldwinsville, New York, the daughter of Phillip Wendell Crannell, a Baptist minister, and Fannie Grout Crannell. She absorbed from both parents great curiosity and an omnivorous taste for literature. Her father, she later commented, was a man with "no racial consciousness." His influence contributed to her later ambition to promote interracial understanding—as she put it, to teach that "folks are folks." During her childhood she spent summers with her mother's family in rural Minnesota, which brought her an appreciation of pioneer life. In 1912 she married Carleton Bell "Carl" Means, a lawyer and businessman who encouraged her to pursue literature. In the next years the couple had one daughter, Eleanor (who would grow up to be the writer Eleanor Hull).

It is not clear when Means began writing for publication. Her first books, a set of fictionalized family stories, recounted the adventures of Janey Grant, a teenager in Wisconsin and Minnesota during the 1870s. In *A Candle in the Mist* (1931), Means's first successful book, Janey experiences boredom with her life, until the disappearance of four thousand dollars entrusted to her father changes her outlook. In the following years Means turned to telling stories of Native peoples and racial and religious minorities, with attention to the problems of prejudice. She exposed these issues primarily through producing novels with young people from those excluded groups—and with girls and young women as her main characters. For example, *Tangled Waters* (1936) is the story of Altolie, a Navajo girl of fifteen who lives in a hogan in Arizona with her mother, stepfather, and step-grandmother. *Shuttered Windows* (1938) features Harriet, an African American teenager from Minneapolis who moves to the Sea Islands of South Carolina to live with her great-grandmother following her mother's death and is shocked by the poverty there. *Whispering Girl* (1941) centers on a Hopi Indian girl. The heroine of *Teesita of the Valley* (1943) is a Mexican American girl living in Denver. All these books were published by a commercial press, Houghton Mifflin.

Means also published a series of works with Friendship Press, the publishing house of the National Council of Churches (then called the Federal Council of Churches). Her first project for council was *Children of the Great Spirit* (1932), a cowritten nonfiction work described in publicity material as a primary school course for children on American Indians. Her next project, the novel *Children of the Promise* (1941), deals with Jewish Americans. One of Means's most-heralded works for Friendship Press was *Across the Fruited Plain* (1940), a kind of mirror version of John Steinbeck's epochal novel *The Grapes of Wrath*. The book tells the poignant story of a once-prosperous mid-Atlantic family, reduced to destitution by the Great Depression, who decide to leave their house behind and travel up and down the East Coast as migrant agricultural laborers.

It was for Friendship Press that Means produced her book *Rainbow Bridge* (1934), illustrated by China-born American writer-artist Eleanor Lattimore. The book was one of the first sympathetic portraits of Japanese Americans in mainstream fiction. It tells the story of Haruko Miyata, a Japanese girl who comes to live in America with her two brothers, her mother, and her father, a brilliant doctor who has been offered a position in an American hospital. The family settles in an unnamed city in Colorado. Haruko attends American school and Christian services and learns American customs, which the book compares at length with Japanese. In one chapter the family heads out to the country to worship with Japanese sugar beet farmers, and Haruko is shocked to discover that the rural families have such slovenly children and ill-kept houses. In the end the Miyata family must decide whether to return to Japan or stay in America.

While the book is certainly dated, in its outlook *Rainbow Bridge* is remarkably progressive for its time. Means presented the Miyatas and other Asians in positive terms and showed respect both for their ancestral cultures and their capacity for good citizenship. While not heavy-handed, the book also does not shy away from a discussion of prejudice. The Miyatas are forced to live in a dingy house in a Japanese enclave of their adopted city—when Haruko passes a nicer street on the way to school, her Nisei friend Gertrude explains that Japanese are not allowed to live there. While the book does not address Japanese exclusion—Dr. Miyata is described as American-born, presumably to explain away how the family could enter the country—there is a discussion of the difficult reception for Asian immigrants at Angel Island. The book also includes a chapter on Tommy Wong, one of the Chinese Americans who befriend the Miyatas and whose family is threatened with deportation.

Following the outbreak of World War II and the wartime removal of West Coast Japanese Americas, Means would throw herself more heavily into offering support. She befriended a set of Nisei who had resettled in Denver and resolved to dramatize their plight in literary terms. (In the Means papers at the University of Colorado are housed a series of questionnaires that Nisei in Denver filled out, giving details of their removal and their daily life in the camps, which the author used as background material.)

The result was Means's young adult novel *The Moved-Outers*. Published by Houghton Mifflin in February 1945, with illustrations by Vera Bartholomew

MacPherson, it was the first full-length published literary work to address wartime confinement. *The Moved-Outers* centers on a Nisei protagonist, Sumiko "Sue" Ohara, a high school senior from Cordova, California, who has a sister and two brothers, one of whom is in the army. After Pearl Harbor, the Ohara family's life is turned upside down. Sue's father is arrested by the FBI, separated from the family, and interned by the Justice Department, while Sue, her second brother, Kim, and their mother are confined first in the holding center at Santa Anita and then in more permanent quarters at the Amache camp in Colorado. After confinement Sue and her mother try to make the best of things, while Kim grows sullen and alienated and gets involved with a "zoot-suit" gang, before he is taken in hand by Jiro Ito, a sympathetic inmate. The book ends in 1943, with Sue's sister Tomi leaving camp to go off to college in Denver and the family questioning their future path.

The Moved-Outers was well received by critics. Writing in the *New York Times*, Ellen Lewis Buell saluted "the timeliness and courage of this book." Barron Beshoar commented in the *Rocky Mountain News* that despite the profusion of official reports and media coverage, "it has remained to Florence Crannell Means to produce the most intelligent and effective piece of writing on the Japanese American evacuation." The book won the annual children's book award of the Child Study Association of America for 1945. It remains Means's best-known work.

Following the publication of *The Moved-Outers*, Means continued her interest in Japanese Americans. In early 1946, shortly after the end of World War II, she published a story as part of the book *Told under the Stars and Stripes*, an anthology of literature by and about minorities. Means's story centers on Hatsuno "Hattie" Noda, a twelve-year old Sansei living in Denver, and her ambivalent feelings toward her great-grandmother, whom she considers "very Japanesey" but whom she comes to appreciate. The story was reprinted in the San Francisco Nisei newspaper *Progressive News*, thereby reaching a Japanese American readership.

After the war Means continued to write multicultural children's books. In *Great Day in the Morning* (1946), a sequel of sorts to *Shuttered Windows*, a Black girl from St. Helena Island goes to Tuskegee Institute and then on to nurse's training. In *Assorted Sisters* (1947) a white family moves to Colorado to head a settlement house and works with nonwhites. *The Rains Will Come* (1954) is the story of a Hopi village. *Alicia* (1953) focuses on Mexican Americans, while *Reach for a Star* (1957) is the story of a young African American woman who goes to college. *Knock at the Door, Emmy* (1956) features a migrant worker family. *Tolliver* (1963) recounts the story of a Negro college graduate torn between ambition and the desire to help his people. *It Takes All Kinds* (1964) is the touching tale of a girl caring for a brother with cerebral palsy. Means also wrote a pair of nonfiction books, *Carvers' George* (1952), a biography of famed African American chemist George Washington Carver, and *Sagebrush Surgeon* (1955). She joined with her husband, Carl, to write *The Silver Fleece* (1950), on the Spanish in New Mexico.

Carl Means died in 1973. That year Florence Crannell Means's last book, *Smith Valley*, was published. Meanwhile, as part of the renewed public interest in wartime Japanese American life, *The Moved-Outers* appeared in a new paperback edition. Failing eyesight curtailed both Means's traveling and writing in the next years. She died in 1980, shortly before her ninetieth birthday.

While Florence Crannell Means's stories and her approach might seem passé to younger, more assertive generations of Asian American readers, at a time of widespread racial hostility toward Japanese Americans and other minorities, her multicultural writings opened many people's eyes, not just to their plight but to their humanity.

AYAKO ISHIGAKI / RADICAL ISSEI FEMINIST WRITER IN 1930S AMERICA

In the years preceding World War II, the Japanese-born writer and progressive activist Ayako Ishigaki lived in exile in New York and Los Angeles. During this time she concentrated on opposing Japanese militarism. In lecture tours around the United States that she made alongside Chinese colleagues, she scored the Japanese occupation of China and called for boycotts of Japanese goods.

Ishigaki was equally forceful as an author, most notably of the semi-fictionalized memoir *Restless Wave*, published in 1940 under the pen name "Haru Matsui." The book described her struggle for independence as a woman within Japan's rigidly hierarchical and patriarchal society, then touched on aspects of her life in the United States. The book received widespread praise from critics, and it appeared on numerous booklists during the war years. (I was proud to coedit a new edition of *Restless Wave*, published by The Feminist Press of the City University of New York in 2004. The new edition of Ishigaki's book was awarded a special citation by the Association for Asian American Studies as a "lost Asian American treasure.")

Still, even before she wrote *Restless Wave*, Ishigaki had made a name for herself as a journalist during the 1930s, writing both in English and Japanese. What is particularly noteworthy about all her writing is the central place the author accorded gender and women's experience, which gives her work a remarkably contemporary tone. Thus, in the various pseudonymous articles and editorials Ishigaki wrote for such left-wing journals as *China Today* and the *New Masses*, she focused on the negative impact of Japan's war in China not just on the Chinese but on the everyday lives of the poor in Japan, especially women. Her practice of "domestic internationalism" was even more marked in the daily Japanese-language column Jinsei Shokan (Woman's Thoughts) that she wrote for the Los Angeles newspaper *Rafu Shimpo* during 1937. In her columns Ishigaki addressed herself to Issei women and portrayed herself as a housewife speaking to other housewives. Using a deliberately simple, chatty style, she discussed household matters and daily activities as a framework through which she introduced analyses of gender discrimination and diffusion of anti-war propaganda.

In the years that followed Japan's 1931 invasion of Manchuria, Ishigaki took a leading role as an organizer and speaker for left-wing antimilitarist groups such as the American Friends of the Chinese People and the American League for Peace and Democracy. During these years Ishigaki also took on a number of different jobs to support herself and her artist husband, working variously as a lampshade factory worker, waitress, and sales clerk.

In 1935 Ishigaki began reporting on Japan for the New York–based progressive publications the *New Masses* and *China Today*. In those articles she demonstrated the class and feminist consciousness that underlay her ideas on international affairs. In one article she reported on slave labor conditions in factories. Peasant girls comprised the largest share of workers. Foremen recruited them as cheap labor by paying their impoverished families seventy yen, representing a year's wages, and falsely promising to educate them in performing the tea ceremony and flower arrangement to help them find husbands. Similarly, in an article in *China Today* on Baroness Shidzué Ishimoto, the feminist and birth control pioneer, Ishigaki praised Ishimoto as "the Margaret Sanger of Japan, carrying on an intensive fight for birth control and struggling to free Japanese women from the grip of feudal bondage in all fields of activity," expressing approval for Ishimoto's socialist sympathies: "The Baroness grew to maturity during the period of Japan's transition from feudalism to capitalism. Factories, machines and skyscrapers sprang up like mushrooms, and thousands of Japanese girls were plunged into the brutality of capitalist exploitation. . . . The ruthless exploitation of the workers in the coal mines came to her as a terrible shock; the poverty and misery among the miners awakened in her a sympathy for the down-trodden and oppressed."

Nevertheless, Ishigaki considered women's rights and democracy to be intimately linked with the struggle against international oppression. The Japanese war machine ran on the exploited labor of the poor, especially women, while militarization silenced opposition and stifled progressive social change. Ishigaki criticized Baroness Ishimoto's failure to connect her reform efforts at home with solidarity against Japan's international aggression in China.

In 1937 Eitaro Ishigaki was hired by the federal Works Progress Administration to paint a Black history mural for a Harlem courthouse. Because of his earnings, Ayako quit her factory job and devoted herself full-time to activism. She decided to base herself in Los Angeles because of the large Japanese American community there. Adopting the pseudonym "May Tanaka," Ishigaki moved west in 1937. Once settled in her new home, she sought a way both to introduce herself into the community and to help support herself. As she later explained, the column she began writing for *Rafu Shimpo* was designed to look at everyday life in Los Angeles from a woman's point of view and then to use such mundane daily scenes to express anti-war ideas.

Ishigaki used her new platform to speak to the community for women's rights and against militarism. She couched her discussions in homey terms. In her April 21, 1937, column, for instance, she described her delight, after so many years on the East Coast, in being able to find authentic Japanese foods such as pickles and soy sauce. However, she used the discussion to make a point about the economic impact of war: "Speaking of the war emergency in Japan, its effects have advanced even to the homes of Japanese away from Japan making strenuous efforts in a strange land. When I was at the market, I heard a middle-aged woman saying, 'The price of soy sauce is up again, [though] it has been up thirty cents more per barrel.'"

Similarly, Ishigaki found ways to bring up the question of women's rights in an indirect fashion. In her April 26 column she decried the images she found of women in Japan magazines as "stupid stuff." Men, she commented acidly, must really fear that women were smarter than them if the only images they were willing to show of women were those doing flower arrangement and the tea ceremony. Her September 13 column was even more daring. Ishigaki presented the case for birth control, commenting, "Just as every woman is free to marry or not, every woman is free to decide whether or not to have children and how many." While she remarked straightforwardly that the decision about whether or not to have children, and how many, was a woman's choice, she placed such a choice in the context of family planning and not sexual freedom: families suffer if mothers lack money to raise their children properly.

In order to gain material for her work, Ishigaki sought out Issei women in the Los Angeles area. Ironically, despite Ishigaki's egalitarian sympathies, she had found it difficult to really connect with workers or country people in Japan because of her elite background. In Little Tokyo, however, all Nikkei were brought together by their shared marginalization, and Ishigaki was able to connect with them on a deep level. She was also interested in the younger generation. As Larry Tajiri later wrote in *Nichi Bei Shinbun*: "Though not a Nisei, Haru Matsui of New York made several succinct observations on the life of the west coast Nihonmachis in her autobiography 'The Restless Wave.' . . . She sympathized with the problems of those bilingual, sometimes bicultural, bipeds, the US Nisei."

Ishigaki's columns gained a great deal of attention. Togo Tanaka, the *Rafu*'s English-language editor, spoke admiringly of them: "Emancipated from the traditional Japanese role of inferior status for women, May Tanaka lashed out in condemnation of the Japanese political system."[1] Sadly, Ishigaki did not think highly of her own efforts. When a captain in the Japanese military made a propaganda tour of California following the Japanese invasion of China in July 1937 and a group of Issei mounted a subscription to purchase an airplane for the Japanese military, Ishigaki decided that her mission had failed, and she returned to New York in September 1937. Not long after, she was commissioned to write the book that emerged as *Restless Wave*.

What is so striking about all of Ishigaki's writings during the 1930s, whether in her magazine articles, newspaper columns, or her book *Restless Wave*, is the way she portrayed herself as ordinary and nonthreatening. Although Ishigaki was clearly an independent-minded upper-class woman with a career, she presented herself as a housewife, talking to other housewives, in ways that simultaneously manipulated and subverted gender and racial expectations of the author as a Japanese woman. Similarly, her arguments relied on deploying domestic imagery, all of which humanized her and made her radical ideas seem less threatening.

After working for the Office of War Information and the US State Department during the wartime period, in 1945 Ishigaki started writing for the New

York Japanese (ultimately bilingual) newspaper *Hokubei Shimpo*. She resuscitated her Jinsei Shokan column, talking about women's rights and international peace. Ishigaki returned to Japan with her husband in 1951, a victim of McCarthy era official harassment. During the decades that followed, she became well-known in Japan, first as a feminist writer and social critic, later as a television commentator and popular author. The rediscovery of Ishigaki's work on both continents allows us not only to celebrate the achievements of a remarkable woman but to see how she challenged stereotypes about Asian women's activism, feminism in popular media, and Issei women's communities.

Chapter 9

THE EUROPEAN NIKKEI COMMUNITY

THE FRENCH (NIKKEI) CONNECTION / JAPANESE AMERICANS IN MIDCENTURY PARIS

The history of the connections that Japanese Americans forged with France during the period before and after World War II, and the nature of their cultural exchange, is an enormous subject. It encompasses such diverse elements as the experience of the Nisei visitors, students, and creative artists who went to Paris and other parts of France (including their interactions with Nikkei from around the world) as well as the visits of French authors to North America and their studies of Japanese communities. My goal here is to scratch a little of the surface of the question, then leave the question for abler hands to develop more fully.

First, beginning in the first years of Japanese settlement in the United States, various Nikkei used the United States as a bridge to France. The theatrical troupe of Otojiro Kawakami, featuring the geisha-performer Sada Yacco, toured the United States in 1899–1900, before traveling on to Europe the following year and making a successful run in Paris. Similarly, after living for three years in the United States from 1903 to 1906, the Japanese expatriate writer Kafu Nagai traveled to Lyon and Paris, where he spent seven months in 1907. His book of sketches of his travels, *Furansu Monogatari* (*French Stories*), was almost immediately banned upon its first publication in 1907. However, the initial edition of his 1908 collection, *Amerika Monogatari* (*American Stories*), which made his name in Japan, included three travel sketches of France.

Another connection that dates from the earliest years of the twentieth century is that of the scholars and journalists in France who wrote about Japanese immigration to North America. Indeed, the very first full-length work about Japanese Americans, at least in any Western language, is the 1908 book *Américains et japonais* (Americans and Japanese) by the orientalist scholar and journalist Louis Aubert. Henri Labroue's book *L'Impérialisme japonaise* (Japanese Imperialism) (1911) discusses Japanese Canadians. There was a further series of works in the 1920s. The expatriate American Prew Savoy's 1923 book, *La Question japonaise aux États-Unis* (The Japanese Question in the United States), supported total exclusion of Japanese immigrants, while the Japanese-born political scientist Macaomi Yoshitomi's 1926 book, *Les Conflits nippo-américains et le problème du Pacifique* (Japanese-American Conflicts and the Problem of the Pacific), opposed it. Perhaps the most eminent French observer to take up the "Japanese question" was the political scientist André Siegfried, whose study of American culture was published in English as *America Comes of Age* in 1928. In a chapter of his book on "yellow" immigration, Siegfried warned that Chinese and Japanese were among the most unassimilable of the larger wave of recent immigrants who threatened to overwhelm American society and alter its character and institutions.

Meanwhile, a galaxy of Nisei creative artists took up residence in France. Painter Henry Sugimoto arrived in France in 1928 and ended up living there for three years, during which time he became close to a circle of Japanese artists. He initially took up painting studies at the Académie Colarossi in Paris, but after one of his paintings was rejected for inclusion by the prestigious Salon d'Automne, he left the Académie and took up residence in the French countryside. One of his landscape paintings was accepted for the 1931 Salon d'Automne. Sculptor Isamu Noguchi likewise arrived in Paris in the 1920s and studied with the famed sculptor Constantin Brancusi. Frances Fitzpatrick Osato, a white woman from Chicago who married the photographer Shoji Osato, took their three children for an extended stay in France in the late 1920s. The eldest child, dancer Sono Osato, was recruited while in France to dance with the Ballets Russes. The Osatos' youngest child, Timothy, had his portrait sketched by the famed post-Impressionist painter Léonard Foujita (Tsuguharu Fujita). Surely the most eminent Nikkei expatriate from America was the actor Sessue Hayakawa. When he made a French film about Japan, *Yoshiwara* (1937), set in the red-light district of Tokyo, it aroused an opposition within Nikkei circles parallel to that caused by his role in the 1915 silent Hollywood film *The Cheat*. The film was officially banned in Japan.

Once war in Europe was declared, in September 1939, there was an exodus of Nikkei to the United States. According to one article, a group of 180 Japanese refugees from Europe set sail for home on a Japanese ship, which docked en route in New York. Along with the passengers were 25 distinguished Japanese artists, led by the painter Minoru Okada, who brought back with them the hundreds of artworks they had produced during their years working in Europe.

A number of Nisei who had been working in Europe also returned. Miné Okubo, who had been traveling through Europe on a Bertha Taussig fellowship, later claimed that she had sailed on the last boat leaving the Continent. Newton Tani, who had moved from San Francisco to Paris to study piano during the 1930s, managed to find his way back to the United States—he would be confined during World War II as a result of Executive Order 9066 and served as director of the Topaz Music School. Tani died in 1989.

Another musician who studied in France was the violinist Masao Yoshida. Yoshida, born in Japan, had come to the United States as a baby and grew up in Alameda. He spent the first part of the 1930s in San Francisco, where he studied with Naoum Blinder, concertmaster of the San Francisco Symphony, before further study and performances in Belgium and France. Caught in Paris at the start of war, he sold his books for food and borrowed money so that he could flee, first to Belgium, then across the English Channel, and finally by ship to the United States. Yoshida would be confined at Topaz during the war, then would become a naturalized US citizen in 1962. Shizuo Kato, a Vancouver-born painter who spent the prewar years studying in Paris, was able to leave Europe on a Japanese ship, the *Kashima Maru*, and return to the West Coast.

Not all refugees stuck in war-torn France were able to get out. Dr. Kenzo Shinohara, who graduated from the College of Medicine of the University of Paris in the late 1930s, was shocked by the coming of war. While en route to Warsaw in summer 1939, he received a summons by the Lille University Hospital to come replace French doctors who had been conscripted for work with the Red Cross. Both Shinohara and his sister-in-law Atsuko Kiyoda—a graduate of LA High School who had moved to Paris to study millinery design—found themselves unable to get back to Los Angeles.

Kiyoda, for her part, married a Jewish Hungarian named George Szekeres and lived with him in Paris under the German occupation. (The couple fled to Hungary in 1943, but George was subsequently arrested as a Jew, sent to forced labor in Russia, and ultimately arrested by the Gestapo—Atsuko finally located her husband in a Displaced Persons camp in Germany at the end of the war.) Atsuko Kiyota Szekeres ended up emigrating to Rio de Janeiro in 1956, by which time she was listed as single.

In the years after World War II, a number of Nisei, notably former GIs, took up residence in Paris. Shinkichi Tajiri and Steve Shigeo Wada each used the GI

Bill to travel to France and study art. John Yoshinaga moved to France to take classes in French civilization in Paris. Robert Chino, a 442nd veteran, decided to reenlist after the war and stay in France and Italy rather than return to Chicago. In the late 1940s Hiroshi Tamura was awarded a two-year fellowship in Paris by the Art Institute of Chicago. Hawaii-born Dorothy Furuya studied for three years at L'Académie Julien in Paris. In 1950 painter Ellen Ochi, a graduate of the Cleveland School of Arts, won a one thousand–dollar Page scholarship to study in Paris. The 442nd veteran Wilson Makabe and Mary Lou Kawasaki were sponsored by Temple University to study at the Sorbonne in 1952. In early 1954 the Hawaii-born anthropologist Dr. Hiroshi Daifuku was appointed as a program specialist in the Museums and Monuments Division of the Department of Cultural Affairs at UNESCO. He would remain in Paris with his family until his retirement in 1980.

One particularly intriguing postwar story is that of Lilli-Anne (Lillian) Oka. Oka, a West Coast Nisei whose family had transplanted to Chicago, was invited by the Marquis de Cuevas to join the Ballet de Monte Carlo in 1949, and she was one of the stars of the troupe's Paris season that year. She subsequently married singer Andre Tcherkassky, returned to the United States, and opened a ballet studio in Kensington, Maryland, where she trained numerous dancers—most notably her daughter Marianna Tcherkassky, who spent a long career as a principal dancer with the American Ballet Theater. In sum, if Paris is where good Americans go when they die, according to Oscar Wilde's famous sally, then it can boast the tombs of countless Nisei.

KIKOU YAMATA / REDISCOVERING THE FIRST NISEI WRITER

Throughout the twentieth century Nikkei writers have dreamed of writing "the Great Nisei novel," a work of literature that would express the Japanese American experience and show off the writing talents of the second generation. Critics have meanwhile drawn attention to existing works as the "greatest." Frank Abe, my friend and collaborator on the anthology *John Okada* (2018), claims the prize for Okada's novel *No-No Boy* (1957). I have several favorite candidates, including Gene Oishi's remarkable work *Fox Drum Bebop* (2014). Others have lauded Japanese Canadian author Joy Kogawa's haunting novel *Obasan* (1976). These debates tend to be confined to North American Nisei writing and do not touch on Latin America or Asia. Certainly, what is not much mentioned in these debates is the work of the first Nisei novelist and one of the most remarkable: the French-born writer Kikou Yamata, who during her long career appealed to readers on both sides of the Atlantic and Pacific and who was alternately beloved and suspected in both her native countries.

Kikou Yamata was born in Lyon, France, on March 15, 1897. She was the daughter of Tadazumi Yamada, a native of Nagasaki. After taking French courses in Japan with the scholar Léon Dury, to prepare him for foreign service, Tadazumi Yamada was invited by the industrialist and collector Émile Guimet (future founder of the renowned Musée Guimet, a museum of Asian civilization in Paris) to come to Lyon, a center of silk manufacturing, and study at the prestigious La Martinière school. Yamada was ultimately appointed Japanese consul at Lyon by the Emperor Meiji. Kikou was the child of his love affair and marriage with Marguerite Varon, a Frenchwoman.

The young Kikou spent her first years in Lyon. However, in 1908, when she was eleven years old, her father brought the family to Japan, settling in Tokyo. There Kikou attended a French school, Sacré-Coeur de Tokyo. During these years she began writing for newspapers as well as for the French magazine *Extrême Orient*. In 1923 Tadazumi Yamada died, and Kikou returned to France with her mother. She moved to Paris, where she began studies in art history at the Sorbonne. Meanwhile, she began frequenting literary salons. Her Japanese manners—she dressed in a kimono and displayed a talent for ikebana—mixed with her fluent French, made her a hit in Parisian society, where *Japonisme* had been a powerful force since at least the days of the Impressionist painters (and of orientalist writers such as Pierre Loti).

Yamata soon began attracting attention for her writings on Japan. Her first book, *Sur des lèvres japonaises* (On Japanese Lips), was published in 1924, the year after her arrival in Paris. A volume of short tales, mixed with poetry and a Noh theater piece, it contained an endorsement in the form of an introduction by the famous French poet and critic Paul Valéry.

The next year Yamata brought out the short novel *Masako* with the well-known French publisher Stock. The title character, Masako, is a young woman with modern ideas who moves into the house of her uncle after her beloved mother's death. There she lives under the moral guardianship of her two aunts. However, she meets a young man, Naoyoshi, whose kisses enchant her, and falls deeply in love. In the end she must defy her aunts in order to marry for love. The novel was an enormous success, thanks in part to its publicity campaign: a portrait of Yamata in kimono was distributed to bookstores, and the author gave a demonstration of ikebana in the show window of the publisher's offices. Since its initial publication, the novel has gone through some twenty-two editions. *Masako* also captivated the attention of Japanese American littérateurs. In 1931–32 Nisei writer Yasuo Sasaki would translate and publish excerpts from *Masako* in his early literary magazine *Reimei*.

Following the success of *Masako*, Yamata branched out into different literary forms. Her book of short stories about young Japanese women, entitled *Le Shoji* (1927), was a minor success. It would appear in English translation with the Dial Press under the title *The Shoji: Japanese Interiors and Silhouettes* (1929). Meanwhile, she published *Vers l'occident*, a slim volume of tales, and *Les Huit renommés* (The Eight Renowned Ones), a travel book about Japan that she produced in collaboration with the celebrated artist Foujita (whose career is discussed in this volume). In 1928 she brought out a partial translation of Lady Murasaki's *The Tale of Genji*, the first French edition of that classic Japanese novel. *Saisons suisses*, the author's reflections on a visit to Neuchâtel, Switzerland, appeared in 1929. It featured illustrations by Conrad Meili, a Swiss painter whom she met during her stay and who became her husband shortly thereafter. Yamata also produced *Shizoula, princesse tranquille*, a slim volume that featured the story of a geisha. It appeared with a portrait of the author by Foujita. Yamata's second full-length novel, *La Trame au milan d'or* (The Golden Kite Frame, appeared in 1930. It is the story of Tazoumi, a young Japanese man from a samurai family who leaves behind Japan, his family and fiancée, and moves to France.

In 1929 Yamata was commissioned by the famous French publisher Gallimard to write a biography of General Nogi, and she spent a year in Japan researching and writing it, during which time she was based in Kamakura. As a result, in 1931 she produced two new books. One was the biography commissioned by Gallimard, which appeared as *La Vie de Général Nogi*. The other, *Japon, dernière heure*, was a traveler's guide to Japan.

Yamata encountered increasing difficulties upon her return from Japan to France in 1931. First, the Great Depression had cut into book sales. More importantly, as Yamata had made her name as a representative (or symbol) of Japan and had even collaborated in the formation of her orientalist image, she was buffeted by the anti-Japanese hostility that followed Tokyo's invasion of Manchuria in 1931, then expanded following the Japanese occupation of China. Yamata's book *Vies des geishas* (1934), a set of stories of geishas, did not sell well. She completed *Mille cœurs en Chine* (A Thousand Hearts in China), a novel set against the Japanese invasion of China, but did not publish it until many years later. As the *Nichi Bei Shimbun* reported in 1935, Yamata also suffered as a result of a plagiarism suit she filed against a Belgian diplomat who had lifted research from her. Not only did Yamata lose her case, but the accused plagiarist's publisher then countersued over her blocking of the rival publication and won damages from her. She did produce a short article on "Japanese Beauty" for the American fashion magazine *Vogue* in 1935.

In summer 1939, just one week before the outbreak of World War II in Europe, Yamata and her husband, Conrad Meili, left France and moved to Japan. During World War II she remained in Japan, where she was suspected because of her mixed-race heritage and French friends. In 1944 Yamata was imprisoned for a time by the wartime Japanese government. Interestingly, during this period she would publish *Au pays de la reine* (In the Queen's Country), a study of women in Japanese culture, which was brought out by a firm in Hanoi, in the Japanese-occupied French colony of Indochina.

In the years after the end of World War II, Yamata remained in Japan. However, after living through the devastation of war and the trials of the US occupation, she returned to France at the outset of the 1950s. Her first postwar novel, *Dame de beauté*, was published in 1951. It is a strange love story that takes place in the ruins of early postwar Japan and centers on the relationship between a young woman, the daughter of a rich banking family, and the husband with whom she has entered an arranged marriage. It would appear soon after in English translation, under the title *Lady of Beauty*, with an introduction by novelist-humanitarian Pearl S. Buck. By chance the Akira Kurosawa film *Rashoman* had won the prize at the Venice Film Festival and in the process had helped create (again) a vogue in France for things Japanese.

After years of silence, Yamata was again sought after for lectures and writings. In 1955 she produced the book *Le Japon des japonaises*, a study of women in Japanese culture. Her next novel, *Trois geishas*, likewise appeared in English translation, as *Three Geishas* (1956). She produced two more novels. The first was *Le Mois sans dieux* (The Month without Gods) (1956). A year later her long-unpublished novel *Mille cœurs en Chine* was at last brought into print. In 1957 Yamata received a signal honor from the French government, which named her as a chevalier of the Legion of Honor. Three years later her final books appeared. *L'Art du bouquet*, an exploration of ikebana, was the culmination of her longtime involvement with that art. *Deux amours cruelles* (Two Cruel Loves), a French translation of Junichiro Tanizaki's book of stories, boasted a preface by the American writer Henry Miller.

Kikou Yamata died in Geneva in March 1975, just days before her seventy-eighth birthday. Her work declined in popularity in the decades after her death—one source says that the author failed to make a provision in her will for control of her author's rights, and so they were frozen in court. Ironically, during this time there was ever-growing mainstream interest in the subjects of her work: the status of women in Japan, particularly the lives of geishas (the latter gaining enormous popularity thanks to Arthur Golden's 1997 novel, *Memoirs of a Geisha*, and its later screen adaptation). Still, Yamata remained a subject of interest to scholars into the new millennium. In 1997 the year of her one hundredth birthday, she was honored by the installation of a commemorative plaque on the wall of her birthplace in Lyon.

AGNES MIYAKAWA / THE *TOAST* OF PARIS

In the years before World War II, West Coast Japanese Americans encountered numerous obstacles to equality, both official and unofficial, and faced great difficulty in making names and careers for themselves outside of their ethnic communities. However, one exceptional individual, the "Nisei songbird," Yoshiko Miyakawa of Sacramento, rose to international celebrity as an opera singer in Paris at the dawn of the 1930s.

Agnes Yoshiko Miyakawa was born in Sacramento, California (the year is unclear, but most sources say 1911). She was one of four children of Tsunesaburo and Haruno Miyakawa (originally Miyagawa). After a career as a salesman and druggist, the elder Miyakawa had distinguished himself by opening the Agnes Hospital (named for his daughter) in Sacramento. Agnes grew up in an accomplished family. Her brothers Jun and Kay Miyakawa both attended Harvard University, where they played on Harvard's varsity baseball team. Another brother, George Miyakawa, became a doctor.

Agnes herself attended Sacramento Junior College. During this time she sang with a Sacramento glee club and also studied voice with a Sacramento-based instructor, Mrs. Charles Brier. Soon the teenager began performing solo. In 1927 she played piano and sang before the Japanese Christian Women's Club for the centenary of Beethoven's death. The next month she sang at Fair Oak Church. In 1928 she performed a recital in Fresno under the auspices of the American Loyalty League (ancestor of the JACL). The program consisted largely of Japanese songs such as "Shikararte" by Hirota and "Jawashima no Ame" by Yamada. Later in the year she toured the northern Pacific cities and sang a concert in Seattle.

In fall 1928, after being the surprise winner of a local contest, Miyakawa

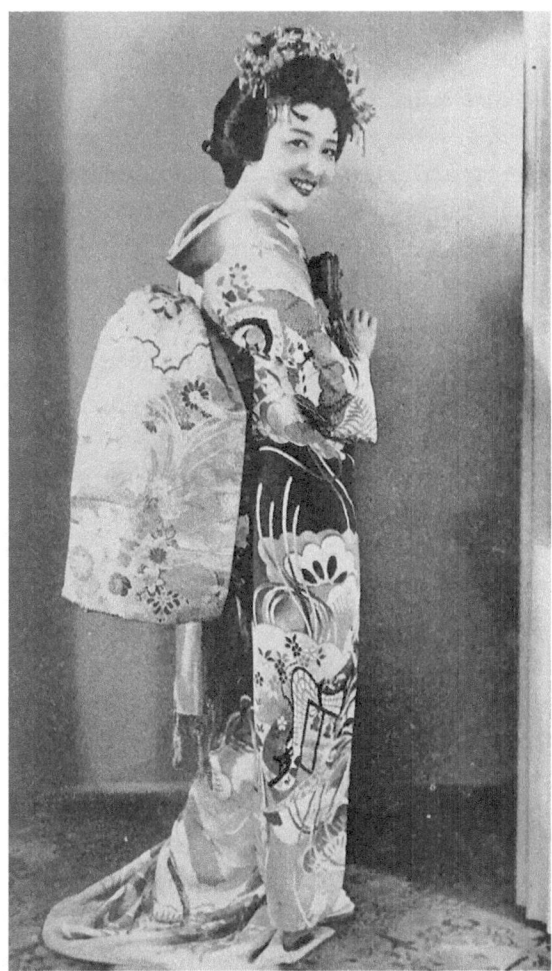

Agnes Yoshiko Miyakawa, from the New York Japan Night program, late 1940s.

gained the right to represent Sacramento in the finals of a national radio audition sponsored by the Atwater Kent Foundation. The competition took place in San Francisco in October 1928. Miyakawa sang "una voce poco fa," from Rossini's *The Barber of Seville*. While she did not win, her talent shone through impressively, and her exploits solidified her desire to study in Europe. Thus, in March 1929, accompanied by her mother, Miyakawa moved to Paris. There she was taken up as a private pupil by Élie Cohen, chef d'orchestre of the National Theater Opéra Comique of Paris. Cohen had previously coached other well-known performers, notably the American opera star Mary McCormic.

In January 1931, at age nineteen, the Nisei soprano made her debut, under the name Yoshiko Miyakawa, at the Opéra Comique in Paris, singing (in French) the lead role of Cio-Cio-San in Giacomo Puccini's opera *Madama Butterfly*. According to one newspaper account, for the final scene, in which a despairing Butterfly kills herself, Miyakawa borrowed her mother's wedding kimono to increase the authenticity and drama. She took a dozen curtain calls, and her ovation lasted twenty-five minutes. According to the *New York Times*, the French critics hailed Miss Miyakawa for having sung "with a charm and freshness of voice rarely, if ever, known before, proving herself a faultless musician and an astonishingly convincing actress." She became a media sensation in Europe and North America. While French newspapers identified her as a "Japanese doll," emphasizing her Asian appearance, she was clear about her own identity. "My parents are Japanese but I am an American."

After her stunning debut as Cio-Cio-San, Miyakawa sang the role four more times. Presumably around the same time, she recorded in French a pair of arias for the Columbia Record company's French label: Puccini's classic aria from *Madama Butterfly*, "un bel di" ("sur la mer calmée" in French) and "Le Jour sous le soleil béni" from the opera *Madame Chrysanthème* of André Messager. She also presented a concert in London.

Even as Miyakawa gained fame in Paris, her father asked her to return to the United States. In May 1931, after almost three years in Europe, she landed in New York, then made her way across the country, performing in Denver. Following her return to the West Coast, she made a concert tour. Her first recital was at the First Reformed Church on Post Street in San Francisco's Chinatown, before an audience of seven hundred people. Miyakawa sang a series of Japanese songs, including "shikararete," then performed *Madama Butterfly*'s aria (in the French version). Soon after, she performed a similar program in Sacramento's Showa Hall. In June, Miyakawa appeared at the Nishi Hongwanji temple in Los Angeles in a concert sponsored by *Rafu Shimpo*. There she presented a program of French, Italian, English, and Japanese songs. She switched costumes through the performance, wearing first a pink dress with rhinestones, then a blue gown, and then a white kimono for the Japanese songs.

In late July 1931 Miyakwa sailed to Japan for a concert tour sponsored by the *Asahi Shimbun* newspaper. She expressed excitement about the tour: "I have sung ever since I can remember hearing the haunting melodies of old Nippon." While on a stopover in Hawaii, she sang a concert at the Pan Pacific Club and signed to record with Nipponophone, Columbia Records' Japanese arm, and a fall 1933 recording of her exists.

Once arrived in Japan, Miyakawa gave concerts in Osaka and Tokyo (including well-publicized benefits she gave to raise money for unemployed Japanese). Soon after, she was signed to a motion picture contract. In early 1933 she made her screen debut, in the Japanese sound film *Warau Chichi* (Smiling Father). The film, a Japanese adaptation of Samuel Butler's novel *The Way of All Flesh*, concerns the trials of a bank clerk, stripped of his money by a gold digger, who sinks to the position of a ragpicker. One day he sees his eldest daughter, played by Miyakawa, in a concert hall showered with acclaim by the admiring throng. When the man visits his estranged family, his daughter does not recognize him. Because of Miyakawa's featured role, the film attracted special interest in the United States, and prints were taken to and shown around West Coast Little Tokyos.

Sometime around the time that Agnes Miyakawa moved to Japan, her family joined her. The elder Miyakawa's hospital, which had faced serious financial trouble amid the Great Depression, went out of business in the early 1930s, and he preferred to start over in his old homeland. Miyakawa's parents settled in Okayama prefecture. There they helped care for Agnes when she was struck by illness and bedridden for several weeks. Brother Kay was ultimately assigned to the Japanese embassy in Hsinking (today known as Changchun) in Japanese-dominated Manchuria.

In November 1933 Miyakawa shocked her fans by getting married. The *Los Angeles Times* headline shouted, "Japanese Diva Wrecks Career—Cupid Wins Singer from Operatic Stage." Her new husband, Richard Takebumi (Takeo) Makiyama, was a mining company executive and the son of a wealthy Japanese sugar magnate. After graduating from McGill University in Montreal, Makiyama had participated in a goodwill tour of the United States. The couple soon had a daughter, Virginia Seiko Makiyama. Still, the marriage was not a happy one—according to an interview with novelist Edward Miyakawa, Agnes's nephew, she contracted syphilis from her husband.

The next few years remain obscure. During a trip to the United States in 1935, Makiyama declared that his wife had retired from the stage and from motion pictures but was still making records. A surviving 78 disc from 1938 features Miyakawa in a program with the Berlin State Opera Orchestra, singing "Le Jour sous le soleil béni." Miyakwa returned to public notice in 1940, when she sang on the *American Salute* program on JZK, Radio Tokyo's overseas outlet. She also sang at a gala of overseas Japanese in Tokyo in November 1940. Articles announced that she would return to the stage as the lead in composer

Koscak (Kosaku) Yamada's opera, variously entitled *Tojin Okichi*, *Yo-ake*, and *Reimei*. Miyakawa was set to play the role of Okichi, the geisha who became common-law wife of Townsend Harris, America's first diplomatic envoy to Japan. It is not clear if the performance ever took place. (Yamada did premiere his opera *Kurofune* that year, on the Black Ships.)

With the coming of the Pacific War, Miyakawa and her family were caught in Japan. Their experience is not recorded. What is certain is that at war's end, Miyakawa was engaged as a secretary to a Colonel Miller, of the occupation Eighth Army, and then to Col. William K. Noel, judge advocate general of the Ninth Corps in Sendai. In late 1946 Agnes (by then single) announced that she would return to the United States and live with her brother George, who operated a medical practice in Charleston, West Virginia. In fall 1947 Miyakawa presented a concert at Charleston's Municipal Auditorium with the Charleston Symphony Orchestra. The following fall, she again concertized with the orchestra. In 1950 she married Ryotaro Minejima (Mineshima) in West Virginia.

Miyakawa seems to have moved to New York after marrying. In April 1949 she offered her first New York recital, at Times Hall. The program mixed French chansons by composers such as Albert Roussel, Claude Debussy, and Gabriel Fauré with Puccini arias. She also was featured at a Japan night benefit concert. In 1951 she gave a radio concert on WNYC's *Hands across the Sea* program, singing Japanese and Ainu folk songs. Meanwhile, she served as an interpreter for a visit by a delegation from Tokyo to Gen. Douglas MacArthur's wife in New York. As far as I have been able to locate, her last concert was a joint recital with mezzo-soprano Nancy Wyner in March 1962 at the Museum of the City of New York. I have found little information on her later life. She met O. P. Moon, a neighbor of her brother George, in Stuart, Florida, and married him. She died on August 30, 1995.

Agnes Yoshiko Miyakwa's star has dimmed to obscurity and her name is now all but forgotten, but she was one of the most renowned West Coast Nisei of her generation.

TOSHIKO HASEGAWA / A NISEI AT LA SCALA

The Nisei soprano Toshiko Hasegawa, who lived in Italy during the 1940s, distinguished herself by her performances of Cio-Cio-San in Puccini's *Madama Butterfly* and other parts, starring at opera houses such as Milan's La Scala.

Born in Sacramento, California, in 1912, Toshio Hasegawa spent her early years in Stockton, where her family ran a dry goods store. According to her own later testimony, she was a tomboy as a child and preferred playing outside to taking music lessons. One day, however, she attended a performance of Verdi's opera *La Traviata* in Sacramento and was so thrilled by the spectacle that she resolved to become an opera singer (according to another media account, she would have preferred a career in drama, but her father thought acting unladylike). After enrolling in the College of the Pacific (today's University of the Pacific), in 1929 she moved to New York to study singing with Arturo Vita. She spent five years doing music training in New York and Boston. In fall 1934 she returned to the West Coast, where she sang a concert on KTAB Radio, then performed a recital, featuring a mix of arias and Japanese songs, on a Christmas program sponsored by the Japan Society of San Francisco. In February 1935 Hasegawa was invited by the San Francisco Opera Association to perform the second act of *Madama Butterfly*, as part of a larger benefit concert. The concert marked the company's first performance by a Nisei. Following her performances, Hasegawa embarked on a recital tour that took her to such nearby cities as Stockton, Santa Cruz, and Watsonville. In her concerts she mixed Japanese folk songs with a repertory of lieder and operatic arias.

Sometime in mid-1935, Hasegawa moved to Milan, Italy, for further training and began studying voice with conductor Angelo Ferrari. In February 1936 she made her European debut using the stage name Cho-Cho-San as a guest artist in Bologna. Shortly thereafter, she sang *Madama Butterfly* and *La Bohème* at Teatr Wielki in Warsaw, Poland. In 1937 she made her French debut in a benefit performance of *Butterfly* at the municipal theater in Enghien, near Paris. The same year she sang in Portugal at the Coliseu de Recreios in Lisbon. In January 1938 she sang *Butterfly* in Palermo opposite tenor Mario Filippeschi, then sang the same role shortly afterward in Monaco at the Theatre de Monte Carlo (situated inside the famous Casino), opposite Enzo Seri. In 1939 she opened the new Arena del Corso theater in Fano, Italy, with a performance of *Madama Butterfly*.

During the late 1930s Hasegawa toured South America four times with Italian opera companies. In November 1936 Hasegawa visited São Paulo and sang *Madama Butterfly* and *La Bohème*. Interviewed by the Japanese Brazilian newspaper *Burajiru Jiho*, she stated that she was especially happy to be in Brazil "because there are so many Japanese here and so at least I can speak Japanese." (In fact, Hasegawa had been to Japan only once, as a child, was unable to read Japanese writing, and mixed her *nihongo* with English.) The journal reported that her most fervent wish was to eat Japanese food while in Brazil, and more broadly to do something for Japan as a future center of world culture. In September 1937 she sang *Butterfly* with the Compania Lirica Italiana at the Teatro Argentino in La Plata, Argentina. In 1940 she was able to leave war-torn Italy and return to South America, where she sang *Butterfly* to great reviews and audiences in São Paulo. A local Japanese newspaper described her as "our dancing princess." After her performance in November 1940 in Rio de Janeiro, the newspaper *Imparcial* raved, "It is a pleasure to hear Toshiko Hasegawa, a perfect artist, who has an admirable vocal timbre that gives the opera of Puccini an uncommon interpretation."

Hasegawa resided in Italy during the war years. While most forms of entertainment were banned by the Fascist government for the duration, opera was permitted, and Hasegawa was able to continue singing and earning money. In 1941–42 she sang in *Madama Butterfly* at the Teatro dell'Opera di Roma (opposite the famed baritone Tito Gobbi as Sharpless) and in Leghorn (Livorno). In 1942 she sang a concert in Venice, appearing for the first time at the famous opera house La Fenice. In 1944 she sang *Butterfly* for the first time in Turin. On multiple occasions she sang in Genoa. She also toured Franco's Spain, a nation allied with Italy. In December 1942 she sang *Butterfly* at the Liceu in Barcelona.

In the latter part of the war period, Hasegawa lived in Milan. When food became scarce, amid the rigors of war and German occupation, she dealt with farmers in the surrounding area to provide herself with sufficient food, especially rice. In 1945, after the area was liberated by the US Army, Nisei GIs from the 442nd Regimental Combat Team were sent to the area. Hasegawa invited them to her home for the Christmas holidays, where she hosted them and made them rice and homemade *tsukemono* (traditional Japanese pickles). Beginning in July 1945, she sang a set of special concerts for the Nisei GIs.

Despite her numerous prewar and wartime engagements and her residence in Milan, it was only after 1945 that Hasegawa was invited to perform at the city's famed opera house, La Scala. One morning in 1946, shortly after completing an engagement in Genoa, Hasegawa was at her home in Milan when a messenger arrived from La Scala to explain that the regular singer engaged to sing Cio-Cio-San that day, plus her understudy, had been taken ill. Could Hasegawa sing the role at that afternoon's performance? Thus it was that she first sang at La Scala and received praise from the management and from conductor Antonio Guarnieri. Following this triumphant appearance, she began to receive more regular engagements. In fall 1948 she returned to South America, where she sang Mimi in *La Bohème* in Rio de Janeiro, opposite the famed tenor Giuseppe di Stefano. In January 1949 she sang Violetta in *La Traviata* at the Teatro Lirico in Turin. The following month she sang *Madama Butterfly* with the municipal opera in Nice, France. In December 1950 she sang Cio-Cio-San in Leghorn (Livorno). It turned out to be a historic occasion because of the appearance of Carlo Bergonzi as Sharpless—it was his last performance as a baritone before he changed to the tenor roles for which he became celebrated.

In 1949, after a fifteen-year absence, Hasegawa returned to the United States to visit her family, who had been confined in the WRA camps following Executive Order 9066 and who had then resettled in Chicago. By that time, she admitted, she spoke Italian better than English. In an interview she gave during her visit, Hasegawa stated, "I would like to sing in the country, but only if I were twenty years younger. I could no longer bear the struggle of making a reputation from the start." She nevertheless agreed to sing a set of arias for the Chicago Japanese American Music Club at a farewell tea in her honor. She added a warning to young singers: "If it were not for my love of acting, I would never have remained on the operatic stage. There is too much politics, too much backbiting. So many singers drop out because of this."

During the first half of the 1950s, Hasegawa continued to perform around Italy, both in *Madama Butterfly* and in other leading roles—one of her favorites was Nedda in Leoncavallo's *I Pagliacci*. She returned to La Scala in May 1951 to perform as Cio-Cio-San, alternating with Licia Albanese. In September 1952 she sang *Butterfly* at the Teatro Alfieri in Turin and then in December sang the same role at the city's famed Teatro Carignano. In 1954 she sang in the role of Cio-Cio-San in Cremona. Most notably, during these years she sang seven times at the Augustus theater in Genoa (fittingly, given her South American tours, the theater where she performed was located on the Corso Buenos Aires).

I have been unable to locate information on Hasegawa's later life. Her career represents a clear example, however, of the opportunities that some exceptional Nisei were able to make for themselves. She died in Chicago in the 1980s.

PIONEERING NISEI SOPRANO TOMIKO (TOMI) KANAZAWA

The pioneering Nisei soprano Tomiko (Tomi) Kanazawa starred throughout the United States and Europe after World War II. She was born in Stockton, California, on July 20, 1915. As a child, she moved to Los Angeles. There she studied both piano and violin. When she was a teenager, her parents discovered her voice and encouraged her to study singing. She attended Jefferson High School in Los Angeles, where she sang in school operettas, then enrolled at Los Angeles City College. In 1932 she performed at a banquet in Los Angeles, capping the biennial convention of the Japanese American Citizens League. The same year she made a radio appearance on KRKD's *Japanese Program* singing Japanese songs.

Around the same time, Kanazawa was granted an audition with the San Carlo Opera Company, then touring the Pacific Coast. San Carlo specialized in productions of Giacomo Puccini's opera *Madama Butterfly*, featuring the celebrated Issei soprano Hizi Koyke. Because of the availability of smaller roles in these productions and because Mme Koyke was known to be generous and respectful of Nisei singers, various sopranos sought auditions with the company every season. The young Tomi Kanazawa was selected as Koyke's understudy. Koyke told reporters that she hoped to introduce her protégé in an East Coast debut. However, Kanazawa remained on the West Coast. In 1937 she undertook a recital tour, with stops at cities such as Bellingham, Washington. In her concerts she mixed Japanese folk songs with a repertory of lieder and operatic arias.

In 1939 Kanazawa, still only twenty-three years old, entered a contest sponsored by the California Recreation Music Committee. She was one of a field of three hundred youthful instrumentalists and vocalists from the Pacific coast. In the end she was awarded first place in the vocalist division at the San Francisco Exposition and won a one hundred–dollar prize. Alfred Frankenstein, the esteemed music editor for the *San Francisco Chronicle*, said: "Miss Kanazawa, who has a bright, clear and highly musical soprano, will learn in time to mix some spirit with her admirable regard for the letter of what she does." Over the next months, she studied music at Chapman College. There she met Leo Müller (Mueller), a European refugee who was a member of Chapman's faculty. She continued to perform on the West Coast. In September 1941 Sueo Serisawa's painting of Kanazawa, *A Portrait of a Singer*, was displayed at the Los Angeles County Fair at Pomona.

Following the declaration of Executive Order 9066, Kanazawa expected to be confined, but friends in New York intervened with offers of sponsorship, and on March 28, 1942, she was able to travel to arrange "voluntary relocation" to New York, where over the next years she worked making artificial flowers and studying music. (One source lists Kanazawa as a graduate of the Curtis

Tomiko Kanazawa, California, *Kashū Mainichi*, late 1930s.

Institute in Philadelphia, but this is unconfirmed.) While in New York, she sang with a quartet in a local synagogue.

Meanwhile, she worked with the activist group Japanese American Committee for Democracy. In May 1945 she made her New York singing debut under JACD auspices, at the famed Carnegie Recital Hall. Partnering with pianist Florence Takayama, she performed a program that included the "Alleluia" from Mozart's "Exsultate Jubilate," the aria "non mi dir" from Mozart's opera *Don Giovanni*, plus selections by Barber, Mahler, Brahms, and Castelnuevo-Tedesco. Meanwhile, Leo Mueller moved east and was engaged as choir conductor and accompanist at the Metropolitan Opera. The two married and remained both personally and professionally involved. In December 1946 Kanazawa made her operatic debut in Scranton, Pennsylvania, singing Cio-Cio-San in *Madama Butterfly*, which would remain her signature role.

Shortly afterward, in February 1948, Kanazawa was engaged by Walter Herbert, conductor-impresario of the New Orleans Opera House, to perform in *Madama Butterfly* in New Orleans. The performances took place under

Herbert's baton on April 8 and 10. It was a notable occasion not only because these were the first postwar performances of Puccini's opera—which had been wildly popular in New Orleans in prewar years but had been banned during the war—but because Kanazawa's leading man was the young tenor Mario Lanza. Lanza would leave shortly thereafter for Hollywood to appear in musical films, and this would be his only lead performance on an operatic stage. On this occasion, however, it was Kanazawa who received the greatest praise. Critic Walter Jenkins of the *New Orleans Times-Picayune* stated that she was most convincing in the role. While he admitted that there were defects in her singing, he lauded the beauty and richness of her voice. *St. Louis News* critic Laurence Oden remarked, "She is to be congratulated for bringing an otherwise ridiculous tragedienne to life for a change." In 1949 she performed a concert tour of the US South with Hungarian tenor Gabor Carelli, giving recitals in such towns as Pauls Valley and Sapulpa, Oklahoma, and Morgan City, Minden, Donaldsonville, Opelousas, and St. Tammany, Louisiana.

During the years that followed, Kanazawa made a number of opera and concert performances around the United States. In 1949 and 1950 she was featured in the Pacific Opera Company's productions of *Madama Butterfly* in Seattle, San Francisco, and Sacramento and also starred as Mimi in the company's production of Puccini's opera *La Bohème*. In 1950 she sang *Butterfly* with the San Francisco Opera. She also performed during these years with local companies in Dallas, Kansas City, Fort Wayne, Portland, Oregon, and Chattanooga, Tennessee. From 1950 to 1956 she sang in the Cincinnati Opera's annual summer series of performances at the Cincinnati Zoo. In 1951 Kanazawa returned to her hometown of Los Angeles and offered a special benefit concert to help raise money for a community center in Little Tokyo. In 1955 she performed in Colorado with the Greater Denver Opera Association. According to *Denver Post* music critic Allen Young, she received an ovation that rocked the theater. Young was enthusiastic: "She uses her voice with intelligence and feeling, an expressive variety of tone, and a remarkable sympathy for the role as Puccini wrote it."

In February 1950 Kanazawa made a landmark television appearance when she performed in "scenes from *Madama Butterfly*," for NBC's program *Television Opera Theatre*, opposite Davis Cunningham as Pinkerton. It was one of the first-ever televised opera performances in the United States and certainly the first televised performance of Puccini's opera. It was seen by millions of spectators.

In 1952 Kanazawa made another landmark appearance in *Madama Butterfly*.

During a Metropolitan Opera tour in Minneapolis, soprano Licia Albanese fell ill, and Kanazawa was invited to substitute for her as Cio-Cio-San. Although this represented Kanazawa's sole Metropolitan Opera appearance and was part of a tour rather than in its New York City home, she had the distinction of being the first nonwhite singer to perform a lead role with the company— three years before famed contralto Marian Anderson broke the Met's color line against African Americans in a supporting role.

Despite her success in the United States, Kanazawa's singing career centered increasingly on Europe. As she explained to a journalist: "European audiences are spoiled because they have grown up with the theater. But they're still appreciative." In 1948 she made her European debut in Budapest, Hungary, and the following year appeared in *Madama Butterfly* with the Vienna Staatsoper. She also sang in France, at the Royal Opera Stockholm, and in Helsinki. In addition to singing *Butterfly* and Mimi, she also sang Pamina in Mozart's *The Magic Flute* and Cherubino in *The Marriage of Figaro*, Leonore in Verdi's *Il Trovatore*, and Liu in Puccini's *Turandot*.

In 1950 Kanazawa made her first concert tour of Sweden, with her husband, Leo Mueller, accompanying. She became a great favorite in Scandinavia, touring almost annually. In 1953 she gave a dozen concerts in Sweden, Norway, and Finland. The following year she gave a "command performance" before the Swedish royal family. In 1959 Kanazawa made one of her last documented performances, performing in a televised program for the United Way.

After her retirement from the operatic stage, Kanazawa spent several years in Halifax, Nova Scotia, where Mueller served as conductor of the Halifax Symphony. The two returned to Vienna in 1976, where Mueller became manager of the Opera Studio of the Vienna State Opera. After her husband's death in 2003, Tomiko Kanazawa Mueller lived in Vienna, where in 2020 she died at 105 years old.

FOUJITA DISCOVERS THE AMERICAS / AN ARTIST'S TOUR
with Seth Jacobowitz

The name of Léonard Foujita (Tsuguharu Foujita) has lost much of its luster today. However, in his heyday in Paris in the 1920s, Foujita was not only the most celebrated Japanese artist in the world but, along with Hollywood star Sessué Hayakawa, was arguably the most famous living person of Japanese ancestry in the Western world.

Born Tsuguharu Fujita in Japan in 1886, the son of a Japanese general, in 1913 he left Japan to seek his career as a painter in Paris, where he changed the spelling of his name to *Foujita* and most often went by his last name alone. Although his debut exhibition encompassed a fascinating range of subjects that included paintings with gold leaf-like backgrounds that fused Christian and Japanese medieval iconographies, he soon settled into his most popular subject matter: portraits of ethereal Parisian nudes and languorous cats. Within the span of several years, he became one of the leading representatives of the circle of modernist painters collectively known as the "School of Paris." Foujita's hallmark style fused elements of Western oil painting techniques with the fine lines and shading of Japanese wood-block prints and sumi-e, India ink brush painting, respectively. Foujita developed a uniquely opalescent white paint he called *grand fond blanc*, which, when overlaid by his perfectly executed black line drawings, imparted an effect that delighted bohemian and bourgeois audiences alike. Yet he also earned considerable notoriety for his flamboyant appearance, with his bowl haircut (a half-century before the Beatles), outsized eyeglasses, tiny mustache, and outrageous costumes, many of which he designed for himself.

After sixteen years in Europe, Foujita began a period of international travel that commenced with his first trip back to Japan, from 1929 to 1931. His triumphant return to Japan, accompanied by his third wife, Youki, occasioned many appreciative commentaries. Renowned novelist Kawabata Yasunari, for instance, made sure to mention Foujita in his own modernist literary masterpiece, *The Scarlet Gang of Asakusa* (1929–30). In the work Kawabata recorded Foujita's presence at the Casino Follies in Asakusa, observing, "Just back from Paris, the accomplished painter Foujita Tsuguharu has come to see the review, accompanied by his Parisienne wife Youki."

After his stay in Japan, Foujita migrated to the United States for a series of gallery exhibitions. In November 1930 Foujita arrived in New York, where he had a show at the Reinhardt Galleries. He remained ten weeks in New York. Among his many interactions with fellow artists during his stay, he made the acquaintance of the famed Japanese-born American modernist Yasuo Kuniyoshi. In January 1931 he moved on to Chicago for a show at the Arts Club.

Upon his return to Paris in March 1931, Foujita found Youki romantically entangled with his friend, surrealist poet Robert Desnos, and abandoned her to him (the two later married). Instead, Foujita resolved to tour Latin America. Ironically, it was at least in part Desnos's enthusiastic visit to Cuba that

Caricature of Foujita by Roy Kawamoto, *Kashū Mainichi*, 1933.

seems to have sparked the idea for Foujita to tour Latin America. Foujita was also inspired to leave France after he received a large tax bill from French authorities for the substantial sums of money he had earned during the 1920s. Foujita made the journey accompanied by a new romantic interest, Madeleine Lequeux, better known as Mady Dormans, a dancer at the Casino de Paris.

Foujita and Mady's first stop was in Brazil. They arrived in Rio de Janeiro for a four-month long stay, conveniently timed to include the two major annual holidays of New Year's Eve and Carnival. The Brazilian modernist community warmly received Foujita as a representative of the School of Paris. The painter Candido Portinari, whom Foujita had known in Paris, hosted him and introduced him to artists such as Emiliano di Cavalcanti and Ismael Nery and the writer Manuel Bandeiras. Their interactions extended not only to witty caricatures and expressions of mutual affection but also an exchange of avant-gardist techniques, including the ultimate homage of imitating one another's painting style. Nery's watercolor of a nattily dressed Foujita and Mady receiving visitors to a gallery exhibition of his work stands out as one of the most elegant records of this brief but intense encounter.

The Brazilian modernist poet, musicologist, and critic Mario de Andrade assessed Foujita's work and praised him deeply in a review for the January 20, 1932 edition of the *Díario Nacional*, saying, "Fujita [sic] represents one of those rare cases, aside from the intellectual arts of the word, of an artist of non-European race and essence, who has succeeded in becoming important from within the European conception of art." Andrade identified what he saw as the central theme of Foujita's work: not the incapacity to faithfully reproduce the essence of European art, but the capacity to purposefully "betray" it. He argued that Foujita was indifferent to merging Japanese and European art, as others so often believed. Rather, he was an artist whose work was characterized by its "extreme silence, shall we say, plastically: a profound emptiness in his paintings and drawings. His sharp lines, the vast, blank surfaces, the true synthesis in its representation of theme, the relative coolness, or placidity of expression. All of these elements of his art, finally, leave me in a state of amazement" (51).

Foujita took advantage of his time to paint. Although he continued to produce familiar works in portraiture, his travels through South America marked a significant departure from his signature style. Not for the first time, or the last, would he court controversy, yet now he dedicated his work toward a wider palette of racial skin tones and social classes. Foujita was predictably drawn to the spectacle of pre-Lenten festivities in *Carnival in Rio de Janeiro* and *À la porte au Carnival* and scenes from the red-light district, such as his painting of four women in dishabille, seen from inside a bordello window, which was simply entitled *Mangue*, after the district itself.

Foujita also captured Rio's vibrant street life, in a marked departure from the modern themes that made his work so coveted by Francophile high society. In *Deux gamins nègres* (Two Black Youths), the young men wear looks of frustrated boredom and stare out beyond the picture plane. In *People in Rio de Janeiro* five Black female figures form a unified composition. Two barefoot little girls stand in the foreground next to a seated young mother with a melancholic expression on her face and hands fidgeting nervously. Two other young women stand ramrod straight with arms akimbo, one with her back turned and the other sternly facing left. Only the little girl at the center of the composition gazes directly at the painter, her head turned slightly, and quizzically, as he sketches them.

So began a new period of experimentation with ethnographic sketches, often done against a neutral beige background. Foujita's impeccable use of line and shading were still in force, but now his attention to intricate fabrics and textiles was directed to depicting indigenous folk garb, rather than the brocade curtains and bed linens of the Parisian boudoir. Foujita enthusiastically pursued this new approach along his travels through South America, and it continued well past his return to Japan in 1933. Some of these later works included such "exotic" subjects as a carnivalesque urban street musician in *Chindon Performer and Serving Maid* (1934) and a tattooed elderly Okinawan woman and her two grandchildren against a sumptuous tropical background in *Okinawan Family* (1938).

Surprisingly, Foujita mostly seems to have flown under the radar of the Japanese Brazilian press during his time in Brazil. The overwhelming majority of the Japanese Brazilian community was concentrated in coffee plantations and agricultural colonies in the interior of São Paulo State. It was still a young community, about one hundred thousand strong, but growing at a frenetic clip in the early 1930s. More than 60 percent of that number had arrived in the previous five years alone. It did not help that Foujita spent most of his time in Rio de Janeiro and only in January belatedly arrived in São Paulo. Not surprisingly, Foujita was not as taken with the gray, commercial metropolis of São Paulo as the enchanting and considerably sunnier Rio de Janeiro. He complained in a letter to Portinari, "Here it is cold and rains," adding, "We very much enjoyed our stay in Rio." In fact, the turmoil of the Great Depression, the immediate consequences of the Manchurian Incident, which had occurred on September 18, 1931, and the larger political situation in both Japan and Brazil dominated the headlines of the ethnic Japanese press. The sole mention of Foujita's visit in the five Japanese dailies appears in the supplementary Portuguese-language section of the *Nippak Shimbun* from January 1, 1932. He is lauded as "one of the idols of Montmartre and Broadway, admired in all the cultured cities of the world."

Despite the lack of publicity attending his visit, Foujita did interact with community members. He met with the young Issei artists Tomoo Handa Tomoo and Yoshiya Takaoka, who went on to cofound the Seibi Group of Nikkei modern artists in 1935, along with Walter Shigeto Tanaka, Kiyoji Tomioka, Yuji Tamaki, Hajime Higaki, and Kichizaemon Takahashi, and the writers Kikuo Furuno and Yoshimi Kimura. Nor did Foujita's influence end there. In 1935 novelist Orígenes Lessa penned a short story about an ill-fated young Issei artist who briefly becomes "the Brazilian Foujita, the national Foujita." Due to the connections he made on his visit to São Paulo, Foujita would receive several promising Nisei artists, including Jorge Mori, in Paris after the war.

After leaving Brazil, Foujita spent the next five months in Argentina, where he was received with almost unbelievable fanfare. According to multiple accounts, sixty thousand visitors flocked to his exhibition, and ten thousand admirers stood in line to receive his autograph. Needless to say, he sold all his displayed works and was directly commissioned for society portraits such as that of Carola Carcano de' Martinez de Oz.

His interactions with the considerably smaller Japanese-language press in Buenos Aires likewise improved upon his experience in Brazil. He drew and signed an illustration of a horse, a popular *gaúcho* theme, for the May 1932 cover of the Buenos Aires–based *Aruzenchin Jihō* (or *El Argentin Djijo*, as it was then spelled in Spanish) and wrote a short article in his own hand congratulating Argentina in commemoration of its independence day. Unlike the better-established Japanese newspapers published in Brazil and the United States, the *Aruzenchin Jihō* was still mimeographed at this time.

After visiting several cities in Argentina, Foujita continued through Bolivia and Peru. In *Japan in Paris,* art historian Emiko Yamanashi cites a section, "Observations of South America," from Foujita's travelogue, *Swimming over Land* (*Chi o oyogu* [1942]): "During my long years of living overseas, I might even say among the unrepeatable experiences of my entire life, if someone were to ask me what lake I liked the best, I would say more than any other one I have ever seen I love Lake Titicaca on the border between Peru and Bolivia, in South America."

This is a fairly typical example of Foujita's public statements, in which he was never prone to divulging his personal sentiments. Yet his works such as *Llama and Four Women* (1933), panned as disappointing by some of his Japanese and Latin American critics, reveals a desire to capture scenes in striking contrast to the spectacles of modern life that his audience had come to expect.

Foujita and Mady arrived in Cuba on October 28, 1932, their only stopover in the Caribbean, before continuing onward to Mexico. Relatively little is recorded from the trip, although it remains open to interpretation whether this was due to the artist's desire to keep Havana's considerable charms to himself or other mitigating circumstances. According to biographer Phyllis Birnbaum, Foujita and Mady's usual bohemian antics caused their fair share of trouble: "A Cuban journalist noted that 'she created more confusion than a cross-eyed traffic cop.'"

After his stays in Brazil, Argentina, Bolivia, Peru, and Cuba, Tsuguharu Foujita resumed his round-the-world tour. In November 1932 he arrived in Mexico City. As an international celebrity in the art world, he was already well-known to Mexican art lovers. As early as 1922, his work had been the subject of a feature article in the newspaper *Excelsior*, "Foujita, Un grande y extraño artista japones, muy apludido en Paris" (Foujita, a Great and Strange Japanese Artist, Much Applauded in Paris).

Foujita originally intended to stay in Mexico City for only one month and to visit with Diego Rivera, whom he had first met in Paris two decades earlier, not long after the Japanese artist's first arrival in the City of Light. In the event he did not reconnect with Rivera, who was working on murals in the United States during early 1933 (notably, the notorious and ultimately destroyed mural that Rivera was commissioned to produce for Rockefeller Center in New York City). Foujita nonetheless enjoyed himself so much in Mexico that he ended up spending seven months there. He found Mexico an inspiring place to work and completed a large selection of canvases. In one later interview, Foujita claimed to have shot several reels of motion pictures in Mexico and added that he intended to use his sketches to illustrate a travel book by Madeleine. (The reels of film, if they existed, seem not to have survived, and no travel book was ever published).

During Foujita's stay in Mexico City, forty of his paintings were displayed in a large-scale exhibition, while art collector Louis Eychenne organized two shows of Foujita's drawings. The artist attended a Christmas reception at the French embassy and was feted at a gala reception hosted by Japan's ambassador to Mexico, Yoshiatsu Hori, and attended by members of the US diplomatic corps. It is not clear how much Foujita connected with local Japanese during his stay—Mexico City was home to some celebrated individuals, including theater director Seki Sano and diplomat-professor Kinta Arai, but the region's total Nikkei population was barely one thousand.

Foujita left Mexico City by train at the end of June 1933 and crossed into the United States. After stopovers in New Mexico and Arizona, he and Madeleine arrived in Los Angeles on July 5, 1933. Beyond the artist's famous eccentric appearance, the couple made a strong visual impact. Interracial marriage was then illegal in California, and mixed-race couples were relatively rare. (Ironically, the middle-aged Foujita and his much younger wife, who stood out in other places due to the difference in their respective ages, resembled many Issei couples.) Foujita announced his plans to the press. "This is my first trip to Los Angeles and I am really delighted to be in such a refreshing climate. I intend to stay here for about two months, after which I will go to the South Sea islands following a brief visit to Japan. I am planning on painting the various Japanese that I find along this Pacific area."

In mid-July, soon after Foujita's arrival, the Dalzell-Hatfield Gallery opened a solo exhibition of eighty-seven of his works, mostly produced during his Latin American trip. They included street scenes and portraits of Indigenous people from Mexico and Bolivia, the inevitable pictures of cats, and Japanese watercolors. Meanwhile, a show of his Mexican landscapes, plus watercolors done on rice paper, was exhibited at the Art Gallery of the Palos Verdes Library. On August 3 Foujita's show moved to the Illsley Gallery at the Ambassador Hotel. It now included some fifteen pieces done in California. On the exhibition's opening day, Foujita gave the first of three special one-day courses to select groups of twenty students of the Art Center school, arranged through Nisei photographer Dave Kurakane. The next day he held an informal reception and lecture before a group of sixty prominent Los Angeles artists and critics. The artist spoke in French on his theories of art and its present trends and made several sketches.

Foujita's stay in Los Angeles received daily coverage in the local Nisei press. The presence of such an international Nikkei celebrity in their orbit was thrilling for locals. Columnist Roku Sugahara pronounced in *Kashū Mainichi*: "When the tumult and the shouting dies, the names of generals, potentates, and statesmen will soon be forgotten. But fine art lives on eternal. Maybe that's why Tsuguharu Foujita has been acclaimed one of the greatest Japanese of the modern era. . . . Lives of great men oft remind us—and so do the lives of great artists. There is just that glamour and drama in the life of Foujita." In *Kashū Mainichi* editor Larry Tajiri reported on a visit from the artist: "We met Foujita yesterday when he came up to the editorial sanctum, and he didn't even vaguely resemble a cat. A wealth of grey-black hair, cut in distinct sharp style Foujita affects, and thin horn-rimmed glasses, represented this famous Parisian artist."

Foujita, though he had worked with California artist Henry Sugimoto in France, was not greatly familiar with Japanese American life at the time of his stay in California. As can be inferred from his initial comments about doing paintings of local Japanese, Foujita may have hoped to find subjects and/or patrons in Little Tokyo, and he made efforts to reach out. Leaders of the Japanese community were invited to his gallery show openings. In late July he spoke at a roundtable on art at the Olympic Hotel, near Little Tokyo. At the request of the Kumumoto kenjin and Tokyo prefectural clubs, he agreed to mount a downtown exhibition especially for the Japanese community. The exhibition opened in a hotel room at the Olympic Hotel on August 24, 1933, and ran for four days. Foujita also agreed to visit the Japanese Amateur Photographers club on August 31 and to review its members' work. Sadly, like the larger visit, these efforts were generally unavailing. In October 1933 Larry Tajiri wrote in *Kashū Mainichi*: "We know that Foujita, the internationally-famous Japanese painter, was disappointed by the lack of enthusiasm in the Los Angeles reception. Paris, Buenos Aires, or Rio was never like this. [There] veritable reams of copy were written of Foujita, his wife, and his cats. In Los Angeles he elicited little response in comparison."

In September 1933 Foujita left for San Francisco. As in Los Angeles, his name and his work were already known. Indeed, just one year earlier, some Foujita works had been included in a show of modern Japanese prints at the city's de Young Museum. A review in the *Oakland Tribune* lauded the works: "It would be safe to say that the average Occidental could not date these within a hundred years if it were not for Foujita. This fellow and his cats are modern revolutionaries to Japan. He chooses western subjects and does them in Japanese."

Foujita's appearance in San Francisco was highlighted by a three-week show at the Courvoisier Gallery, which combined his Latin American works with a separate room of Parisian nudes. The opening was not without a dramatic flair. According to one report, on the weekend before the show's Monday premiere, neither the artist nor his pictures had arrived, so gallery owner Guthrie Courvoisier took a night plane to Los Angeles, bundled Foujita and some of his pictures into the return flight, and landed just in time to hang them for the opening. Several days later Foujita returned to Los Angeles to pick up Madeleine and take her to San Francisco with the remainder of his baggage.

The Courvoisier Gallery show was a success and was held over for a fourth week. In an article in the *Oakland Tribune* (which featured the trenchant sub-headline "Nudes, Peons and Cats Vie for Interest in S.F. Gallery Display"), critic H. L. Dungan noted: "Foujita has used more color in most of his Mexican pictures then in his French. There are portraits or full length figures of men and women. He has departed from the Rivera-Orozco tradition that all Mexicans must appear in a paint[ing] as solid as board, clothes and all. He has given the Mexican the lightness of the Japanese touch without depriving him of his character or characteristics." Foujita was feted by local artists and intellectuals. In October he spoke before the city's elite Commonwealth Club.

As in Los Angeles, Foujita's tour was heavily covered by the local Nisei press. However, whether because he already knew individuals such as Henry Sugimoto or just because Bay Area Nikkei were generally more sophisticated, Foujita seems to have had an easier time connecting with the community than in Little Tokyo. He was the guest of honor at a sukiyaki party at the Yamato Hotel in September. *Shin Sekai* journalist Welly Shibata described the visitor positively: "Individual. Intensely so, yet contrary to general expectations, he is not eccentric. Confident, yet unassuming... interesting, cosmopolitan, and possessor of a whimsical sense of humor, [he] proves to be a regular fellow."

Shibata recounted being invited by Henry Sugimoto to join him and the Foujitas on a trip to Golden Gate Park. Foujita was enchanted by the Japanese Tea Garden, which made him homesick. When they went to the park's aquarium to view the fish, the artist's presence drew a crowd.

> Always an object of attention in a crowd, many of whom evidently recognize Foujita, for his tortoise-shell rimmed glasses and the bangs are conspicuous badges of individuality, he is sometimes just a little weary, perhaps, to be an eternal cynosure. But he wears his mantle of fame modestly, graciously. The applause has not lessened his interest in his fellow human beings, nor in the world in general. Perhaps that is the reason why, despite his graying hairs, his spirit seems very young. "Au revoir," said Foujita in French to us as we parted. "Sayonara," said his wife in Japanese.

Tsuguharu and Madeleine Foujita sailed to Japan in November 1933. Madeleine died in Japan three years later. In 1939 Foujita traveled once more to Paris but soon returned to Japan. There he abandoned his established artistic style and began a series of brutally heroic war paintings. In 1938 the Imperial Navy Information Office supported his visit to China as an official war artist. After Pearl Harbor he lent his artistry to supporting Japan's war effort against the Allies in World War II. His monumental painting *Final Fighting at Attu* (1943) depicts gallant Japanese soldiers in a final stand against US forces. Similarly, *Compatriots on Saipan Island Remain Faithful to the End* (1945) glorifies the mass suicide by Japanese soldiers and civilians following the American invasion of the Pacific island.

Following the end of the war, Foujita was publicly denounced in Japan for his propaganda works. (Ironically, under the American occupation, a set of his wartime paintings was seized by the United States government, which later offered them on "indefinite loan" to the National Museum of Modern Art in Tokyo.) With his reputation permanently stained in Japan, in 1949 Foujita left his native land for the last time, accompanied by his Japanese wife, Kimiyo. On the invitation of Gen. Douglas MacArthur, the American proconsul, he traveled to New York, where he worked for a year. When he planned an exhibition of his works, Yasuo Kuniyoshi opposed the holding of the show, labeling Foujita a fascist and imperialist.

In 1950 Foujita returned to France. Apart from his brief visit in 1939, he had been away for nearly twenty years. There he worked once again to reinvent himself. In 1955 he became a French citizen, taking the Western name Léonard Foujita (in honor of Leonardo da Vinci). Two years later he was awarded the Legion of Honor by the French government. He took up residence in Villiers-le-Bâcle, a town southwest of Paris. Under the sponsorship of René Lalou, director of Mumm champagne, he converted to Catholicism and shifted his focus to religious art. He devoted much of his attention in his last years to designing a chapel in Reims and producing stained glass and frescoes for it. The Chapel of Our Lady Queen of Peace (better known as the Foujita Chapel) was completed in 1966, two years before his death in Switzerland.

EPILOGUE

Dear Reader, thank you for coming along on this tour of the unknown. I hope that you found the pieces in this volume both diverting and enlightening. I have often been asked how I began writing popular history. I explain that my involvement follows from my longtime interest in producing scholarship that could reach readers beyond the academy. As a graduate student, I worked for popular encyclopedias and experimented with producing historical articles for newspapers and magazines, even a daily legal newspaper, the *New York Bar Journal*. In fact, my very first published work in Asian American history was a feature in the *Pennsylvania Gazette*, the alumni magazine of the University of Pennsylvania, on Penn's exclusion of Nisei students during World War II.

Although I became widely known as a historian of Japanese Americans after the publication in 2001 of my first book, *By Order of the President*, the real turning point in my career came in 2004, when the right-wing commentator Michelle Malkin published a book purporting to justify the wartime confinement of Japanese Americans. I joined forces with my friend Eric Muller on a series of blog posts refuting Malkin's arguments. In the process I discovered not only the power of social media, then still largely in its infancy, but the importance of using my historical research to connect with real-life communities and their concerns. True, this was nothing new for historians: as Alice Yang has shown, the generation of scholars who were active during the 1970s and 1980s, including Roger Daniels and Peter Irons, provided important support to the Japanese American redress movement. However, it was not something that I had previously taken for granted nor that I sensed history departments valued in hiring and tenure decisions.

In the wake of the debate with Malkin, my friend Chizu Omori, a filmmaker and columnist for the *Nichi Bei Times*, encouraged me to think about writing a historical newspaper column, and she recommended me to the *Nichi Bei*'s English-language editor, Kenji Taguma. Kenji expressed to me that he felt the need for his paper to address new issues and audiences and thought I might help provide something different. I was especially qualified from this point of view, as I was a professionally trained scholar with research interests in diverse aspects of Japanese American history. What is more, I was an outsider to the community, both as a non-Japanese and as a New Yorker living in Montreal. For this reason, while I might not have the same kind of understanding of events that a community insider would, I could more easily write about delicate subjects, particularly the lives of LGBTQ+ Japanese Americans. I joked that I had an advantage over "insider" writers because none of my readers would call up *my* mother to complain about my columns! (The joke gained extra pungency from the fact that my late mother, Toni Robinson, had actually been my professional collaborator.)

I started my *Nichi Bei Times* column, The Unknown Great and the Great Unknown, in April 2007. I settled into publishing on a more or less monthly basis, though without a fixed schedule. I was delighted by the positive response that I received from readers. Then, in mid-2009, barely two years after I had started, the newspaper folded. I was convinced that my life as a columnist had come to its end. Instead, Kenji Taguma made the brave decision to create a nonprofit organization and spin off his own (all-English) publication, *Nichi Bei Weekly*. I gladly accepted Kenji's invitation to move my column to the new publication, and I published my first piece there in February 2010.

At first I published columns in the new *Nichi Bei Weekly* on a monthly basis, and by the end of 2012, I had enough material to collect into a book-length manuscript made up of the best of the new columns, plus those I had produced for the defunct *Nichi Bei Times*. This collection saw print as *The Great Unknown* (2016). In the next years, though, the economics of the newspaper forced Kenji to impose limits on the size and frequency of my columns. As the *Nichi Bei Weekly* changed into a biweekly publication—its title notwithstanding—and expanded its news coverage, he had less space to give me. My columns became smaller, and they were no longer accompanied by images as they had been previously. I did continue my long-standing practice of writing for the *Nichi Bei*'s annual New Year's edition and also contributing an annual LGBTQ+ history article around Pride Week. However, apart from those two set occasions, there were sometimes gaps of weeks or months between the appearance of my Great Unknown columns.

Because I was less busy with *Nichi Bei Weekly*, I undertook other public writing projects in order to take up the slack. I was a major contributor to, and associate editor of, the online *Densho Encyclopedia*. I worked for a time as a columnist for the monthly Japanese Canadian newspaper *Nikkei Voice*. On the invitation of Professor Duncan Ryūken Williams, I produced a series of articles on mixed-race Japanese Americans (two of which are reprinted in this collection) for his now-defunct website, hapajapan.com. While these gigs were all quite rewarding, each was a limited-term assignment.

It was Yoko Nishimura of the Japanese American National Museum who provided a second home for my writing. Over the preceding years I had contributed a few pieces to JANM's blog, *Discover Nikkei*, mostly reports on various Japanese American and Japanese Canadian conferences that I had attended. On her invitation I now agreed to do a monthly column, and I began my new assignment in September 2017.

From the outset the arrangement worked admirably. The editors of *Discover Nikkei* allowed me greater flexibility as far as word counts, and they welcomed multipart columns, so I could write more in depth. Best of all, I could select images from among JANM's rich visual resources to accompany my posts. At the same time, I still enjoyed doing my Great Unknown columns for *Nichi Bei Weekly*, and I started the series on Japanese American classical musicians that appears in these pages. In 2019 I prepared a new book of collected pieces, selecting works from all the various publications in which I had published. It appeared as *The Unsung Great: Portraits of Extraordinary Japanese Americans* (2020).

I come now to the most sensitive and personal part of my story. The lion's share of this volume was produced during the period from 2019 to early 2022. Like so many people, I faced multiple troubles during these years, whose impact was magnified by the COVID pandemic. I mourned a dear friend who took his own life, experienced a series of painful breaks with friends who began erupting in sudden rage or coldness, and faced feelings of isolation and lassitude. My home city of Montreal went through extended periods of curfew and closure of nonessential businesses. True, I was fortunate in that I remained healthy and employed and was able to teach and write from home. Yet restrictions on international travel, accompanied by limitations on in-person contacts and shuttering of libraries and archives, not only hampered my professional work but brought long-term separation from loved ones. Once I was at last permitted to travel to the United States in fall 2021, I spent a good deal of time at the bedside of my beloved father, whose health was failing and who was in and out of the hospital.

In these difficult times I laid aside more extended scholarly projects and concentrated on my short pieces. There were good reasons for this. First, on the practical side, I found my columns less challenging to produce. Even with no in-person access to archives, I could put together texts by drawing on previously acquired material in my files and unearthing information through virtual research. Also, the writing itself did not require as much concentration. Most importantly, I found that doing columns provided me a vital feeling of solace and gratification.

Another big change for me was that whereas in the past I had generally worked alone on my columns, I shifted my practice and began writing with various collaborators. I found that teaming up with a partner (especially a younger scholar whom I could help mentor through our joint efforts) made the work easier and more intriguing. One bright young historian, Jonathan van Harmelen, became my chief collaborator.

A watershed moment came in early 2022, when *The Unsung Great* was awarded honorable mention (a "silver medal" in terms of the award Olympics) for the History Book prize of the Association for Asian American Studies. I considered it an affirmation by my professional colleagues of the importance of the kind of writing I do and of my goal to reach community audiences and the general public with my writing. So, with that encouragement, I continue my explorations of the Unknown Great.

ACKNOWLEDGMENTS

Writing a book can be a lonely enterprise at the best of times. As I've described, this volume is the child of confinement and isolation. I am thus especially grateful for the friends and colleagues who kept me going. First, I thank again Kenji Taguma and the staff of the *Nichi Bei Weekly*, most notably Heather Horiuchi and Tomo Hirai, for giving me my start and for their encouragement. I thank them, as well as Yoko Nishimura and Vicky Murakami-Tsuda of the Japanese American National Museum; Brian Niiya and Nina Wallace of Densho; and Duncan Williams of Hapajapan, first for commissioning my work, then granting me permission to reprint it. I thank Roxane Ando, Kay Bromberg, Kiyo Knight, Janine Macbeth, Bobby Matsudaira, Emily Murase, Maryka Omatsu, Mayumi Takasaki, and June Wheeler for assistance with photos.

I am naturally obliged to University of Washington Press, to my editor Mike Baccam and to editor-in-chief Larin McLaughlin, who agreed to publish this book and who guided the manuscript with an apparent effortlessness that hid actual effort.

I am greatly indebted to my collaborators in this volume: Peter Eisenstadt, Christian Heimburger, Seth Jacobowitz, Matthieu Langlois, Zacharie Leclair, Brian Niiya, James Sun, and Bo Tao. They agreed to work with me and then allowed me to publish our joint work here. I wish to pay special tribute to my chief collaborator, Jonathan van Harmelen. Since 2019 Jonathan has published some twenty columns with me, in addition to producing dozens of solo writings. Not only does Jonathan contribute his share of research and writing to our joint productions, but his knowledge and enthusiasm stimulate my own. Thus, even though Jonathan cowrote only a fraction of pieces in this volume, his name appears beside mine on the title page in tribute to our enduring partnership. Jonathan himself wishes to thank Frank Abe; Clark Alejandrino; Patricia Arra; Will Buchholtz; Leonard Butingan; Jingjie Alva Dai; Tetsuo and Betty Furukawa; Arthur Hansen; Lynne Horiuchi; Lawson Fusao Inada; Matthieu Langlois; Peter Mellinger; Gwen Muranaka; Brian Niiya; Yoko Nishimura;

Chizu and Emiko Omori; Daniel Rodriguez; Tascha Shahriari-Parsa; Tomás Summer-Sandoval; Giotta Tajiri; Stefan, Susan, and Christopher van Harmelen; Helena Wall; Samuel Hideo Yamashita; Karen Tei Yamashita; Alice Yang; and Hong Yang.

Beyond those who directly contributed to the making of this book, I wish to single out some of the friends and loved ones who have offered me support and caring these last years and put up with my zeal for Nikkei history. For help and friendship, I salute Frank Abe, Pierre Anctil, Aditya Bhattacharjee, Jérôme Bosser and Marie-Natacha Papillon, Christopher Bram, Steven Capsuto, Ben Carton, Connie Chiang, Floyd Cheung, Hadrien Chino, Elena Tajima Creef, Dominic D'Amour, Takako Day, Quentin de Becker, Ken Feinour, Francois Furstenberg, Jason Gillingham, Louis Godbout, Sheila Hamanaka and Russell Dale, the late Roger Daniels, Arthur Hansen, Robert Hayashi, Lynne Horiuchi, Karen Inouye, Pahul (Alex) Josan, Catherine Ladnier, Matthieu Langlois, Shirley Geok-Lin Lim, Lei Liu, Guillaume Marceau, Marco Mariano, Valerie Matsumoto, Paul May, John Meehan, Sean Metzger, Jeremy Meyer, Robert Moulton, Takeya Mizuno, Phuong and Betty Nguyen, Brian Niiya, Chizu and Emiko Omori, Tsung-Hsien Pan, Olivier Peloquin, Michael Prior, Adam Rabiner, Jonathan Fortin, Bruno Ramirez, Robert Schwartzwald, Ronn Seely and David Latulippe, Gabriel Séguin, Charles Senay, Stevie Souvenir, Chris Suh, James Sun, David Tacium, Shelley Tepperman, Dorothy Williams, Mark Williams, Shirlette Wint, Frank Wu and Juneyup Yi. Family members Jono Mainelli, Michael Massing, Hannah Perez Postman, Neal Plotkin and Deborah Malamud, Melissa Plotkin, Jocelyn and Adam Rigel, Ariella Robinson and Gray Tolhurst, Ed Robinson and Ellen Fine, Heng Wee Tan, and the members of the Sandler, Post, and Mackey-Baker clans merit my gratitude and devotion. Last but most, Xiaolin Zhu, although far away, brings calm joy into my life.

NOTES

INTRODUCTION

1. Definition of *cosmopolitan*, *Merriam-Wester Dictionary*, accessed November 15, 2022, https://www.merriam-webster.com/dictionary/cosmopolitan.
2. See, for example, Shana Bernstein, *Bridges of Reform: Interracial Civil Rights Activism in Twentieth-Century Los Angeles* (New York: Oxford University Press, 2011); Diane Fujino, *Heartbeat of Struggle: The Revolutionary life of Yuri Kochiyama* (Minneapolis: University of Minnesota Press, 2005); Scott Kurashige, *The Shifting Grounds of Race: Blacks and Japanese Americans in the Making of Multiethnic Los Angeles* (Princeton, NJ: Princeton University Press, 2008); Daryl Maeda, *Like Water: A Cultural History of Bruce Lee* (New York: New York University Press, 2022).
3. See, for example, Paul Spickard, *Mixed Blood: Intermarriage and Ethnic Identity in 20th-Century America* (Madison: University of Wisconsin Press, 1989); Paul Spickard, *Japanese Americans: The Formation and Transformations of an Ethnic Group*, rev. ed. (New Brunswick, NJ: Rutgers University Press, 2009); Duncan Ryūken Williams, ed., *Hapa Japan: History*, vol. 1 (Los Angeles: Kaya Press / Ito Center Editions, 2017).
4. Amy Sueyoshi, *Queer Compulsions: Race, Nation, and Sexuality in the Affairs of Yone Noguchi* (Honolulu: University of Hawai'i Press, 2012); John Howard, *Concentration Camps on the Home Front: Japanese Americans in the House of Jim Crow* (Chicago: University of Chicago Press, 2008); Eric C. Wat, *The Making of a Gay Asian Community: An Oral History of Pre-AIDS Los Angeles* (Lanham, MD: Rowman & Littlefield, 2001); Eric C. Wat, *Love Your Asian Body: AIDS Activism in Los Angeles* (Seattle: University of Washington Press, 2021).

HISAYE YAMAMOTO AND THE CATHOLIC WORKER

1. Sarah D. Wald, *The Nature of California: Race, Citizenship, and Farming since the Dust Bowl* (Seattle: University of Washington Press, 2016), 105, https://books.google.com/books?id=ewQgDAAAQBAJ.

2. Copies of the *Catholic Worker* from Hisaye Yamamoto's personal collection are in the possession of Matthieu Langlois.
3. Wald, *Nature of California*, 105.
4. Yone U. Stafford, "Pacifist Conference at Peter Maurin Farm," *Catholic Worker*, October 1953, 2.
5. Hisaye Yamamoto, Small Talk, *Los Angeles Tribune*, September 3, 1945, 12.
6. Hisaye Yamamoto, Small Talk, *Los Angeles Tribune*, August 20, 1945, 14.
7. Hisaye Yamamoto, intro. King-Kok Cheung, *Seventeen Syllables and Other Stories* (Latham, NY: Kitchen Table—Women of Color Press, 1988), 60.
8. Yamamoto, *Seventeen Syllables*, 81.
9. Dorothy Day, *The Duty of Delight: The Diaries of Dorothy Day*, ed. Robert Ellsberg (Milwaukee: Marquette University Press, 2008), 169.
10. Dorothy Day, On Pilgrimage, *Catholic Worker*, November 1953, 2 and 4; Dorothy Day, "Peter Maurin Farm," *Catholic Worker*, June 1954, 2; and Dorothy Day, On Pilgrimage, *Catholic Worker*, July–August 1955, 3.
11. Wald, *Nature of California*, 109.
12. Dorothy Day, On Pilgrimage, *Catholic Worker*, May 1954, 8.
13. Dorothy Day, "Mid-Summer Retreat at Maryfarm," *Catholic Worker*, July–August 1954, 6.
14. Vivian Cherry, in Dorothy Day, *Dorothy Day and the Catholic Worker: The Miracle of Our Continuance*, ed. Kate Hennessy (New York: Fordham University Press, 2016), 62.
15. Hisaye Yamamoto, Small Talk, *Los Angeles Tribune*, September 3, 1945, 12.
16. Yamamoto, *Seventeen Syllables*, 85.

CLASSICAL MUSIC IN THE WRA CAMPS

1. "Center Residents to Hear World Famous Music," *Fresno Grapevine*, 1, no. 20, July 29, 1942, https://ddr.densho.org/ddr-densho-190-20.
2. United States, War Relocation Authority, "Programs of Recorded Classical Music, Programs and Notes (handwritten)," BANC MSS 67/14c, folder R4.22, Bancroft Library, University of California, Berkeley, https://oac.cdlib.org/ark:/13030/k6rj4rqs/?brand=oac4.
3. Mae Kanazawa Hara interview segment, July 15, 2004, Densho Digital Repository, http://ddr.densho.org/interviews/ddr-densho-1000-168-1.
4. *Manzanar (CA) Free Press*, February 21, 1945.

T. JOHN FUJII

1. I am indebted to Junhan Yu for getting me a copy of the book.

FLORENCE CRANNELL MEANS

1. See Eric Saul's website, "Eric Saul—Historian, Museum Director," accessed March 26, 2023, www.easaul.com.

AYAKO ISHIGAKI

1. Togo Tanaka, cited in Kaori Hayashi, "History of the *Rafu Shimpo*: Evolution of a Japanese-American Newspaper, 1903–1942" (master's thesis, California State University, Northridge, 1990), 277.

SELECTED BIBLIOGRAPHY

ARCHIVES

Densho Digital Repository, http://www.densho.org
Bill Hosokawa Papers, Denver Public Library
Mike Masaoka Papers, J. W. Marriott Library, University of Utah
Carey McWilliams Papers, Hoover Institution, UCLA, Claremont Colleges
Isamu Noguchi Papers, Isamu Noguchi Foundation, New York City
Japanese American National Museum, Los Angeles
Miné Okubo Papers, Riverside Community College
Norman Thomas Papers, New York Public Library
War Relocation Authority Files, RG 210 National Archives, Washington, DC
Minoru Yasui Papers, University of Colorado Denver, Auraria Library
Yuji Ichioka Papers, Charles E. Young Research Library, UCLA

BOOKS AND ARTICLES

Abe, Frank, Greg Robinson, and Floyd Cheung, eds. *John Okada: The Life and Rediscovered Work of the Author of* No-No Boy. Seattle: University of Washington Press, 2018.

Azuma, Eiichiro. *Between Two Empires: Race, History, and Transnationalism in Japanese America*. New York: Oxford University Press, 2005.

Bernstein, Shana. *Bridges of Reform: Interracial Civil Rights Activism in Twentieth-Century Los Angeles*. New York: Oxford University Press, 2011.

Birnbaum, Phyllis. *Glory in a Line: A Life of Foujita, the Artist Caught between East and West*. New York: Faber and Faber, 2006.

Bosworth, Allan R. *America's Concentration Camps*. New York: Norton, 1967.

Chang, Gordon H., Mark Dean Johnson, Paul J. Karlstrom, and Sharon Spain, eds. *Asian American Art: A History, 1850–1970*. Stanford: Stanford University Press, 2008.

Chiang, Connie Y. *Nature behind Barbed Wire: An Environmental History of the Japanese American Incarceration*. New York: Oxford University Press, 2018.

Chuman, Frank F. *The Bamboo People: The Law and Japanese-Americans*. Del Ray, CA: Publisher's Inc., 1976.

Daniels, Roger. *Asian Americans: Chinese and Japanese in the United States since 1850*. Seattle: University of Washington Press, 1988.

———. *Prisoners without Trial: Japanese Americans in World War II*. New York: Hill and Wang, 1993.

Dunaway, David King. *How Can I Keep from Singing: Pete Seeger*. New York: McGraw-Hill, 1981.

Eisenstadt, Peter. *Against the Hounds of Hell: A Life of Howard Thurman*. Charlottesville: University of Virginia Press, 2021.

Fujii, Tatsuki. *Singapore Assignment*. Tokyo: Nippon Times, 1943.

Fujino, Diane. "The Indivisibility of Freedom: The Nisei Progressives, Deep Solidarities, and Cold War Alternatives." *Journal of Asian American Studies* 21 (2018): 171–208.

Girdner, Audrie, and Anne Loftis. *The Great Betrayal*. New York: Macmillan, 1969.

Hansen, Arthur A., ed. *Japanese American WWII Evacuation History Project*. 5 vols. Westport, CT: Greenwood Press, 1992.

Hathaway, Heather. *That Damned Fence: The Literature of the Japanese American Prison Camps*. New York: Oxford University Press, 2022.

Hirasuna, Delphine. *The Art of Gaman: Arts and Crafts from the Japanese American Internment Camps, 1942–1946*. Berkeley, CA: Ten Speed Press, 2005.

Hirsch, Jerrold *Portrait of America: A Cultural History of the Federal Writers' Project*. Chapel Hill: University of North Carolina Press, 2003.

Hosokawa, Bill. *JACL in Quest of Justice*. New York: William Morrow, 1982.

———. *Nisei: The Quiet Americans*. New York: William Morrow, 1969.

Houston, Jean Wakatsuki, and James D. Houston. *Farewell to Manzanar: A True Story of Japanese American Experience during and after the World War II Internment*. New York: Bantam, 1973.

Ichioka, Yuji. *The Issei: The World of the First Generation Japanese Immigrants, 1885–1924*. New York: Free Press, 1988.

Ikeda, Stewart David. *What the Scarecrow Said*. New York: Regan Books, 1996.

Irons, Peter. *Justice at War*. New York: Oxford University Press, 1983.

Isherwood, Christopher. *A Single Man*. New York: Macmillan, 1964.

Ishigaki, Ayako. *Restless Wave: My Life in Two Worlds*. With an afterword by Greg Robinson and Yi-Chun Tricia Lin. New York: The Feminist Press, 2004.

Kashima, Tetsuden. *Judgment without Trial: Japanese American Imprisonment during World War II*. Seattle: University of Washington Press, 2003.

Kawakami, Iwao. *The Parents and Other Poems*. San Francisco: Nichi Bei Times, 1947.

Kelen, Leslie G., ed. *This Light of Ours—Activist Photographers of the Civil Rights Movement*. Vancouver: University of British Columbia Press, 2012.
Kikumura-Yano, Akemi, ed. *Encyclopedia of Japanese Descendants in the Americas: An Illustrated History of the Nikkei*. Walnut Creek, CA: Rowman & Littlefield / AltaMira Press, 2002.
Macbeth, Hugh. *Justice for All Humanity: Colored America Answers the Challenge of Pearl S. Buck*. Pamphlet. Los Angeles: United Races of America, 1942.
McWilliams, Carey. *Prejudice: Japanese-Americans: Symbol of Racial Intolerance*. Boston: Little, Brown, 1944.
Means, Florence Crannell. *The Moved-Outers*. Boston: Little, Brown, 1945.
Miyake, Perry. *21st Century Manzanar*. Los Angeles: Really Great Books, 2002.
Miyamoto, Kazuo. *Hawaii: The End of the Rainbow*. Rutland, VT: Charles Tuttle Publishing, 1964.
Mochizuki, Ken. *Beacon Hill Boys*. New York: Scholastic, 2004.
Muller, Eric L. *American Inquisition: The Hunt for Japanese American Disloyalty during World War II*. Chapel Hill: University of North Carolina Press, 2007.
Nagahara, Shoson. *Lament in the Night*. Translated by Andrew Leong. Los Angeles: Kaya Press, 2012.
Nakagawa, Karl S. *The Rendezvous of Mysteries*. Philadelphia: Dorrance Press, 1928.
Niiya, Brian, ed. *Japanese-American History: An A to Z from 1868 to the Present*. New York: Facts on File, 1983.
Nishi, Setsuko. *Facts about Japanese-Americans*. Pamphlet. Chicago: American Council on Race Relations, 1946.
Ohta, Takashi, and Margaret Sperry. *The Golden Wind*. New York: Boni, 1929.
Oishi, Gene. *Fox Drum Bebop*. Los Angeles: Kaya Press, 2014.
———. *In Search of Hiroshi*. Rutland VT: Charles Tuttle, 1987.
Okada, John. *No-No Boy*. 1957. Reprint, Seattle: University of Washington Press, 1977.
Okimoto, Daniel I. *American in Disguise*. New York: Walker/Weatherhill, 1971.
Omura, Bunji. *The Last Genro, Prince Saionji, the Man Who Westernized Japan*. Philadelphia: Lippincott, 1938.
Oyabe, Jenichiro. *A Japanese Robinson Crusoe*. Edited by Greg Robinson and Yujin Yaguchi. Honolulu: University of Hawaii Press, 2009.
Piehl, Mel. *Breaking Bread: The Catholic Worker and the Origin of Catholic Radicalism in America*. Philadelphia: Temple University Press, 1982.
Revoyr, Nina. *Southland*. Los Angeles: Akashic Books, 2003.
Robinson, Greg. *After Camp: Portraits in Midcentury Japanese American Life and Politics*. Berkeley: University of California Press, 2012.
———. *By Order of the President: FDR and the Internment of Japanese Americans*. Cambridge: Harvard University Press, 2001.

———. *A Tragedy of Democracy: Japanese Confinement in North America.* New York: Columbia University Press, 2009.

Robinson, Greg, ed. *Pacific Citizens: Larry and Guyo Tajiri and Japanese American Journalism in the World War II Era.* Urbana: University of Illinois Press, 2012.

Robinson, Greg, and Robert S. Chang, eds. *Minority Relations: Intergroup Conflict and Cooperation.* Oxford: University Press of Mississippi, 2016.

Rutkowski, Sara, ed. *Rewriting America: New Essays on the Federal Writers' Project.* Amherst: University of Massachusetts Press, 2022.

Seigel, Shizue. *In Good Conscience: Supporting Japanese Americans during the Internment.* San Francisco: Asian American Curriculum Project, 2006.

Shaffer, Robert. "Cracks in the Consensus: Defending the Rights of Japanese Americans during World War II." *Radical History Review* 72 (June 1998): 84–120.

Shirota, Jon. *Pineapple White.* Honolulu: Ohara Publications, 1972.

Sieg, Gerald Chan. *The Far Journey.* Savannah; Poetry Society of Georgia, 2002.

Takahashi, K. T. *The Anti-Japanese Petition: Appeal from a Threatened Persecution."* Montreal: Montreal Gazette Press, 1897.

Tamagawa, Kathleen. *Holy Prayers in a Horse's Ear.* Edited by Greg Robinson and Elena Tajima Creef. 1932. Reprint, New Brunswick, NJ: Rutgers University Press, 2008.

Thomas, Will. *The Seeking.* Revised ed. 1953. Reprint, Boston: Northeastern University Press, 2013.

Tokunaga, Yu. *Transborder Los Angeles: Cultivating Japanese and Mexican Relations, 1924–1942.* Berkeley: University of California Press, 2022.

Tsuzaki, Mutsumi. *Mokkin deizu: Hiraoka Yōichi "ten'i muhō no ongaku jinsei."* Tokyo: Kōdansha, 2013.

United States Commission on Wartime Relocation and Internment of Civilians. *Personal Justice Denied.* 1982. Reprint, Seattle: University of Washington Press, 1997.

United States Department of the Interior. War Agency Liquidation Unit. *People in Motion: The Postwar Adjustment of the Evacuated Japanese-Americans.* Washington, DC: USGPO, 1947.

Uyeda, Clifford I. *Suspended: Growing Up Asian in America.* San Francisco: National Japanese American Historical Society, 2000.

Wat, Eric C. *The Making of a Gay Asian Community: An Oral History of Pre-AIDS Los Angeles.* Lanham, MD: Rowman & Littlefield, 2001.

Williams, Duncan Ryuken. *American Sutra: A Story of Faith and Freedom in the Second World War.* Cambridge: Harvard University Press, 2018.

Yamamoto, Hisaye. *Seventeen Syllables and Other Stories.* New Brunswick, NJ: Rutgers University Press, 2001.

Yamata, Kikou. *Lady of Beauty.* New York: John Day, 1951.

Yoneda, Karl G. *Ganbatte: Sixty Year Struggle of a Kibei Worker*. Los Angeles: UCLA Asian American Studies Center Press, 1983.

Yoshida, George. *Reminiscing in Swingtime: Japanese Americans in American Popular Music, 1925–1960*. San Francisco: National Japanese American Historical Society, 1997.

———. *Musicians from a Different Shore: Asians and Asian Americans in Classical Music*. Philadelphia: Temple University Press, 2008.

THE JAPANESE AMERICAN PRESS

Bandwagon (New York City)
Catholic Worker (New York City)
Chicago Shimpo (Chicago)
Continental Times (Toronto)
Crossroads (Los Angeles)
Doho (Los Angeles)
Gyo-Sho: A Magazine of Nisei Literature (English Club of Cornell College)
Hawaii Hochi (Honolulu)
Heart Mountain Sentinel (Cody, WY)
Hokubei Mainichi (San Francisco)
Hokubei Shimpo / New York Nichibei (New York City)
JACD News Letter (Japanese American Committee for Democracy, New York City)
JACL Reporter (Japanese American Citizens League, Salt Lake City)
Japanese American Courier (Seattle)
Japanese American Review (New York City)
Kashū Mainichi (Los Angeles)
Manzanar Free Press (Manzanar, CA)
New Canadian (Vancouver and Toronto)
New World Sun (*Shin Sekai*) (San Francisco)
Nichi Bei Shimbun (*California Japanese-American News*) (San Francisco)
Nichi Bei Times (San Francisco)
Nisei Weekender (New York City)
Northwest Times (Seattle)
Pacific Citizen (Salt Lake City and Los Angeles)
Rafu Shimpo (Los Angeles)
Scene (Chicago)
Trek (Topaz, UT)

CREDITS

CHAPTER 1   *African American Allies*

"Erna P. Harris: Champion of Equality," *Discover Nikkei*, November 26, 2019.
"Japanese Americans and the Macbeth Legacy," *Discover Nikkei*, November 13, 2019; *Nichi Bei Weekly*, September 26, 2019.
"Seeking Will Thomas: A Friend of the Nisei," *Discover Nikkei*, May 6, 2020.
"Howard Thurman and Japanese Americans: Toward the Blessed Community" (with Peter Eisenstadt), *Discover Nikkei*, June 2–3, 2021.

CHAPTER 2   *Japanese Americans and Interracialism*

"From Kenny Murase to Kenji Murase: The Journey of a Nisei Writer, Scholar, and Activist," *Discover Nikkei*, September 14–15, 2020.
"Mari Sabusawa Michener, Champion of Civil Rights and Supporter of the Arts," *Discover Nikkei*, January 27–28, 2021.
"Way Down in Egypt Land: Tamio Wakayama, Civil Rights Photographer," *Discover Nikkei*, March 11–12, 2020.
"Paul Takagi: A Fearless Advocate," *Discover Nikkei*, June 13, 2019.
"Toshi Ohta Seeger: The Power behind the Music," *Nichi Bei Weekly*, March 4, 2021.

CHAPTER 3   *Japanese Americans and African Americans: Word and Places*

"Stepping Over the Color Line: Nikkei at Historically Black Colleges and Universities," *Discover Nikkei*, September 30, 2019.
"African American Scratches on a Nikkei Canvas: Black Characters in JA Literature" (with Brian Niiya), *Discover Nikkei*, January 23, 30, February 6, 13, 2022.
"The Japanese American Press and the History of the 'N-Word'" (with Jonathan van Harmelen), *Discover Nikkei*, August 23, 2021.

CHAPTER 4   *The Queer Heritage of Japanese Americans*

"K. T. Takahashi: Transnational Writer and Activist," *Nichi Bei Weekly*, June 21, 2021.
"Not Just *A Single Man*: Christopher Isherwood's Nisei Connections," *Discover Nikkei*, June 26, 2017.

"*Tondemonai*: Recovering a Groundbreaking Asian American Play," *Nichi Bei Weekly,* May 30, 2013.

"Randy Kikukawa and 1980s Asian American Gay Activism," *Nichi Bei Weekly,* June 20, 2019.

"The JACL's Shift to Support for LGBT Equality," *Nichi Bei Weekly,* June 18, 2020.

CHAPTER 5   *In Good Faith*

"Laying Down the Law of Love: The 1936 American Tour of Dr. Toyohiko Kagawa" (with Bo Tao), *Discover Nikkei,* March 12, 2021.

"Hisaye Yamamoto and the Catholic Worker" (with Matthieu Langlois), original essay for this volume.

"The Undiscovered History of Japanese Americans and the Church of Jesus Christ of Latter-day Saints" (with Christian Heimburger), *Discover Nikkei,* January 30–31, 2019.

"Nikkei and the Peace Churches: Mennonites and Brethren" (with Zacharie Leclair), *Nichi Bei Weekly,* August 13, 2020.

CHAPTER 6   *Mixed-Race Stories*

"Kinjiro Matsudaira: Mayor of Edmonston, Maryland" (with Jonathan van Harmelen), *Discover Nikkei,* May 5, 2021.

"Bernard Spencer Miyaguchi: Ice Skater Extraordinaire," Hapa Japan Project.

"Edith de Becker Sebald: Diplomat," Hapa Japan Project.

"The Enigma of Marion Saki," *Discover Nikkei,* November 16, 2021.

"Ruth Sato Reinhardt: From Chorus Girl to Jazz Momma," *Discover Nikkei,* January 10–11, 2022.

CHAPTER 7   *Music*

"Yoichi Hiraoka, Issei Xylophone Virtuoso" (with Jonathan van Harmelen), *Nichi Bei Weekly,* November 21, 2019.

"Classical Music in the WRA Camps" (with Jonathan van Harmelen), *Nichi Bei Weekly,* October 10, 2019.

"Akira Kikukawa and the Japanese American Orchestra" (with Jonathan van Harmelen), *Nichi Bei Weekly,* September 10, 2020.

"Juilliard-Trained Songbird Mariko Mukai Ando Defied Expectations" (with Jonathan van Harmelen), *Nichi Bei Weekly,* October 8, 2020.

"Nisei Singer and Civil Rights Activist Ruby Hideko Yoshino" (with Jonathan van Harmelen), *Nichi Bei Weekly,* November 5, 2020.

CHAPTER 8 *Literature and Journalism*

"T. John Fujii: Collaborator or Cosmopolitan?" *Discover Nikkei*, August 18–19, 2020.

"Bunji Omura: New York Japanese Antifascist Writer and Publicist" (with Jonathan van Harmelen), *Discover Nikkei,* November 11, 2020.

"Iwao Kawakami's Intriguing Elegy for Topaz," *Nichi Bei Weekly*, May 7, 2020.

"Eddie Shimano and Gerald Chan Sieg" (with James Sun), extract from Greg Robinson and James Sun, "Eddie Shimano and Gerald Chan Sieg: Asian American Writers in the FWP," in *Rewriting America: New Essays on the Federal Writers' Project*, ed. Sara Rutkowski, chap. 11 (Amherst: University of Massachusetts Press, 2022).

"Florence Crannell Means, the Woman behind *The Moved-Outers*," *Discover Nikkei*, March 15, 2019.

"Ayako Ishigaki: Radical Issei Feminist Writer in 1930s America," *Discover Nikkei*, October 20, 2020.

CHAPTER 9 *The European Nikkei Community*

"The French (Nikkei) Connection: Japanese Americans in Midcentury Paris," *Discover Nikkei*, October 28, 2019.

"Kikou Yamata: Rediscovering the First Nisei Writer," *Discover Nikkei*, October 14, 2019.

"Agnes Miyakawa, the Toast of Paris," *Nichi Bei Weekly*, January 1, 2019.

"Toshiko Hasegawa, a Nisei at La Scala," *Nichi Bei Weekly*, April 25, 2019.

"Pioneering Nisei Soprano Tomiko (Tomi) Kanazawa," *Nichi Bei Weekly*, February 21, 2019.

"Foujita Discovers the Americas: An Artist's Tour" (with Seth Jacobowitz), *Discover Nikkei*, January 7–8, 2021.

EPILOGUE

Nichi Bei Weekly, May 12, 2022.

INDEX

Italicized page numbers indicate illustrations.

activists and activism: Black, 1–10, 13–25, 53; Japanese American Committee for Democracy, 29, 52, 159, 215; labor, 47, 99, 103, 107–8; LGBTQ+, 84, 91–97. *See also* Japanese American Citizens League

African Americans: literature and, 4, 84–87, 191, 193; music and musicians, 144, 151, 159, 163; Nisei collaboration with, 26–29, 34, 38, 43–45, 49, 186; Nisei depictions of, 23, 60–75; racism and, 75–79, 217. *See also* Harris, Erna P.; Macbeth, Hugh; Thurman, Howard

Alameda, CA, 160, 165, 201

Amache camp, 16, 33, 163, 193

American Civil Liberties Union (ACLU), 6–7

American Council on Race Relations (ACRR), 33–35

Ando, Mariko Mukai, 157–60, *158*

Angelou, Maya, 12

Animal Crackers (film), 135

assembly centers, 120. *See also* Fresno Assembly Centers; Santa Anita Assembly Center; Tanforan Assembly Center

Atlanta University, 55, 58

Baldwin, James, 64, 77

baseball, 24, 28, 58, 112, 206

basketball, 23, 160

Berkeley, CA, 4, 50, 89, 100

birth control, 195–96

British Columbia, 39–42, 64

Buddhism, 78, 155, 165

California, 3, 6, 78, 87, 107, 115, 152 174, 197, 223; state assembly, 18. *See also* Northern California; Southern California

camp newspapers. See *Denson Communiqué*; *Heart Mountain Sentinel*; *Manzanar Free Press*; *Poston Chronicle*; *TREK*

Canada, 12, 39–42, 80–82

Catholicism, 100, 227

Catholic Worker, The, 103–10, 186

Catholic Worker movement 103–10

Chicago, 33–36, 50, 61, 65 120, 137

Chicago Defender, 1, 19

Chicago Tribune, 39, 144

China, 15, 50–51; Japanese invasion of, 15, 82, 125, 183, 189–90, 226; Nisei opposition to Japan's invasion of, 25, 190, 194–97, 204

Chinese Americans, 168, 175; depictions of, 4–5, 9, 20, 25; and the Federal Writers' Project, 186–90; and performing arts, 51, 85, 87, 90, 155; writers, 182

249

Chuman, Frank, 8
Church of Jesus Christ of Latter-day Saints, 110–18, 40
Church of the Brethren, 120–21
civil rights: African American, 1–10, 14–22, 60; Japanese American, 32–54, 104, 160; LGBTQ+, 87–97
Columbia University, 29, 30, 51, 174–77

Day, Dorothy, 105–7, 109–10
Denson Communiqué, 185
Dewitt, John, 6

East West Players, 88–90
Edmonston, MD, 122, 124–25
Eisenhower, Dwight D., 131, 59
Executive Order 9066, 33, 39, 64, 163, 185, 201, 213–14; African American reactions to, 1–2, 6, 13; criticism of, 114, 118, 120, 172

Farewell to Manzanar (book, Houston and Houston), 70
Farewell to Manzanar (film), 150
Federal Bureau of Investigation (FBI), 52, 130, 142, 158, 193
Federal Writers' Project (FWP), 177, 182
Fellowship of Reconciliation, 2, 14–22, 102, 106
Filipino Americans, 5, 18, 20–21, 49, 182
Fisk University, 55–59
football, 74, 78
Foujita, Tsuguharu, 200, 204, 217–27, 219
442nd Regimental Combat Team, 47, 95, 172, 202, 212
France, 71–72, 199–205, 213, 217, 219, 224, 227

Fresno, CA, 23, 25, 27, 113, 162, 206
Fresno Assembly Center, 151, 153
Fresno Bee, 25, 27
Fujii, T. John, 165–73

Gandhi, Mahatma, 14, 19, 22, 98–99
Gila River camp, 72

Hampton Institute (later Hampton University), 55, 56–59
Harris, Erna P., 1–4
Hasegawa, Toshiko, 210–13
Hatsumi (film), 45
Hawai'i, 36, 38, 68–70, 76, 78, 85, 99, 111, 112, 115, 117, 122, 208
Hayakawa, Sessue, 200, 217
Heart Mountain camp, 115
Heart Mountain Sentinel, 116
Himes, Chester, 11, 86
Hirabayashi v. U.S., 7
Hiraoka, Yoichi, 146–50, 153, 155
historically Black colleges and universities (HBCUs), 55–60. *See also* Atlanta University; Fisk University; Hampton Institute; Howard University; Morehouse College
Honda, Harry, 34
Hosokawa, Bill, 39, 60, 116, 165, 167, 171, 173, 178
Houston, Jeanne Wakatsuki, and James Houston, 70
Howard University, 14–16, 27, 55–56, 58–59

Isherwood, Christopher, 84–87
Ishigaki, Ayako, 194–98
Issei, 42, 51, 101, 150; academics, 173,

177–78; artists, 148, 150, 214, 221, 223; Christians, 58, 111; imprisonment of, 3, 32, 114–15, 180, 190; leaders, 26; women, 195, 198

Japanese American Citizens League (JACL), 25–26, 113–15, 173; and African Americans, 1, 7–8, 17–18, 59, 87; LGBTQ+ activism, 95–97; women and the JACL, 33–39, 160–164, 206
Japanese American Committee for Democracy (JACD), 29, 51–52, 159, 186, 215
Japanese American National Museum, 45, 231
Japanese Canadians, 39, 42–46, 64, 65–67 82, 83, 200
Jerome camp, 73, 152, 185
Juilliard School of Music, 157–62

Kagawa, Toyohiko, 98–103, *101*
Kanazawa, Tomoko, 213–17, *215*
Kashu Mainichi, 90, 103, 165, 219, 223–25; fiction, 23–24, 64, 76; music reviews, 157, 215
Kawakami, Iwao, 178–82
Kido, Saburo, 17, 59, 173
Kikukawa, Akira, 153–56
Kikukawa, Randy, 91–95
King, Martin Luther, Jr., 22, 53
Kobe, Japan, 99, 126, 128–29
Korean Americans, 87–89
Korean War, 130, 168
Korematsu v. U.S., 7

Last Genro, The (Omura), 176–78
LGBTQ+ activism, 84, 91–97
Los Angeles, 31, 68, 70, 74, 112, 148; artists, 223–25; civil rights activists, 5, 8, 12, 13, 16, 114; journalism in, 2–3, 23, 65, 77, 104, 106, 110, 155–57; LGBTQ+ activism in, 92, 94; in literature, 74, 84, 183, 194–97; music, 148, 155–57, 201, 208–9, 213–16; theater, 87–90
Los Angeles Times, 3, 90, 155–56, 209
Los Angeles Tribune, 1–4, 65, 103–6, 186
Louisiana, 58, 168, 216

Macarthur, Douglas, 130, 131, 210, 227
Macbeth, Hugh, Jr., 5–10, *6*
Macbeth, Hugh, Sr., 5–9, 20
Mako (actor), 88–90
Manchuria, 78, 175, 195, 204, 209, 221
Manzanar camp, 8, 47–50, 70, 74–75, 89–91, 120, 150, 152–53, 164
Manzanar Free Press, 47, 153
Maryland, 122, 124–25, 129–30, 202
Masaoka, Mike, 113–15
Matsudaira, Kinjiro, 122–26, *124*
Means, Florence Crannell, 11, 190–94
Mennonites, 118–21
Mexican Americans, 3, 28, 84, 191, 193
Michener, James A., 35–39
Michener, Mari Sabusawa. *See* Sabusawa, Mari
Military Intelligence Service (MIS), 47, 168
Mills College, 16, 20, 66
Minidoka camp, 115
Miyaguchi, Bernard Spencer, 126–28
Miyakawa, Agnes, 206–10, *207*
Morehouse College, 14
Mormonism, 110–17. *See also* Church of Jesus Christ of Latter-day Saints.
Montreal, Quebec, 80–82, 153, 179, 209, 230–31
Moved-Outers, The (Means), 192–94

Murase, Kenji/Kenny, 15–16, 23–32, 24, 59, 63, 67, 76
musicians, 50–54, 71, 150–56, 168, 231

Nakagawa, Karl S., 60–61
National Association for the Advancement of Colored People (NAACP), 17, 159
Native Americans, 28, 56, 67, 190, 224.
New Canadian, 29, 64–65
New World Sun/Shin Sekai Asahi Shinbun, 78, 183, 226
New York City, 32, 51, 107, 133, 137, 223; LGBTQ+ activism in, 91, 95; in literature, 71, 73; musicians, 148, 163, 217
New York Herald Tribune, 82, 125, 188
New York State, 14, 46, 51–54, 102
New York Times, 136, 141, 159, 163, 176, 178, 188, 193, 208
Nichi Bei Shinbun, 112, 125, 179, 185, 197, 204; music reviews in, 148, 161; short stories in, 24–26, 63, 166
Nippu Jiji, 76, 111, 125
Nisei: artists, 220–24; musicians, 146–56; singers, 157–62, 206–17; students, 27, 31, 58–59, 119, 157, 199, 229; writers, 23–32, 50, 60–78, 105, 165–73, 182–86, 202–6
Nisei Writers and Artists Mobilization for Democracy (NWAMD), 26–27, 184–85
Nishi, Setsuko Matsunaga, 34, 65
Nomura, Mary Kageyama, 150, 164
Northern California, 18, 32

Oakland, CA, 16, 26, 29, 160–62, 166, 182
Office of Naval Intelligence, 129–30
Office of Strategic Services, 128, 130, 197
Office of War Information, 185, 197
Oh, Soon-Tek, 71, 87–90
Oishi, Gene, 71–72, 202
Okada, John, 11, 66–67, 172, 202
Okubo, Miné, 180, 201
Omatsu, Maryka, 40, 45
Omura, Bunji, 173–78, 174
Oregon, 30, 115, 118, 216
Oyabe, Jenichiro, 56–57, 57
Oyama, Joe, 29, 63, 67, 77–78
Oyama, Mary, 78, 183
Oyama v. California, 7

Pacific Citizen, 29, 34, 65, 115, 138, 164, 173. See also Tajiri, Larry
painters, 51, 85, 150, 184, 200–204, 218–27
Partisan Review, 105
Pearl Harbor, HI, 114, 158, 172, 226; Japanese Americans, 6, 12, 26, 51, 129, 170; in literature, 86, 179; treatment of Japanese Americans in, 148, 177, 193
Philadelphia, 28–29, 45, 51, 72, 136, 140, 176, 215
playwrights, 4, 87–91, 164
Pomona College, 165–66, 172
Poston camp, 3, 16, 27–29, 64, 67, 103–4
Poston Chronicle, 28, 103–4

queer, 80–97

Rafu Shimpo, 24, 26, 52, 63, 68, 77–78, 90
Reagan, Ronald, 49
redress, 43, 45, 95–96, 229
Regan v. King, 7
Reinhardt, Ruth Sato, 137–45
resettlement, 2, 18, 28, 34–35, 40, 120, 143, 159, 163, 186
Restless Wave (Ishigaki), 194–97

Rohwer camp, 152
Roosevelt, Eleanor, 19
Roosevelt, Franklin D., 6, 100, 161

Sabusawa, Mari, 32–39
Sacramento, CA, 47, 61, 112, 206–8, 210–11, 216
Saki, Marion, 131–37, *132*
San Francisco, 114, 118, 125, 225; activists, 6–10, 16–22, 27–32, 47, 49, 98, 100; African Americans, 16–18; Chinatown, 4; LGBTQ+ in, 92–94; in literature, 12, 62, 76, 82, 89, 176, 182–84, 193; musicians, 141, 160–62, 201, 207–8, 211, 214
Sansei, 43, 73–74, 91, 104, 193
Santa Anita Assembly Center, 14–15, 185
Seattle, 31, 45, 127, 177, 179, 206, 216; Japanese Americans, 57, 157–159, 182; in literature, 66, 74
Sebald, Edith deBecker, 128–31, *131*
Seeger, Toshi Ohta, 50–54
Shimano, Eddie, 29, 182–86
Sieg, Gerald Chan, 186–90
Singapore, 38, 166–73
Singapore Herald, 166–67, 170–71, 173
Single Man, A (Isherwood), 84–87
Southern California, 2, 97–102, 182–83
Stanford University, 48, 88, 162
Student Nonviolent Coordinating Committee (SNCC), 42, 45
Sugihara, Ina, 32–33, 65
Sugimoto, Henry, 220, 224–26

Tajiri, Guyo, 45, 112, 178–80
Tajiri, Larry, 27, 45, 60, 65, 114, 172, 184, 186; prewar journalism of, 165–70, 197, 224–25

Takagi, Paul, 46–50
Takahashi, K. T., 80–84
Takasaki, Mayumi, *40*, 43–46
Takei, George, 88
Tamagawa, Kathleen, 61–62
Tanaka, Togo, 197
Tanforan Assembly Center, 167
Tatsuno, Dave, 20
Temple Univeristy, 28–29, 31
Thomas, Elbert, 113–14
Thomas, Norman, 6, 8–9
Thomas, Will, 10–13, *11*
Thurman, Howard, 14–22, *15*
Tondemonai (Oh, play), 87–90
Topaz (Tatsuno, film), 20
Topaz camp, 115–16, 150, 152–53, 163, 167, 178, 180, 182, 201
TREK, 64
Truman, Harry S., 130
Tule Lake camp, 2, 27, 47, 90–91, 119–20, 151

University of California, Berkeley, 5, 15, 26, 33, 47–50, 89, 93, 156, 161–62
University of California, Los Angeles, 5, 24, 88, 155, 169
University of Chicago, 36, 182
University of Colorado, 190, 192
University of Iowa, 183
University of Minnesota, 30, 179
University of Nebraska, 28
University of Paris, 176, 201
University of Southern California, 154
University of Texas, Austin, 37–39
University of Utah, 113
University of Washington, 30, 157
Utah, 152, 163, 181; Mormonism, 110–17

Index 253

Vancouver, BC, 39, 40, 42–46, 64, 201

Wakayama, Tamio, 39–44, *40*
War Relocation Authority (WRA), 9, 59, 64, 72, 118, 181, 213; music education, 150–52; resettlement program, 20, 47, 152, 163
War Relocation Authority Camps. *See* Amache camp; Gila River camp; Heart Mountain camp; Jerome camp; Manzanar camp; Minidoka camp; Poston camp; Rohwer camp; Topaz camp; Tule Lake camp
Washington, DC, 55–57, 97, 134; African Americans, 6, 14, 16, 18, 27; Japanese Americans, 33, 122, 129–30
Washington Post, 188
Washington State, 157, 182, 214
Whittier College, 14

Wirin, A. L., 6–7
Works Progress Administration (WPA), 177, 182, 196
World War I, 94, 99, 119
World War II, 17, 21, 58, 94, 142, 205; literary depictions of, 8, 64, 68, 107, 171, 190–94; military service, 47, 129, 159, 177, 202, 210, 212; religious groups and, 14, 114, 188

Yale Divinity School, 99
Yamamoto, Hisaye, 4, 24, 103–10, *104*
Yamamoto, Hugo, 65, 67
Yamamoto, Tak, 94, 96–97
Yamashita, John, 20–22
Yamata, Kikou, 202–6
Yamauchi, Wakako, 4, 65
Yoneda, Karl, 49, 122, 178
Yoshino, Ruby Hideko, 160–64, *161*

THE SCOTT AND LAURIE OKI SERIES
IN ASIAN AMERICAN STUDIES

From a Three-Cornered World: New and Selected Poems, by James Masao Mitsui
Imprisoned Apart: The World War II Correspondence of an Issei Couple, by Louis Fiset
Storied Lives: Japanese American Students and World War II, by Gary Okihiro
Phoenix Eyes and Other Stories, by Russell Charles Leong
Paper Bullets: A Fictional Autobiography, by Kip Fulbeck
Born in Seattle: The Campaign for Japanese American Redress, by Robert Sadamu Shimabukuro
Confinement and Ethnicity: An Overview of World War II Japanese American Relocation Sites, by Jeffery F. Burton, Mary M. Farrell, Florence B. Lord, and Richard W. Lord
Judgment without Trial: Japanese American Imprisonment during World War II, by Tetsuden Kashima
Shopping at Giant Foods: Chinese American Supermarkets in Northern California, by Alfred Yee
Altered Lives, Enduring Community: Japanese Americans Remember Their World War II Incarceration, by Stephen S. Fugita and Marilyn Fernandez
Eat Everything before You Die: A Chinaman in the Counterculture, by Jeffery Paul Chan
Form and Transformation in Asian American Literature, edited by Zhou Xiaojing and Samina Najmi
Language of the Geckos and Other Stories, by Gary Pak
Nisei Memories: My Parents Talk about the War Years, by Paul Howard Takemoto
Growing Up Brown: Memoirs of a Bridge Generation Filipino American, by Peter Jamero
Letters from the 442nd: The World War II Correspondence of a Japanese American Medic, by Minoru Masuda; edited by Hana Masuda and Dianne Bridgman
Shadows of a Fleeting World: Pictorial Photography and the Seattle Camera Club, by David F. Martin and Nicolette Bromberg
Signs of Home: The Paintings and Wartime Diary of Kamekichi Tokita, by Barbara Johns and Kamekichi Tokita

Nisei Soldiers Break Their Silence: Coming Home to Hood River, by Linda Tamura

A Principled Stand: The Story of Hirabayashi v. United States, by Gordon K. Hirabayashi, with James A. Hirabayashi and Lane Ryo Hirabayashi

Cities of Others: Reimagining Urban Spaces in Asian American Literature, by Xiaojing Zhou

Enduring Conviction: Fred Korematsu and His Quest for Justice, by Lorraine K. Bannai

Asians in Colorado: A History of Persecution and Perseverance in the Centennial State, by William Wei

The Hope of Another Spring: Takuichi Fujii, Artist and Wartime Witness, by Barbara Johns

John Okada: The Life and Rediscovered Work of the Author of No-No Boy, edited by Frank Abe, Greg Robinson, and Floyd Cheung

The Unsung Great: Stories of Extraordinary Japanese Americans, by Greg Robinson

Becoming Nisei: Japanese American Urban Lives in Prewar Tacoma, by Lisa M. Hoffman and Mary L. Hanneman

Contemporary Asian American Activism: Building Movements for Liberation, edited by Diane C. Fujino and Robyn Magalit Rodriguez

The Unknown Great: Stories of Japanese Americans at the Margins of History, by Greg Robinson with Jonathan van Harmelen

www.ingramcontent.com/pod-product-compliance
Lightning Source LLC
Chambersburg PA
CBHW030532230426
43665CB00010B/855